A SOARING SPIRIT

TimeFrame 600-400 BC

EUROPE: ROMANS AND CELTS

GREECE

TimeFrame 600-400 BC

THE PERSIAN EMPIRE

INDIA

CHINA

Other Publications:
MYSTERIES OF THE UNKNOWN
FIX IT YOURSELF
FITNESS, HEALTH & NUTRITION
SUCCESSFUL PARENTING
HEALTHY HOME COOKING
UNDERSTANDING COMPUTERS
LIBRARY OF NATIONS
THE ENCHANTED WORLD
THE KODAK LIBRARY OF CREATIVE PHOTOGRAPHY
GREAT MEALS IN MINUTES
THE CIVIL WAR
PLANET EARTH
COLLECTOR'S LIBRARY OF THE CIVIL WAR
THE EPIC OF FLIGHT
THE GOOD COOK
WORLD WAR II
HOME REPAIR AND IMPROVEMENT
THE OLD WEST

For information on and a full description of
any of the Time-Life Books series listed above,
please write:
Reader Information
Time-Life Customer Service
P.O. Box C-32068
Richmond, Virginia 23261-2068
or call: 1-800-621-7026

This volume is one in a series that tells the story
of humankind. Other books in the series
include:
The Age of God-Kings
Barbarian Tides

A SOARING SPIRIT

TimeFrame 600-400 BC

BY THE EDITORS OF TIME-LIFE BOOKS

TIME-LIFE BOOKS, ALEXANDRIA, VIRGINIA

Time-Life Books Inc.
is a wholly owned subsidiary of
TIME INCORPORATED

FOUNDER: Henry R. Luce 1898-1967

Editor-in-Chief: Henry Anatole Grunwald
Chairman and Chief Executive Officer:
J. Richard Munro
President and Chief Operating Officer:
N. J. Nicholas Jr.
Chairman of the Executive Committee:
Ralph P. Davidson
Corporate Editor: Ray Cave
Executive Vice President, Books:
Kelso F. Sutton
Vice President, Books: George Artandi

TIME-LIFE BOOKS INC.

EDITOR: George Constable
Executive Editor: Ellen Phillips
Director of Design: Louis Klein
Director of Editorial Resources:
Phyllis K. Wise
Editorial Board: Russell B. Adams Jr., Dale
M. Brown, Roberta Conlan, Thomas
H. Flaherty, Lee Hassig, Donia Ann Steele,
Rosalind Stubenberg, Kit van Tulleken,
Henry Woodhead
Director of Photography and Research:
John Conrad Weiser

PRESIDENT: Christopher T. Linen
Chief Operating Officer: John M. Fahey Jr.
Senior Vice President: James L. Mercer
Vice Presidents: Stephen L. Bair,
Ralph J. Cuomo, Neal Goff, Stephen
L. Goldstein, Juanita T. James, Hallett
Johnson III, Carol Kaplan, Susan
J. Maruyama, Robert H. Smith, Paul
R. Stewart, Joseph J. Ward
Director of Production Services:
Robert J. Passantino

Editorial Operations
Copy Chief: Diane Ullius
Production: Celia Beattie
Quality Control: James J. Cox (director)
Library: Louise D. Forstall

Correspondents: Elisabeth Kraemer-Singh
(Bonn); Maria Vincenza Aloisi (Paris); Ann
Natanson (Rome). Valuable assistance
was also provided by: Mirka Gondicas
(Athens); Philip Cunningham, Jaime
A. Florcruz, Jane Zhang (Beijing);
Caroline Alcock, Caroline Lucas,
Christine Hinze, Linda Proud (London);
Josephine du Brusle (Paris); Elizabeth
Brown, Christina Lieberman (New York);
Ann Wise (Rome); Traudl Lessing
(Vienna).

TIME FRAME

SERIES DIRECTOR: Henry Woodhead
Series Administrator:
Philip Brandt George

Editorial Staff for *A Soaring Spirit*
Designer: Dale Pollekoff
Associate Editors: Jim Hicks (text), Robin
Richman (pictures)
Writers: Stephen G. Hyslop, Ray Jones,
Brian C. Pohanka, David S. Thomson
Researchers: Patti Cass, Barbara Sause,
Trudy Pearson, Connie Strawbridge
(pictures)
Assistant Designer: Alan Pitts
Copy Coordinator: Vivian Noble
Picture Coordinator: Renée DeSandies
Editorial Assistant: Patricia D. Whiteford

Special Contributors: Ronald H. Bailey,
Brian McGinn, Charles Phillips, Bryce
Walker (text); Cathy Sharpe Cooke, Ann-
Louise G. Gates, Oobie Gleysteen
(research)

CONSULTANTS

Europe:
LAWRENCE OKAMURA, Assistant Profes-
sor of Ancient History, University of
Missouri, Columbia, Missouri

Greece:
JOSIAH OBER, Professor of History, University of Michigan, Ann Arbor, Michigan

JOHN CAMP, Andrew W. Mellon Professor of Classical Studies, American School
of Classical Studies, Athens

WILLIAM B. DINSMOOR, JR., American
School of Classical Studies, Athens

JOHN M. MANSFIELD, Department of
Classics, Goldwin Smith Hall, Cornell
University, Ithaca, New York

India:
GREGORY POSSEHL, University of
Pennsylvania Museum, Philadelphia

Persia:
DAVID F. GRAF, Assistant Professor of
History, University of Miami, Coral Ga-
bles, Florida

STEVEN W. HIRSCH, Associate Professor
of Classics and History, Tufts University,
Medford, Massachusetts

KATHRYN GLEASON, Department of
Landscape Architecture, University of
Pennsylvania, Philadelphia

FRIEDRICH KREFTER, former assistant director of the first scientific expedition excavating Persepolis

**Library of Congress Cataloging in
Publication Data**

A Soaring spirit.
  Bibliography: p.
  Includes index.
  1. History, Ancient. I. Time-Life Books.
D57.S69 1987   930   87-18018
ISBN 0-8094-6408-X
ISBN 0-8094-6409-8 (lib. bdg.)

Time-Life Books Inc. offers a wide range of fine
recordings, including a *Rock 'n' Roll Era* series.
For subscription information, call 1-800-621-
7026, or write TIME-LIFE MUSIC, P.O. Box
C-32068, Richmond, Virginia 23261-2068.

CONTENTS

1 Persia at the Crest 9

Essay: The Embattled Greeks 39

2 The Hellenic Unfolding 51

Essay: The Flowering Voice of Poetry 85

3 Dawn of the Romans 97

Essay: Creating an Ideal Beauty 119

4 Enlightenment in the East 143

Essay Dwellings for the Dead 161

Chronology 168

Acknowledgments 173

Picture Credits 174

Bibliography 172

Index 170

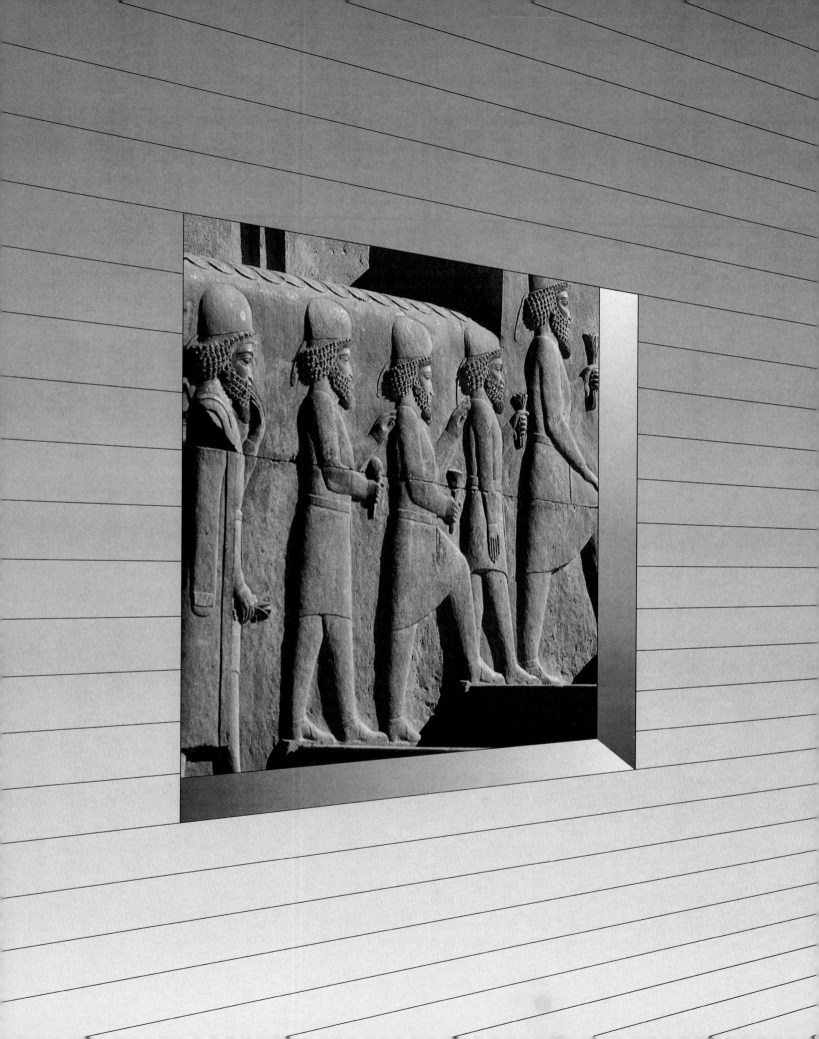

PERSIA AT THE CREST

Every year, as the days grew longer and spring quickened the land, the caravans set out from the far reaches of the known world — pack horses from Anatolia and Thrace, camel trains from Bactria and Arabia, armies of porters from the thousand-mile-long oasis of the Nile, chariots from Assyria, bullock carts from the gold-rich tributaries of the Indus River. They all headed for the same destination, carrying an imperial ransom in gems, precious metals, ebony, ivory, rare furs, and textiles. Some groups brought animals: antelopes from Libya, prize stallions from Armenia. The caravan from Babylon transported a particularly exotic shipment — 500 young eunuchs.

From every corner of the empire, the processions moved along a network of imperial highways to converge, shortly before the spring equinox, at Persepolis — a dazzling, monumental complex of palaces, cavernous pillared halls, and thick-walled treasury buildings that stood in isolated splendor on the high, dusty Iranian plateau. There officers from all the subject states and satrapies of the Persian empire would present their New Year's "gifts" — actually the exact quantity and nature of the annual tributes had been specified by the imperial government — to their supreme overlord, the King of Persia, the Great King, King of Kings, the mightiest ruler in the world.

No one had ever controlled such an enormous sweep of territory or so much wealth as the man who sat on the Persian throne. The nobles of Egypt, the satraps of Mesopotamia and Asia Minor, the nomad chieftains of the eastern deserts, and the rajas of India all paid tribute to the Persian emperor. At its zenith, around the beginning of the fifth century BC, Persia ruled nearly two million square miles of mountain and steppe, sand waste and fertile river plain, and about ten million subjects. The total value of annual imperial revenues was the equivalent of almost a million pounds of silver.

The Persians' achievement represented a significant step forward for civilization — and not simply because of their dumbfounding wealth or the sheer size of their empire. To run their vast domain, they developed new, enlightened techniques for governing large areas and disparate populations. Brutal power and terror like that employed by, say, the Assyrians in their heyday probably could not have successfully welded together a realm as large as the Persians'; although fear had its uses in empire building, it usually soon led to resentment and rebellion. Persian rule interfered little with the normal administration or daily life of a subject nation. Persian kings demanded their taxes, of course, but they also promoted increased economic activity that left many countries and people in the empire better off than they were before the Persians arrived. The entirely new dimension in prosperity and governmental grace that characterized their rule was not a happenstance. It resulted from an effort to improve the way human society was organized, to make it work better — and not only for the powerful. Persia's King Darius I said that he staunchly supported the rule of law "so that the stronger does not smite nor destroy the weak."

The desire for improvement during this period — roughly 600 to 400 BC — was not exclusive to the Persians, nor was it confined to the field of government. In fact, new ideas, attitudes, and beliefs aimed at securing a better life, or a better understanding of life, bubbled up in many parts of the world. It was as if humanity was being moved by a universal spirit to aspire to greater things, to lift itself onto a higher plane of existence. Although the spirit was universal, it nonetheless inspired a multiplicity of varying notions. The Greeks, for instance, were in this same era developing a political philosophy far different from that of the autocratic Persian kings: democracy. The Greek emphasis on the rights and potential of the individual led to a political life marked by debate and dissension, and contributed to constant squabbling and even warring among Greece's jealously independent city-states. But it also encouraged exquisite accomplishments in art and other intellectual pursuits, and it fed a pride and sense of righteousness that proved telling weapons when the Greeks were threatened, as the Persians would one day learn.

While the Greeks were elevating the individual to a new level of nobility, other philosophers, prophets, and mystics were proposing completely different ways for human beings to improve their relationships with nature, society, or the gods. Several of the world's great religions and systems of ethical behavior were born or significantly shaped in this era. One was the Persians' Zoroastrianism, among the earliest faiths to proclaim a single god and to promise reward or punishment in the afterlife for a person's deeds on earth. Jewish spiritual leaders, meanwhile, living in exile in Persian-ruled Babylon, were exposed to some of those ideas as they refined the laws and beliefs of Judaism. In India, a nobleman who had given up his wealth and family for an ascetic's life experienced a flash of spiritual understanding that earned him the title of Buddha, "the Enlightened One." The force of his discovery would radiate outward through South and East Asia and eventually make him a god. And in isolated China there evolved two philosophies for living that acquired more influence than most religions — indeed, that came to be regarded by many as religions. Taoism, which stressed the joy to be found in yielding, in accepting the unity of human beings and the universe, and Confucianism, with its emphasis on morality and duty, would fundamentally influence Chinese life, society, and government for the next 2,500 years.

In western Europe, meanwhile, the people of a new, bustling city that sprawled across seven hills near the Tiber River were in the early stages of making what amounted to a religion out of the state itself. These Romans had gods to whom they paid elaborate homage, but as the centuries passed, the most truly revered object of their devotion would be Rome, the place and the political entity. And during this era they would be confronted by another vigorous European people — wild, free-spirited Celts — who were intent on destroying Rome and its infant civilization.

The ancestors of the Persians had migrated to the Iranian plateau in the waves of Indo-European tribes that descended the steppes of southern Russia beginning around 2000 BC. They were among the Aryans (from which came the name Iranians) who arrived around 1000 BC. Most likely they trekked in through the bleak wastes of Turkestan, then turned west below the Caspian Sea to reach the snowy flanks of the Zagros Mountains. A related Iranian group, the Medes, found a permanent homeland nearby in the rolling uplands of the northwestern Iranian plateau. But the Persians continued south and after many generations came to rest in the region they called Parsa, on the mountainous southwestern rim of the plateau.

It was not a land that inspired much confidence. To the north and east stretched the dreary salt wastes of the central plateau. To the south, along the Persian Gulf, was a sweltering landscape of sand and rubble that held little promise. Prospects were better to the northwest, where the mountains sloped down to a fertile plain watered by a lower branch of the Tigris River. But that area had long been held by the Elamites, whose small but powerful kingdom had maintained its independence for 2,000 years, longer than any state in history.

So the Persians made do with what they had. In the back country on the fringe of Elam there was land enough to live on. They could grow wheat in the folds between the mountains and graze their flocks of fat-tailed sheep on the slopes above, moving up each spring in the wake of the retreating snow, and down again to the flats in autumn. For several hundred years, life in Parsa followed the same uneventful pattern. Then, toward the middle of the seventh century BC, a series of political convulsions began to reshape the structures of power throughout the region. Elam fell to the massed cavalry and lofty siege towers of the Assyrians. Its capital, Susa, was thrown into desolate ruin and abandoned to the lizard and locust. Soon after, Assyria itself, having dominated the Middle East for several centuries, faced a serious challenge.

Under Darius I, the Persian empire *(outlined area)* **reached its peak soon after 522 BC. Extending from the Nile to the Indus, from the Black Sea to the Persian Gulf, this vast realm included the rich agricultural lands of the Fertile Crescent, the mineral-laden hills of Asia Minor, and the wealthy Ionian and Phoenician trading centers on the Mediterranean. To help bind together these holdings, Persia's kings built the famous Royal Road, which stretched nearly 1,700 miles from the imperial city of Susa, near the center of the empire, to Sardis in Lydia.**

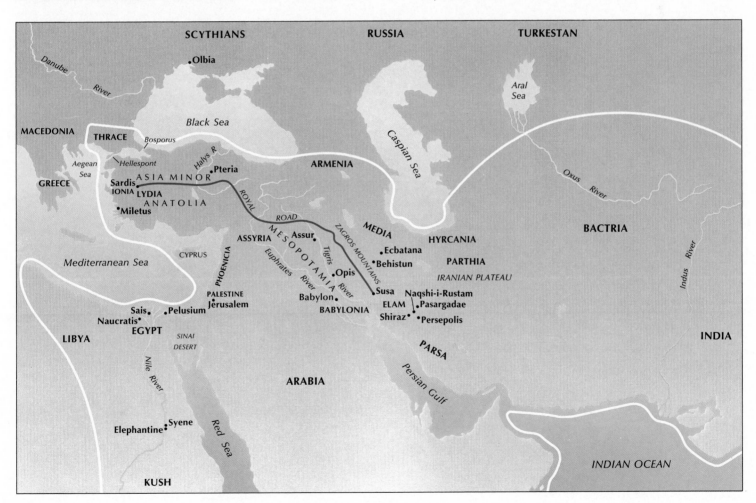

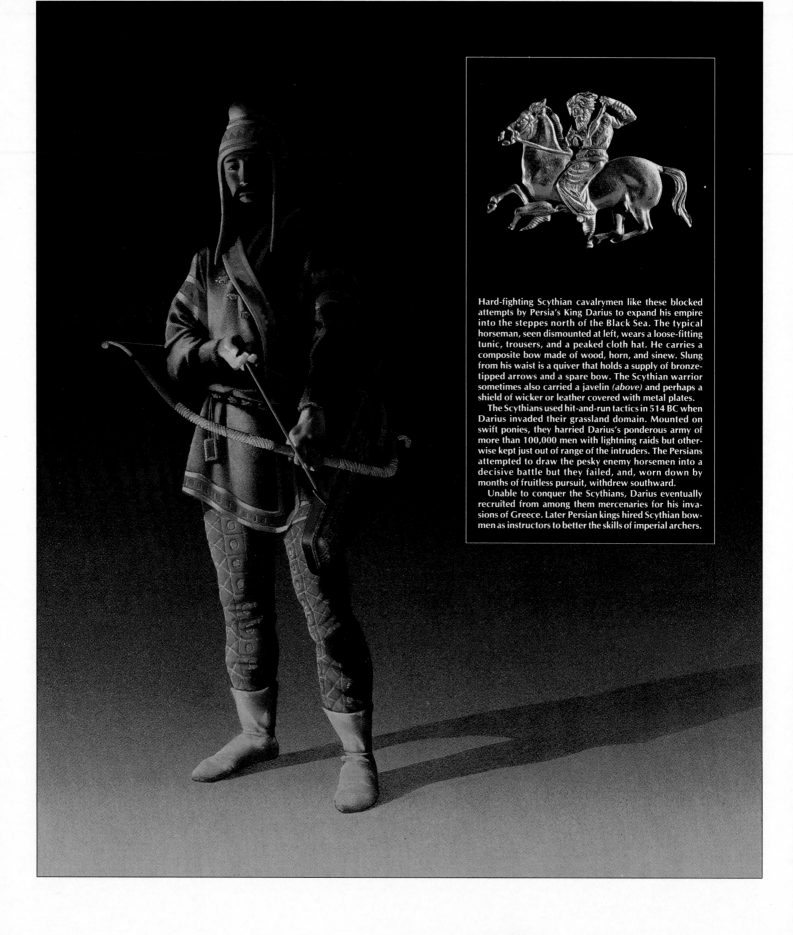

Hard-fighting Scythian cavalrymen like these blocked attempts by Persia's King Darius to expand his empire into the steppes north of the Black Sea. The typical horseman, seen dismounted at left, wears a loose-fitting tunic, trousers, and a peaked cloth hat. He carries a composite bow made of wood, horn, and sinew. Slung from his waist is a quiver that holds a supply of bronze-tipped arrows and a spare bow. The Scythian warrior sometimes also carried a javelin *(above)* and perhaps a shield of wicker or leather covered with metal plates.

The Scythians used hit-and-run tactics in 514 BC when Darius invaded their grassland domain. Mounted on swift ponies, they harried Darius's ponderous army of more than 100,000 men with lightning raids but otherwise kept just out of range of the intruders. The Persians attempted to draw the pesky enemy horsemen into a decisive battle but they failed, and, worn down by months of fruitless pursuit, withdrew southward.

Unable to conquer the Scythians, Darius eventually recruited from among them mercenaries for his invasions of Greece. Later Persian kings hired Scythian bowmen as instructors to better the skills of imperial archers.

Prominent among the challengers were the Medes, who had evolved in their Zagros mountain territory from a nomadic tribal society to a strong, stable monarchy. The Median monarch ruled from a hilltop citadel at Ecbatana, said to be surrounded by seven concentric walls, the innermost two being plated in silver and gold. According to the Greek traveler and historian Herodotus, no one was allowed to laugh or spit in the royal presence, and all communication between supplicants and the king was through an intermediary. The king of the Medes in the closing years of the seventh century BC was Cyaxares, perhaps the finest military leader of the era. He reorganized the Median armed forces, substituting disciplined units of spearmen, archers, and cavalry for the old-style armies of loosely organized warriors raised by tribal levies.

In 615 BC, Cyaxares attacked Assyria's principal religious center, Assur, throwing down its walls and slaughtering most of its inhabitants. Then the Medes joined forces with the Babylonians to lay waste to Nineveh, the Assyrian capital, after which they pursued and utterly destroyed the fleeing Assyrian army. The allies divided the Assyrian empire. The Babylonians took southern Mesopotamia, Syria, and Palestine, and the Medes most of the rest. Egypt, which had played a supporting role, secured its own independence. Nomadic Scythians, who had come down from the steppes to lend a hand, galloped home with their saddlebags stuffed with booty.

Cyaxares now laid claim to a great swath of territory that stretched from eastern Anatolia to the Caspian, and south through ancient Elam and the land of the Persians. For all the pomp of the Median court, Cyaxares most likely ruled his domain in the manner of a feudal overlord rather than as an absolute monarch, being the final arbiter and commander among the princes of Parsa, who paid him homage and tribute.

In Anatolia, Cyaxares' lands abutted the rich and aggressive nation of Lydia. The Lydians controlled most of western Asia Minor. In their grip were the land trade routes to Europe, the sea passage from the Black Sea to the Aegean Sea, and the Greek city-states of the Ionian coast. They mined gold and silver in the nearby Mount Tmolus region and panned the precious metals from a river that ran through their capital city of Sardis. They also had designs on the Median holdings to the east. Hostilities between the Lydians and the Medes broke out in 591 BC and dragged on for five difficult years. Just when it became obvious that neither side could win conclusively, an apparent miracle occurred. As the two armies hacked away at each other — astronomers later set the date at May 28, 585 BC — the midday sky darkened, and night appeared to fall. It was a solar eclipse, which had been predicted years earlier by a Greek philosopher, Thales of Miletus, but which the combatants took to be a sign of the gods' displeasure. Abashed, they laid down their spears and walked away.

Both parties were thoroughly fed up with the war in any case. So was Babylonia, which had watched its profitable Lydian trade dwindle alarmingly during the conflict. At Babylon's urging a treaty was drawn up setting the border between the two combatants at the Halys River. Then Cyaxares' son and heir, Astyages, sealed the compact by marrying the daughter of the Lydian monarch. For the first time in many generations an interlude of peace descended upon the Middle East. Power was balanced among the Medes, the Lydians, and the Babylonians. So the situation remained for some thirty-five years, until it was disrupted by the driving ambition of another Iranian leader: the vassal prince of Parsa.

Parsa had long been a minor factor in the Middle Eastern equation. Its ruling house, the Achaemenians, had owed allegiance first to the Elamites, then briefly to the Assyrians, before the Medes. But the ties to Media were particularly strong — not only because of their shared Aryan heritage but in consequence of a political marriage. Soon after Astyages assumed the Median throne in 585 BC, he arranged a marriage between his daughter Mandane and the Achaemenid ruler Cambyses, a man "of good family and quiet habits." The following year Mandane produced a son, Kurush — who in future ages would be known to the world by the Greek form of his name, Cyrus.

All kinds of fanciful stories later grew up about Cyrus's birth and early years. Some people said he was not of royal birth at all, but the son of a shepherdess and a Persian bandit. Others held that he had been abandoned in the mountains as a babe and was suckled by a she-wolf. Herodotus recorded one such tale. He related that shortly before Cyrus was born, his royal grandfather Astyages had a dream in which a vine sprouted from Mandane's loins, sending out tendrils that enveloped all Asia. The king called his priests for an explanation. They told him that the vine was Mandane's future son, who would grow up to conquer first Media, then all the lands beyond.

Astyages was determined to nip this threatening growth in the bud. He ordered his chief steward, Harpagus, to carry the newborn Cyrus into the wilderness and slay him. But seeing the child's extreme beauty and nobility, Harpagus could not bring himself to do the deed. Instead, he gave the infant to a mountain herdsman, who raised him as his own. Later, when Astyages learned he had been duped, he imposed a dreadful punishment. He ordered Harpagus's own son to be killed and dismembered, and then served him up for dinner to the father, who did not know what he was eating until the lid was lifted from the final course — his son's head.

Whatever the circumstances of his early years, Cyrus undoubtedly acquired a Persian boy's basic education, which by tradition was learning "to ride a horse, to draw a bow, and to speak the truth." In reality the curriculum was only slightly broader, including using other weapons in addition to bows and arrows, fighting on foot as well as on horseback, and survival training in the wilderness. Cyrus grew to manhood toughened by the desert life, strong with spear and bow, wise beyond his years, and charged with ambition. Succeeding his father in 559 BC, he quickly unified the tribes of Persia, which had drifted apart. To establish Persia's credentials as a civilized nation, he moved into Elam, rebuilding the old Elamite seat of Susa to serve as his administrative capital. And he soon began to show more independence than a well-behaved vassal should. He conducted a diplomatic exchange with Babylon, for instance — much to the dismay of Astyages, who saw his worst fears coming true.

Astyages' own rule, meanwhile, had become increasingly wayward and tyrannical, causing ripples of discontent among his subjects. A silent opposition began to develop among the Medes — led, understandably, by the steward Harpagus. So when Astyages sent an army in 550 BC to put down his upstart grandson, the outcome was virtually already decided. The two forces met on a bleak gravel plain near Pasargadae, the ancestral Persian capital, and scarcely had an arrow been shot before the main body of Median troops defected. Astyages was seized by his own generals and taken in chains to Cyrus. Instead of beheading his royal captive (the usual fate of a vanquished king), the Persian commander displayed a generosity in victory that would distinguish his entire career. Although he stripped Astyages of his rank and titles, he spared his life. Then he marched in triumph to Ecbatana to take charge of the Median empire.

In addition to its lands, Cyrus acquired all the institutions of the Median state: its bureaucracy of officials and scribes, its powerful army, its august protocols of kingship. He left them intact. Median officials were allowed to keep their posts, where they worked with newly appointed Persian counterparts in apparent harmony. Then Cyrus set about extending his territory farther. His first target was Lydia, the Medes' old enemy to the west. In the years since the battle of the solar eclipse, Lydia had prospered. So packed with gold were its royal treasuries that its ruler, Croesus, was seen as the personification of extravagant wealth. Perhaps this hoard was what tempted Cyrus. Or perhaps he sought an outlet to the Mediterranean. Indeed, his first step was to send envoys to the Greek cities of the Ionian coast in hopes of stirring them into revolt against their Lydian overlord.

Croesus had imperial ambitions of his own. Eyeing the lands east of the Halys River that were denied him by the old treaty with Media, he plotted his campaign. Like many a prudent monarch of that era, he consulted a soothsayer. And not just any soothsayer, but the best money could buy: the oracle at Delphi, in Greece. His emissaries arrived at Delphi with a shipload of donations that included 1,000 pounds of gold bars and statuary and all his wife's necklaces. Asked whether Croesus should go to war, the oracle's response seemed well worth the fee. He would "destroy a great empire," declared the sibyl, the priestess through whom the god Apollo spoke. The Lydian ruler never thought to ask precisely which empire the sibyl meant. Confident of victory, he marched his troops into Median territory in 547 BC.

Meanwhile, Cyrus had led his army of Medes and Persians across the northern rim of Mesopotamia. He met the enemy at the fortress town of Pteria near the Halys, where they battled from dawn until dusk with neither side gaining the upper hand. The next morning Croesus, deciding that he was outnumbered, did an about-face and retreated to Sardis, the Lydian capital. Warfare in the ancient world tended to be a seasonal activity. Armies mobilized in the spring, then disbanded in the autumn so that the conscripts could return home to tend their flocks and plant their crops of winter wheat and barley. It was now late in the year, when hostilities would normally cease. Croesus began paying off his soldiers and making arrangements for the next season's campaign. He lined up several allies — the Babylonians, the Egyptians, and the Spartans of Greece — to send reinforcements in four months' time.

Among the last and most important conquests of the Persian king Cyrus was Babylon, perhaps the world's greatest commercial center at the time. As shown above, the city's seven-storied ziggurat — recorded in the Bible as the Tower of Babel — dominated an enclosed sacred precinct located near a bridge spanning the Euphrates. Opposite the ziggurat, another huge temple housed the statue of Marduk, most esteemed of the Babylonian gods. Cyrus proved a tolerant conqueror: When he entered Babylon in 539 BC, he ordered his troops to show respect for the city's temples and religious customs.

But Cyrus had no intention of waiting. Pausing just long enough for the Lydians to disband, he marched to Sardis. He arrived so swiftly that, as Herodotus put it, "he was his own messenger." Croesus hastily recalled what troops he could and sent them to face the attackers. In the front ranks rode the Lydian cavalry divisions, famous for their courage and horsemanship, and for the lethal effect of their long, iron-tipped spears. The cavalry charged. Then, abruptly, it stumbled into disarray. For Cyrus had hit upon a remarkably effective tactic. He had mounted his cavalry on camels, and the scent of those strange beasts so terrified the Lydian horses that they turned tail and fled. After this debacle, Croesus withdrew to his citadel at Sardis. The city, a supposedly impregnable hilltop fortress, fell within two weeks. At last Croesus understood the true import of the Delphian sibyl's message. He had indeed destroyed an empire: his own.

Cyrus spared the Lydian king and even took him into his entourage as an adviser.

Leaving a governor in charge of affairs at Sardis, Cyrus then turned to deal with the Greek communities of Ionia. Earlier, when he had tried to open negotiations with the Ionians, his ambassadors had been summarily turned away. So this time he sent soldiers, who subdued each city in turn. The Persian leader never did have much patience with Greeks, in any case. They were a depraved and dishonest race, he was said to have observed, whose tawdry marketplaces were "set apart for people to go and cheat each other under oath."

Over subsequent years Cyrus consolidated his holdings on the Iranian plateau and extended his rule to the east. Having installed his cousin Hystaspes as governor of Parthia and Hyrcania, lands southeast of the Caspian Sea and just east of Median territory, he pushed on into Bactria, which much later would be part of Afghanistan. He then swung north through the Asian steppes, besting one nomadic tribe after another, and crossed the Oxus River into Turkestan. At the next desert watercourse,

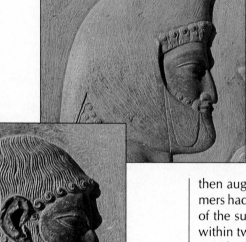

Mede

Ionian

today's Syr Darya, he called a halt. Declaring this cheerless hinterland to be his northern boundary, he built a string of fortresses to secure it. He had extended the Persian reach halfway across the Asian continent. There is an imperative of conquest suggesting that a nation, once embarked on a course of empire, must continue expanding, or else it will decline. Cyrus was not the kind of man to rest content with present victories. The most important center of Middle Eastern culture, Babylonia, still retained its independence, though it lay half enveloped by Persian territory. So Cyrus turned there next.

In the decades since its victory over Assyria, Babylonia had prospered as never before. It controlled the avenues of trade south into Arabia and west through Syria and Palestine to the Mediterranean coast. Its ancient institutions, based on a temple culture that dated back more than 2,000 years, were charged with new vitality. Its moneylenders had developed an extensive banking system, centered at first on the temple treasuries, then augmented by the private holdings of wealthy merchants. Babylonian astronomers had managed without benefit of clocks or telescopes to work out the movements of the sun, moon, and planets; one practitioner calculated the length of the year to within twenty-six minutes. The twelve signs of the zodiac, which divide the heavens into thirty-degree segments, were a Babylonian concept.

Babylon was the greatest metropolis in the Middle East, with a population of as many as 200,000. King Nebuchadnezzar, who had ascended the throne in 604 BC, had surrounded the city with massive brick walls so broad at the top that a row of houses crowned each rim, with a street between them wide enough for a chariot and four horses. The immense royal palace rose terrace above terrace like a man-made mountain, each opulent tier spilling over with ferns, flowers, and trees: Babylon's Hanging Gardens, regarded by the Greeks as one of the world's seven wonders.

But Nebuchadnezzar's death in 562 BC had brought on a period of discontent. His successor, Nabonidus, neglected state affairs and frittered away his energies and wealth on an unorthodox religious cult, that of the moon god Sin, which thoroughly alienated the powerful priesthood of the nation's chief god, Marduk. Furthermore,

Indian

Nabonidus left the capital for eleven years on a military expedition to the Arabian Peninsula. While he was gone, his religious duties — important obligations if Babylonia was to continue receiving Marduk's protection — went unfulfilled. The crown

prince Belshazzar, placed in charge, apparently was no better a national leader than his father. One evening during a palace revel, the Bible recounts, a disembodied hand wrote a warning on the wall: *Mene, mene, tekel upharsin* — "You are found wanting, your kingdom is finished." Nabonidus hurried back to resume command, but his presence did not help matters.

At this juncture the Persian armies rumbled into Babylonia. There was a bloody clash near the city of Opis, but on the whole Cyrus seems to have been greeted as a liberator. One of the nation's provincial governors, Gobryas, switched to the Persian side, and Cyrus sent him ahead to the capital with a detachment of troops. Gobryas took the city on October 13, 539 BC, "without a battle," according to a chronicler. Cyrus himself arrived sixteen days later, marching in triumph through the massive Ishtar Gate, with its great bronze doors wide open and sunlight glinting from its resplendent bas-reliefs, while a cheering populace threw garlands at his feet.

Cyrus played the conquering hero with his usual panache. Taking the title King of Babylonia, he presented himself as the nation's rightful heir, selected to rule by none other than the god Marduk. He worshiped daily at Marduk's temple, thus winning the support of the priests. He kept Babylonian bureaucrats at their jobs, entrusting them to run the nation as before. Commerce continued to thrive without interruption. The Persian king may not have dealt as generously with Nabonidus as he had with other defeated enemies. Some chroniclers said the Babylonian monarch was sent into exile to live out his days as a private citizen, but others recorded that Cyrus had him executed. The leaders of Babylonia's former dependencies hastened to Babylon to declare their loyalty to the new ruler. Among them came the kings of Phoenicia, whose powerful warships and maritime cities of the Syrian coast dominated the entire Mediterranean. They were an important addition to Cyrus's list of acquisitions. In a decade of steady campaigning, his armies had shown themselves to be unstoppable; now he was also master of a naval force whose superiority was contested by none.

Cyrus administered his expanded realm with the same tact and generosity that distinguished his moments of victory. Wherever possible he kept local governments in place, demanding only a pledge of fealty and tribute. Even as king of Babylonia he rested his hand lightly on the

The faces shown on these pages were carved on the stone facades of staircases at Persepolis, the ceremonial capital established by Darius I. These men were among a group of officials who, representing more than twenty nations, marched through the city each spring in a splendid parade held to celebrate the Persian New Year. The procession ended at the foot of the king's throne in his apadana, or audience hall, where each vassal delegation paid homage to the King of Kings.

Persian

Cilician

Scythian

Scythian offering a stallion

Bactrian leading a camel

Cilicians with two prize rams

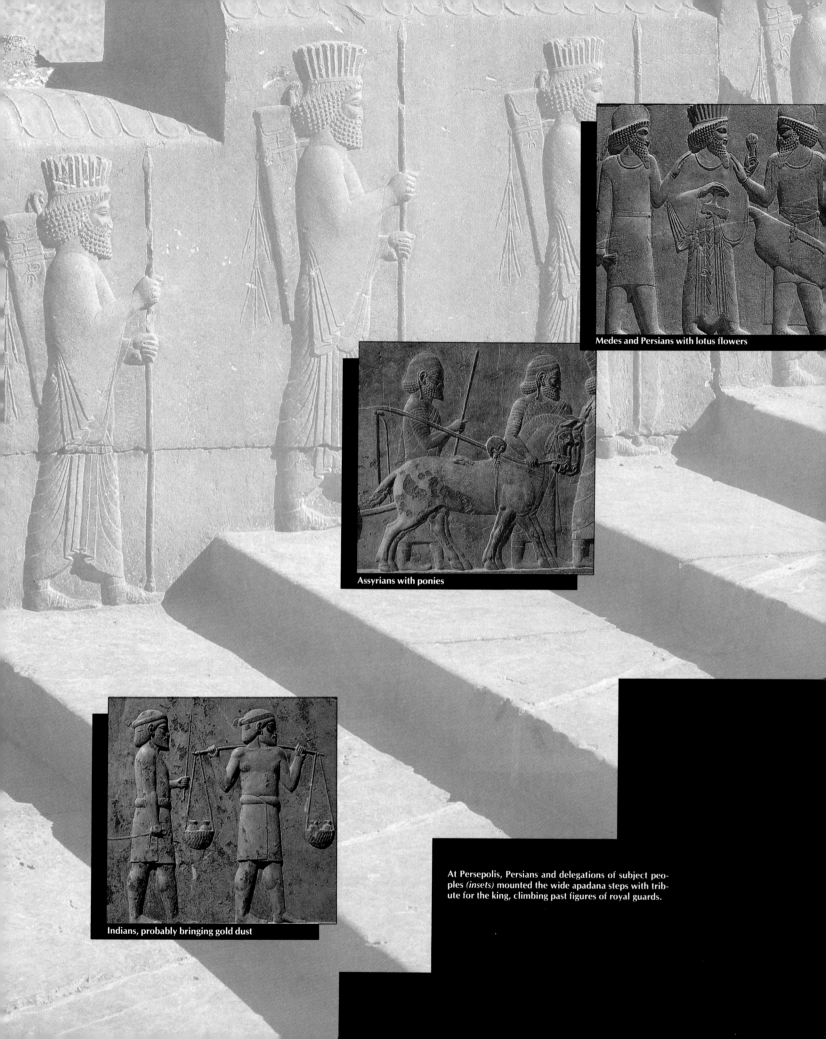

Medes and Persians with lotus flowers

Assyrians with ponies

Indians, probably bringing gold dust

At Persepolis, Persians and delegations of subject peoples *(insets)* mounted the wide apadana steps with tribute for the king, climbing past figures of royal guards.

instruments of power. In the Greek cities of Ionia, he supported local rulers who were compliant with his imperial designs. In most cases he displayed a remarkable tolerance for local customs and institutions.

Among the beneficiaries of Cyrus's enlightened rule were the people of Judah, many of whom were living in forced exile at Babylon when the Persians won control of the city. The Jews' situation was not entirely desolate. Their merchants shared in the city's humming commercial life, and Jewish scribes could aspire to comfortable positions in Babylonian government. The biblical hero Daniel was portrayed as a favorite adviser of King Nebuchadnezzar. But the exiles looked back to a time, not so many years earlier, when they had occupied their own independent kingdom in the Judean hills of Palestine. It had been a small, relatively inconsequential state, roiled by internal strife and greatly reduced from the glory days under kings David and Solomon in the tenth century BC. But it remained the Promised Land of the Hebrew people, bequeathed them by their god Yahweh, whom they had worshiped in Solomon's glittering temple at Jerusalem. "By the rivers of Babylon, there we sat down, yea, we wept when we remembered Zion," the psalmist lamented.

The vision of Jerusalem's fall retained a special poignancy. Shortly after his conquest of Assyria, the victorious Nebuchadnezzar had sent his chariots to claim the tiny nation as part of the spoils. The Jewish ruler, Jehoiakim, had resisted, and as a result was carted off to Babylon in 597 BC, along with a large number of Judea's elite. His successor, Zedekiah, continued to plot for independence. It was a foolhardy mistake, as the prophet Jeremiah was quick to point out. In thundering tirades, Jeremiah denounced the idolatry and corruption he saw at every hand and predicted the kingdom's impending destruction, only to find himself confined to prison for demoralizing the populace. But Jeremiah was right. In 586 BC, the Babylonian chariots rolled in again, this time in savage reprisal. The invaders stripped the temple of its gold, then burned it to the ground along with most of the city. Zedekiah, taken captive, was forced to witness the flogging and execution of his entire family. Then his eyes were put out and he was transported in chains to Babylon. Thousands of people from Jerusalem — men, women, and children — were also carried into exile.

ornate Lydian armbands

The Jews enjoyed full rights in Babylon, but their yearning for their homeland ran deep. It gave Cyrus the opportunity to win the loyalty of a people who could strengthen his hold over distant Palestine. In 537 BC, he decreed that the exiles could return home. Some 40,000 eventually did so, trudging the 1,000 miles from Babylon to Jerusalem with their families and belongings, determined to rebuild the city to its former glory. In their pack train they carried the gold and silver looted from the temple, which Cyrus had returned to them, along with an imperial stipend for constructing a new house of worship. For generations afterward the Jews hailed Cyrus as the Persian Messiah.

With a gratefully loyal nation settled in Palestine and his reputation enhanced, Cyrus controlled the land corridor between his Asian empire and the tempting grain lands of the Nile Valley. The way was now open to another military venture of major consequence: the conquest of Egypt. But as Cyrus was laying out his strategy, trouble erupted along Iran's northeast border.

A tribe of steppe-roaming nomads, the Massagetae, led by a warrior queen named Tomyris, was marauding along the Per-

Median bowl, possibly of precious metal

lion cub from Susa

Assyrian bowls, perhaps
silver or gold

costly Ionian yarn for textiles

Darius awaits his gifts *(insets)*, mere tokens of
larger tributes delivered directly to his treasury.

sian frontier between the Caspian and Aral seas, and in 530 BC, Cyrus hurried north to repel the raiders. It was the only battle he ever lost. He was killed, along with most of his men, and was carried back to Pasargadae, the site of his first great victory. The pallbearers laid his body in a plain stone mausoleum, which the emperor had designed himself to resemble the wooden tombs of his nomadic ancestors. For generations afterward, Persian priests sacrificed a horse at the spot each month in his honor.

The empire passed to Cyrus's eldest son, Cambyses. As governor of Babylonia under his father, Cambyses had become an experienced administrator. Now he intended to show his mettle on the battlefield. He marched south through Palestine with an imperial army that included Greeks from Ionia, troops from Anatolia and Cyprus, perhaps some Jews and Babylonians, along with his Mede and Persian regulars. A fleet of Phoenician warships probably sailed in parallel down the coast. Egypt's best general, a Greek mercenary, went over to the Persian camp with the secrets of the Egyptian defense system. And a pact of friendship was forged with the tribes of Arabia, who supplied the army with camel skins of water for their march through the Sinai desert.

The object of Cambyses' aggression — rich, ancient, deeply conservative Egypt — was itself a conglomerate of races and cultural strains. There were Greek traders living at Naucratis on the Nile Delta, Jewish emigres at Syene and up river at Elephantine, and blacks from Nubia in the southern deserts. Greek mercenaries stiffened the backbone of the Egyptian army. At the moment Egypt was enjoying renewed self-confidence and vigor. From their seat of power in the Delta city of Sais, its pharaohs had restored much of the nation's former eminence in the last century or so, since wresting independence from Assyria. Egypt held sway over the Nile Basin as far south as Napata, the old Nubian capital in the central Sudan. The coast of Libya was under its control, along with the Sinai, and the desert highlands east to the Red Sea.

The Saite pharoahs had augmented their majesty with a program of public works and other ventures. Necho II, who ruled from 610 to 595 BC, began construction of a canal between the Nile and the Red Sea. The project reportedly cost the lives of 120,000 laborers before it was finally abandoned. Necho also sent a fleet of Phoenician ships to explore the nether reaches of the African coast. The mariners headed south through the Red Sea and into the Indian Ocean, rounded the Cape of Good Hope, and after three years sailed back into the Mediterranean, having circumnavigated the continent, a stunning feat of maritime exploration. The present ruler, Ahmose, refurbished the city of Sais with monumental temples, giant statuary, and triumphal gateways. Commerce flourished, and prosperity reached new heights.

Ahmose was a brash and lively leader — "fond of his joke and glass," Herodotus reported — and in his younger days had been a skilled campaigner. But he was now an old man, and as the Persian armies approached he breathed his last. His son and successor, Psamtik III, was no match for the invaders. The Persians gobbled him up at the Battle of Pelusium in 525 BC, and once again Egypt was in foreign hands.

As victor, Cambyses at first conducted himself in the liberal tradition of his father. He honored native customs, paid homage to local gods, and employed Egyptians to administer the government. At the same time he took the title of pharaoh, a virtually godlike position that commanded the devotion of all subjects. But when he tried to expand his African territory, he began to have trouble. He first planned an assault on the Phoenician city of Carthage on the North African coast, but had to call it off when the Phoenician sailors who manned his navy refused to fight their kinsmen. When he sent a large force of soldiers to seize an Egyptian oasis in the western desert, a sandstorm blew up, and his men perished. Finally, he set his sights on Nubia, an independent black nation of the Upper Nile known also as the Kingdom of Kush.

Few northerners ever ventured into Kush, and those who did brought back tales of a wondrous race blessed with great nobility and wealth beyond measure. The people of Kush were "the tallest and handsomest in the whole world," it was said. They bathed in violet-scented fountains, feasted on nothing but meat and milk, lived to be 120 years old, and on dying were buried in coffins of dazzling crystal. Gold in Kush was so common, it was reported, that prisoners in local jails were bound in gold chains. The reality at Meroe, the Kushite capital, fell considerably short of these legends, but Cambyses never found out. As his ill-prepared army trudged south along the Nile, its provisions ran out, reducing the troops to eating their pack animals. Finally, amid reports of cannibalism among the ranks, a shaken Cambyses ordered a withdrawal.

The Great King became increasingly haughty and despotic, according to Herodotus, acting in a manner that showed he "was completely out of his mind." (Herodotus came along eighty years later and got most of his information from Egyptian priests, who were no doubt biased against the conquerer.) Cambyses was said to be subject to fits of rage: In an outburst against his pregnant wife, who also happened to be his sister, he kicked her to death. When news arrived from Persia that an insurrection had broken out, Cambyses started home to deal with the crisis. But during the journey he died from a wound that his detractors claimed he inflicted upon himself.

Following Cambyses' death, political turmoil swept Persia, and from its midst a distant royal cousin — Darius, son of the Achaemenid satrap of Parthia — rose to assume the imperial throne. To legitimize his reign, Darius inscribed the details of his succession on a bare rock face at Behistun in the Zagros Mountains. The message was written in three languages — Old Persian, Elamite, and Akkadian — and described a bizarre train of events that is partly confirmed by other sources. According to the inscription, a usurper who claimed to be the emperor's younger brother, Smerdis, seized the throne while Cambyses was in Egypt. The usurper made himself enormously popular by suspending taxes and war levies. He was also strongly supported by the hereditary Iranian priesthood, the Magi. According to one account, the real Smerdis was already dead, having been slain by Cambyses before his departure to prevent just such a palace coup. The man on the throne was a rank impostor, a near look-alike named Gaumata. What was more, Gaumata was himself a member of the Magi caste, almost all of whom were Medes. If so, his accession would have meant the end of the Achaemenid dynasty and its replacement by a Magi theocracy.

Darius moved quickly to unseat him. Striding into the pretender's camp in Media, Darius and six other Persian noblemen dispatched the attendant guards and eunuchs. Then Darius thrust his spear through the would-be emperor's heart, severed his head, and carried it outside to display to the crowd. Possession of the palace did not automatically mean sovereignty over the empire, however. Rebellion flared up in almost every province, and Darius spent nearly two years hurrying from one trouble spot to the next in an effort to establish his control. Rival kings declared their independence in Elam and Babylonia, and while Darius was dealing with them other challenges arose in the eastern deserts. Skillfully deploying his forces, balancing clemency with stern reprisals, he eventually brought the rebels to heel. He generously rewarded loyal vassals, but punishment for the upstarts was bloody and swift. When he captured a Median pretender named Farvartish, a descendant of Cyaxares, Darius cut off his nose and ears, tore out his tongue, and then had him impaled. After he restored peace in

With its lofty, fluted columns and massive, ramplike stairways, the apadana of Darius I dominated the city of Persepolis, the ceremonial heart of the Persian empire. The bas-reliefs along the staircases recorded the pageantry of the festival of the spring equinox — the beginning of the Persian year — when as many as 10,000 of the king's subjects journeyed from their far-flung nations, bearing gifts to honor him.

521 BC, the new Great King began stretching the borders of the empire, conquering northwest India as far east as the upper Indus River.

Darius was a leader in the heroic mold of Cyrus the Great, with a natural command of his people's loyalty. "Whatever I said to them, by night or day, they did," he remarked. His popularity stemmed from both his strong personality and his innate sense of justice. "I am a friend of the right," he declared. "I am not hot tempered. What things develop in my anger, I hold firmly under control. I am a good fighter." His military skill was indeed considerable, but it was as a politician and administrator that Darius's achievements were most memorable. He brought a remarkable degree of unity to the sprawling lands of the Persian empire, with their diverse languages and ethnic strains, their different laws and customs and economic systems, and their competing religions. The result was a cultural cross-fertilization and an exchange of trade goods and wealth that raised the standards of civilized life for everyone.

Administration of the empire depended on an adroit balancing act between local self-government and centralized control. Cyrus had erected the framework, with his tolerance for local usages and beliefs. But Darius expanded and strengthened it into a lasting, well-ordered governmental structure. His realm was divided into twenty large provinces, or satrapies, each run by a satrap appointed by the crown. Though Darius might on occasion name a local nobleman to the post, most satraps were members of the Persian aristocracy. Wherever possible, however, they ruled through the administrative apparatus that was already in place before the Persians took charge, and subdivi-

The wealth and splendor of the Persian kings was displayed in Persepolis's monumental public buildings, whose gold-leafed roof timbers were supported by limestone columns such as the one illustrated at left. About sixty-five feet tall, the fluted columns stood on cylindrical stone bases and were topped by massive capitals carved in the shape of bulls' heads (inset) or mythical horned lions.

sions within the satrapies tended to be governed by natives. Greeks stayed in charge of the Ionian cities, for instance, and Jews ran Jerusalem.

The satraps were more like viceroys than governors. They lived in regal style, maintained their own courts, and were supported by vast agricultural estates. They collected taxes, passed laws, and occasionally kept their own private armies. In time many satrapies became hereditary fiefs, so that their rulers became in effect subkings under the umbrella of imperial power. Having granted broad authority to the satraps, Darius devised a system to keep them in line. They and lesser local rulers were assigned Persian secretaries who monitored their actions and reported back to the emperor. A garrison of imperial troops, with a chain of command that in peacetime bypassed the satrap and ran straight to the king, was stationed in each province.

Should a satrap overstep his authority, retribution was sure to follow. Reports came back that the satrap of Sardis, a Persian named Oroetes, supported by a bodyguard of 1,000 Persian soldiers, was displaying an unacceptable degree of independence. Rather than send an army to dislodge him, Darius used a subtler tactic. He dispatched an envoy with several sealed imperial documents. Some were only routine messages, but when the envoy had the satrap's secretary read them aloud at the Sardis court, the men of the bodyguard listened to the emperor's words with obvious deep respect. Then the secretary read two imperial orders directed to the soldiers. The first bade them to quit serving Oroetes. They promptly laid down their spears. The second called for Oroetes' immediate execution. On hearing it, the soldiers drew their swords and killed the satrap on the spot.

The local ordinances of each province remained in effect, administered by native judges and officials. In some cases, the laws were codified for the first time under Persian rule. Of all his achievements, Darius was proudest of his role as protector of the law. Indeed, Persian law enforcement was renowned for its fairness, impartiality, and consistency — as the Old Testament described it, "the law of the Medes and the Persians that may not be altered."

Darius restructured the tax code on more rational lines. Vassal states had always paid tribute to the empire in the form of money or produce, but the collections tended to be haphazard, and often the sum demanded bore no relation to the nation's ability to pay. So Darius had his officials measure the agricultural lands in each region and gauge the crops over a period of years. The tax was figured accordingly, at about twenty percent of the normal annual yield. Other revenues accrued from industrial and mining tariffs, port duties, water fees, commercial fees, and sales taxes. In each satrapy, a Persian treasurer collected the money, reserved a portion for local government expenses, and sent the rest to Darius. Some of the national contributions were staggering. Babylonia paid 1,000 talents — about thirty-three tons — of silver annually, enough to support the imperial army for four months out of twelve. India provided even more: 23,760 pounds of gold dust washed from the stream beds of the Indus River tributaries. North Arabia paid with 6,600 pounds of frankincense, a resin valued for its fragrance. Only Parsa, the Persian homeland, was exempt from taxes and fees.

To speed the transport of this tribute and to knit together the margins of his realm, Darius built a network of highways that in scope ranked among the foremost engineering feats of the ancient world. Before the days of empire, travelers from one Middle Eastern city to another plodded along rough caravan trails in constant fear of bandits, blizzards, sandstorms, wild animals, and other wilderness dangers. Cyrus had begun to improve these tracks, but Darius brought the road system to completion. His most famous and heavily traveled route was the 1,700-mile royal road that led from Sardis across Anatolia and Mesopotamia to the royal capital at Susa. An army of laborers and soldiers worked year round to patrol and maintain it. Most of the road was hard, packed earth. Rough stretches were leveled, and paving stones were laid where needed. The route included seven ferry crossings, at least four heavily guarded checkpoints to keep track of who was going where, and 111 inns spaced a day's journey apart. Other highways branched out across the Iranian plateau to Bactria and India, and south through Palestine to Egypt.

If the ease and speed of ordinary travel increased under Darius, it was nothing compared with the lightning-fast efficiency of his royal messenger service, which carried documents between the satrapies and the central government. This relay system had riders and fresh horses posted at intervals along each major route. A rider would gallop from one station to the next, a distance of perhaps fifteen miles, then pass the satchel of royal mail to the next messenger. These riders set a standard of reliability

Travelers on Persia's Royal Road from Susa to Sardis arrive at a way station to refresh themselves. Situated at intervals of about fifteen miles — roughly one day's walk — these hostelries offered lodging to the messengers, merchants, and dignitaries who traveled the vast domain, and a walled corral to protect their horses and pack animals from predators.

for postal service that would still be respected two and a half millennia later, when the U.S. Post Office would base its motto on Herodotus's words about the Persian messengers: "Nothing stops these couriers from covering their allotted stage in the quickest possible time — neither snow, rain, heat, nor darkness."

Besides improving administrative control, the highway system helped generate a dramatic upsurge in economic activity. It was said that if Cyrus was father of the empire, and Cambyses its tyrant, then Darius was its shopkeeper. Darius did more than anyone to increase the realm's material well-being. He took a direct, personal interest in the details of trade and production. The most bountiful regions were the rich flood plains of Babylonia and Egypt's Nile Basin, where huge estates worked by serfs yielded bumper crops of wheat, barley, flax, millet, sesame, and dates. The landowners most often were Persian noblemen who held their acreages in recompense for service to the crown. The system had arisen over time from land payments to the armed forces: An archer was awarded a "bow" of property (the basic unit), a horseman the equivalent of several bows, and a charioteer still more. But high officials would be granted enormous domains. Often the nobles would leave these holdings in the hands of local overseers while they availed themselves of the easy pleasures of life at court.

However dilatory some noblemen may have been, the Great King turned the power of the state to boosting crop production. He sent engineers into Babylonia to renew the irrigation ditches that crisscrossed the flood plain between the Tigris and the Euphrates. In the arid reaches of the Zagros Mountains and the Iranian plateau, water for farming had to be transported from highland springs through miles of semidesert. To keep it from evaporating en route, the Persians dug long subterranean aqueducts, called *qanats*. Shafts reached down from the surface at intervals to enable the laborers to remove excavated earth and for maintenance. During Darius's reign, existing qanats were cleaned and shored up, and new ones were dug to reach additional farmlands.

The emperor was constantly urging estate owners to experiment with crops and farming techniques. He had his agents collect and forward packets of seeds from satrapy to satrapy, so that fruit trees native to the Zagros might be grown in Anatolia, and grapevines from Iran tried out in Damascus. Under Darius, rice from India was introduced into Mesopotamia, sesame into Egypt, pistachios into Syria. When Persian armies crossed into Europe they would plant alfalfa seeds from Media to obtain fodder for their horses. Doves and peacocks, both Asian fowl, would soon follow.

While fields and orchards bloomed, another kind of flowering occurred in trade and commerce. One of Darius's most fruitful reforms was to standardize the currency. For centuries, most transactions took the form of barter, goods for goods. Laborers were commonly paid in kind — so much meat, barley, wine, or olive oil for a day's work. When gold or silver was used, whether in small shops or wholesale commodity exchanges, each bar and nugget had to be weighed on a scale and assessed for purity. This cumbersome system first changed in Lydia under, appropriately enough, the wealthy Croesus, who conceived the notion of striking gold coins of uniform size and value. By Darius's time a number of other states had adopted the idea, but some currencies were of dubious worth. Darius's contribution was to prohibit the coining of gold by anyone but his royal minters, and then to impose a standard value for each coin. The so-called gold darics, each bearing the emperor's image, became the premier currency of the age, accepted without question as far away as central Europe.

The reach of the Persian coins testifies to the dramatic increase in worldwide commercial traffic during Darius's rule. Regions that had never traded with each other

before — Babylonia and mainland Greece, for example — began to do so now. With a sound common currency, a network of roads that allowed goods to move cheaply and safely, and a uniform set of weights and measures that Darius also imposed, the empire became an enormous common marketplace. From India came spices, gold, pearls, and gemstones. The mines of Anatolia shipped out silver, copper, and iron. Flax and papyrus from Egypt, textiles from Carthage and Corinth, purple dyes from Phoenicia, carpets from Iran, shields from Attica and swords from the Black Sea, timber from Lebanon and the forests of Thrace: All of these goods became widely available.

Luxury items had always been important and profitable to traders, but now improvements in transportation enabled merchants to deal increasingly in products for everyday use. Great quantities of grain were moved about by sea. Cheap textiles, leather sandals, iron tools, and household articles such as pottery and utensils were widely distributed. The benefits of trade filtered down from the wealthier classes to the artisans and farm workers. Indeed, the state was much concerned with the welfare of its poorer members, and Darius passed laws regulating working hours and wages.

With each transaction, tax money flowed into the imperial coffers. Darius used some of it to continue improving the commercial infrastructure. With his road system in place, he turned to shipping. Seaports took shape along the sweltering sand flats of the Persian Gulf. One ambitious undertaking saw the completion of the old Egyptian canal, left abandoned by the pharaoh Necho nearly a century earlier. The new channel, 90 miles long and 150 feet wide, was opened with much fanfare around 500 BC. A convoy of merchant ships from the Indian Ocean could now sail up the Red Sea, across the Egyptian desert to the Nile, and from there to the Mediterranean. The emperor also underwrote several Persian voyages of exploration: one downstream from the sources of the Indus, another into the Aegean, and one more down Africa's west coast.

And the money kept pouring in. With more wealth than even he knew what to do with, Darius began to embellish the various seats of imperial power. By this time he had not one capital but four. The original Achaemenid center was Pasargadae, on the barren plain where Cyrus had conquered the Medes and where he now lay buried. It was primarily a ceremonial site, a compound of palaces, religious structures, and lush gardens. Here Darius had been crowned king, here he married the first of his six wives — Cyrus's daughter, Atossa. The business of government took place largely at Susa, the old capital of Elam, which Cyrus had begun rebuilding. Darius continued the task with an ambitious program of construction. He designed a magnificent palace for

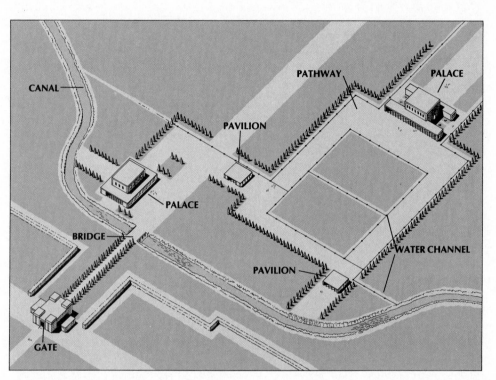

A lush oasis in the arid Persian plain, Cyrus the Great's garden at Pasargadae *(left)* was laid out in a geometric design *(above)*. More than 3,000 feet of carved limestone channels carried water through the garden, spilling into small basins every fifty feet. The channels were purely decorative; irrigation was by open ditches. Plants, chosen for fragrance as well as for appearance, included fruit and cypress trees, aromatic wild grasses, and native flowers — lilies, roses, jasmine. Pasargadae set the style for the gardens of other rich and noble Persians. For all levels of society, a garden was the closest thing to heaven; the word *paradise* comes from *pairidaeza,* Persian for "walled garden."

himself, which he had adorned with carved stone columns, rare inlaid woods, and bas-relief tiles in the Babylonian style. "A splendid work was ordered," he allowed, "very splendid did it turn out." Susa was well positioned at the empire's geographic midpoint, but in summer it became uncomfortably hot. So during the dog days, Darius and his court of mountain-bred nobles would retire north to Ecbatana, the old Median capital. Here they could hunt lions, practice their skills with spear and arrow, and attend when necessary to affairs of state.

But Darius required a city of his own devising, more distinctly Persian than Ecbatana or Susa, more lavish than Pasargadae, and imposing enough to convey the majesty and sweep of his power. The spot he chose was on the Iranian plateau some thirty miles north of where the city of Shiraz one day would stand. There a low bench of earth rose above the plain, its back to a mountain ridge, and upon this he erected the colonnades and battlements of Persepolis. The effect was as monumental in its way as Egypt's pyramids or the gardens of Babylon. Persepolis was a place of ceremony, like Pasargadae, a vast stage set for enacting the rites of imperial prestige. It was here that the vassal lords and their bearers from all parts of the realm arrived each new year to prostrate themselves before the King of Kings and deliver their gifts. The site's natural earth platform was extended and buttressed with a sheathing of cut stone, and faced with a grand double stairway. The nobles bringing tributes would climb these steps and proceed through a triumphal arch flanked by two massive stone bulls. They would cross a broad plaza, ascend more steps, and stand at the portico of the soaring *apadana*, or audience hall. Before them Darius sat enthroned, robed in purple and gold, a golden scepter in his hand, his booted feet resting on a golden stool, a purple canopy above his head. Rare unguents perfumed his manicured beard. Gold, silver, and precious stones cascaded from his neck, ears, and wrists.

Around the plaza stood palaces, barracks, and administrative buildings. There were also huge vaults, for Persepolis was one of the empire's repositories of wealth. (Susa was the other main treasury.) A force of scribes and accountants at Persepolis kept track of the swelling piles of coin, bullion, and artifacts. There were rooms full of carved gilt furniture, of gold and crystal chalices, of fine armor and costly textiles. Each piece was itemized, every disbursement recorded on both parchment and clay tablets.

The scribes kept records in several languages, reflecting the diversity of cultures within the realm. Accounts at Persepolis were set down in Elamite, since most clerks came from Susa. Written on clay tablets in cuneiform script, Elamite was one of the region's oldest tongues, with no known relation to any other. Most regular state business was conducted in Aramaic, a Semitic dialect from Syria that had become the lingua franca of the ancient Middle East. Babylonians might use their own language, Akkadian, and the court nobility probably spoke an Aryan derivative known as Old Persian. The multilingual nature of the empire could be clearly seen in the pronouncements of Darius on monuments throughout the realm. He used three languages: Elamite, Akkadian, and Old Persian. For the latter his scribes had to invent a special script, Darius's nomadic ancestors having neglected to devise a system of writing.

Whenever the emperor moved between capitals he was accompanied by a prodigious retinue of bureaucrats and court attendants. The company included a secretary in charge of administration, a chamberlain who dealt with protocol, a ceremonial cupbearer, a taster to make sure no one had poisoned the imperial dinner, a royal charioteer, a pair of noblemen who carried the royal spear and bow, a coven of Magi priests, scores of nobles and royal offspring, a cadre of military commanders, and a

THE ATTRACTIONS OF BEASTS

In the ancient world, nothing was so potent and magical as a wild animal, and in the eyes of the ancients, beasts of the field and forest came to embody characteristics of humankind. The bull, for example, was seen as a symbol of virility and power; the lion stood for kingly triumph and majesty. And fanciful beasts concocted in the imagination from elements of various animals loomed large in the spiritual realm. So magnetic were the mystical qualities of all these creatures that they became prime subjects for artists and artisans, as the images here and on the following pages demonstrate.

The Persians, and the peoples influenced by their culture, were particularly fond of portraying animals. Persian artists were inspired by the ibexes of the Median mountains, the horses and oxen that grazed in the plains around Pasargadae, and the sea creatures brought to shore by fishermen of the Ionian coast. The sculptors, whose human figures were stiff and formal, took much freer delight in their animal subjects; they portrayed creatures of the natural world in flowing motion and in exquisite detail.

The limestone head of a griffin (above), symbol of the sun, combines the features of a lion and a bird of prey. Below, a lion tears at a bull in an oft-repeated motif of Persian kings. This one appears in a bas-relief from Darius's palace at Persepolis.

Sea monsters like this beast, a Scythian clothing ornament, were regarded as embodiments of evil.

This Chinese creature, a crane with the antlers of a deer, conveyed longevity.

This gold panther inlaid with stone emblazoned the breastplate of a Scythian warrior.

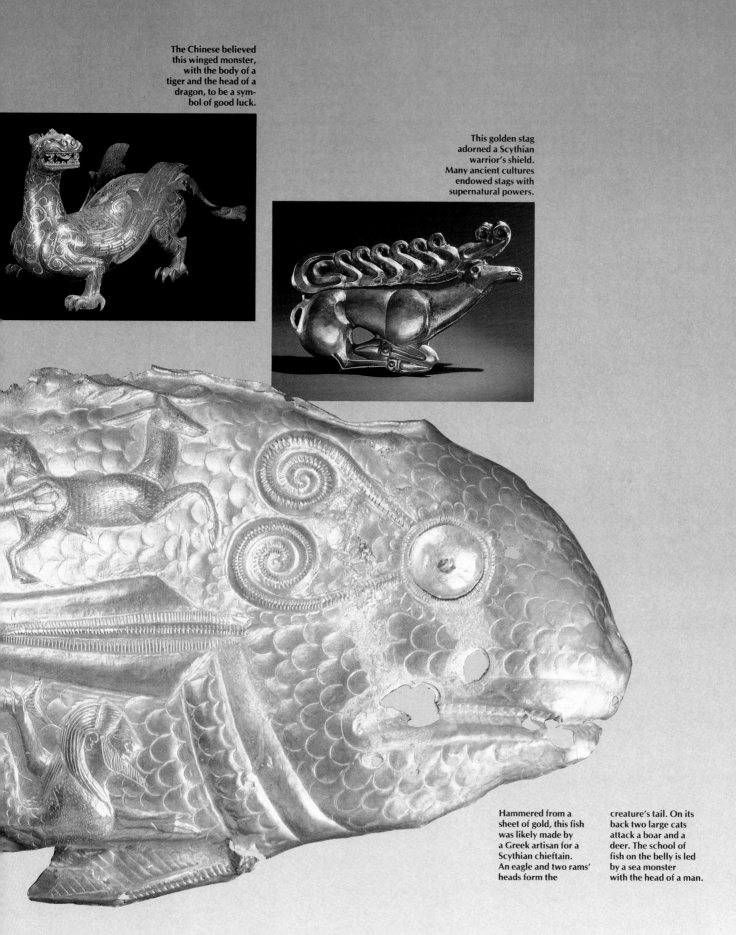

The Chinese believed this winged monster, with the body of a tiger and the head of a dragon, to be a symbol of good luck.

This golden stag adorned a Scythian warrior's shield. Many ancient cultures endowed stags with supernatural powers.

Hammered from a sheet of gold, this fish was likely made by a Greek artisan for a Scythian chieftain. An eagle and two rams' heads form the creature's tail. On its back two large cats attack a boar and a deer. The school of fish on the belly is led by a sea monster with the head of a man.

Symbolic of strength
and swift passage, these
winged horses at one
time stood atop an
Etruscan temple.

thousand-man bodyguard. The six Persian noblemen who had helped Darius slay the usurper of the throne formed an inner cabinet of close advisers. Darius might also bring along his six wives and his 360 concubines, together with the eunuchs attending them.

It was quite a departure from the empire's younger days. A generation earlier, just before Cyrus and Croesus met in battle, a wise man had warned the Lydian monarch: "You are preparing to fight against men who dress all in leather — both breeches and everything else. So rough is their country that they eat as much as they have, and never as much as they want. They drink no wine, but only water. They have no good things at all, not even figs for dessert." Now, the imperial kitchens regularly served such delicacies as roasted camel's flesh and ostrich breasts to 15,000 at a sitting. Nights were filled with singing and dancing, and the wine flowed like the Tigris in spate.

The very concept of royalty had changed. In earlier days the king was regarded as the first among equals. When Darius assumed the imperial mantle, all pretense of equality evaporated. The Great King reigned supreme, with life-and-death power over all his subjects. All property was at his disposal, although in practice it was held in fief by vassals. His body was sacrosanct. His word was law. He could do no wrong.

Persian kings — at least Darius and his successors, and perhaps Cyrus and Cambyses too — embraced a state religion. They conquered in the name of a supreme being, Ahuramazda, the Wise Lord, creator of heaven and earth — although, pragmatically, they did not require others to worship him. In the dim Aryan past Ahuramazda had been one of many nature deities, all revered without preference by the Magi priests. The rites of worship had included animal sacrifice, a fire ceremony, and the quaffing of a sacred, hallucinogenic beverage, haoma. But sometime around or before 600 BC — perhaps as early as 1200 BC — there came forth from the windy steppes of northeastern Iran a mysterious prophet who utterly transformed the Persian faith.

The prophet was Zarathustra — or Zoroaster, as the Greeks would style his name. Ahuramazda had appeared to Zoroaster in a vision, in which the god had revealed himself to be the one supreme deity, all-seeing and all-powerful. He represented both light and truth, and was creator of all things, fountainhead of all virtue. Ranged against him stood the powers of darkness, the angels of evil and keepers of the lie. The universe was seen as a battleground in which these opposing forces contended, both in the sphere of political conquest and in the depths of each man's soul. But in time light would shine out, scattering the darkness, and truth would prevail. A day of reckoning would arrive in which the blessed would achieve a heavenly salvation, while all others would find themselves roasting in fiery purgatory.

The concept of a single, all-powerful god was not entirely new. Egypt had flirted with the notion in the fourteenth century BC under the pharaoh Akhenaten, and the Jews had been tending toward it for centuries. But Zoroaster gave monotheism a powerful new impetus. And his view of moral struggle — light against darkness, truth versus falsehood — was a spiritual innovation of profound importance. In an immediate sense it may have reflected the natural animosity between a visionary reformer and the tradition-bound Magi priesthood. Zoroaster condemned animal sacrifice, for example, and elevated the fire cult to symbolic eminence as a sacrifice of purity and truth. But it was on an ethical level that he achieved his real triumph, by promoting a standard of virtuous behavior that illuminated the best years of Persian rule.

Zoroastrianism underwent many changes over time, and its essential monotheism was eroded by a proliferating hierarchy of saints and demons. Some of its rituals struck contemporaries as downright eccentric: its apparent fire worship, conducted on lofty,

37

open-air towers; the absence of the usual temples and idols; a reverence for nature so pervasive that orthodox Zoroastrians exposed their dead on mountaintops rather than pollute the earth with burial. But the abstract core of Zoroastrian belief survived intact, and deeply affected Middle Eastern religious thought. It touched the Jewish scribes in Babylon who were editing and reworking the ancient texts of Mosaic law, gave them new concepts of heaven and hell, and charged them with a new sense of individual responsibility before a single true god — ideas that later passed into Christianity.

Belief in a heavenly afterlife for good people and torment for evil-doers may have been partly responsible for the moral treatment that Achaemenid kings accorded subject nations. But since the Persians did not seek converts to Zoroastrianism, the religion was not of itself a motive for the conquests that created and expanded the empire. The impetus for Persian military adventures came from the same age-old drives — for security, power, territory, and wealth — that inspired other expansionist nations before and after the Persians. The most crucial instrument of Achaemenid expansion was the army, built around an elite corps of highly trained Median and Persian warriors known to the Greeks as the Ten Thousand Immortals — so called because whenever a man fell in combat he was immediately replaced by another, thus keeping the regiment up to strength. The standing army was much larger than just the Immortals, however. Garrisons of Persian regulars were stationed at key points throughout the realm. In times of national stress, the emperor would call up additional levies from the satrapies, native units that were organized and deployed according to their own regional methods of fighting. To supplement these, later Persian kings also used the treasury to hire mercenaries, including phalanxes from various Greek states.

By 514 BC, Darius was ready to use his mighty war machine for the purpose of imperial expansion once again. Already ruler of much of Asia and Africa, he turned his attention this time to Europe. His immediate intentions were to subdue the warlike tribes of Thrace and Macedonia and the nomadic Scythians who dwelled in the region of the Danube River. By doing so, he could gain control of the shipping lanes — and thus of the flow of grain — from the Black Sea to the Aegean. Darius assembled more than 100,000 men and 300 to 600 ships for the expedition, had a pontoon bridge flung across the Bosporus, a narrow body of water that separates the two continents, and proceeded to launch the first organized military invasion of Europe by Asians.

Macedonia submitted, and the Persian armies marched through Thrace virtually unopposed. But the Scythians were another matter. Every time Darius launched an assault, the mounted enemy would loose a devastating flight of arrows, then fade out across the plain. Furthermore, when he least expected it, guerrilla bands on horseback would thunder down from nowhere to pick off small detachments and stragglers in his baggage train. He seemed to be battling phantoms. At one point, when the two adversaries met face to face for what the Persians thought would surely be an honest fight at last, the Scythian cavalry suddenly wheeled and galloped off in another direction — in pursuit of a hare that had wandered into view.

Frustrated beyond endurance, Darius went home. But he left behind a force that maintained an imperial presence in Thrace, virtually at the Greeks' back door. In Cyrus's time the Greeks had seemed unimportant, and he had experienced no trouble adding their Ionian city-states to his empire. Now, although Greece was still a disunited region of independent states, some of those states had grown markedly in wealth and power. Greeks were a factor that even the Great King, King of Kings, would have to deal with, as Darius and his successors would find in the years ahead.

THE EMBATTLED GREEKS

Undergirding the stunning cultural achievements of the Greeks was an unsurpassed talent for warfare. Armed struggles in the ancient world depended largely on brute strength: At sea, swift galleys propelled by hundreds of oarsmen collided with shattering impact; on land, masses of infantry clashed in ferocious melees. The Greeks did not shy away from such shock tactics, but they brought to them an unprecedented level of discipline. Their galley crews pulled together with uncanny precision, and their infantrymen marched and fought as one in the phalanx, a massive formation that called for absolute steadiness on the part of each member. All this was made possible by the Greek warrior's fierce allegiance to his city and to his comrades, reinforced by a code that impelled men in battle to seek death before dishonor.

Such combative élan helped the outnumbered Greeks to repulse the Persians in a series of epic encounters *(pages 40-45)*. But once that threat was contained, the Greeks fell to fighting among themselves *(pages 46-49)* — employing stratagems perfected in the earlier conflicts.

The superiority of the Greeks at close-in fighting was made painfully clear to the Persians at the battles of Marathon and Plataea. The hoplites, as Greek infantrymen were called, had stronger body armor than their Persian counterparts, sturdier shields, and longer spears. But more to the point, they fought with machinelike efficiency in phalanxes up to twelve ranks deep, the soldiers in each rank pressing so close together that their shields presented an almost unbroken wall. Facing such a prospect, the Persians learned why the phalanx was the most fearsome engine of war known to the ancient world.

Even in defeat, however, the diverse Persian army taught the Greeks an important lesson. Throughout the conflicts, the hoplites were harried by the enemy's wide-ranging cavalry and pelted by arrows loosed by masses of bowmen. Afterward, the city-states of Greece began to recruit mounted troops, to train bowmen, and to field units of swift, light infantry called peltasts after their wicker shields, or peltae.

When Greeks began slaughtering Greeks in the long fratricidal struggle known as the Peloponnesian Wars, both sides — one led by Athens and the other by Sparta — increasingly employed cavalry and missile-launching auxiliaries. The great battle at Mantinea was largely a classic struggle between hoplites, but the siege of Syracuse was another matter. There the final Athenian defeat — one of the most terrible disasters in military annals — came largely at the hands of Syracusan archers, soldiers using powerful slingshots, and other troops flinging short dartlike spears. The lowly peltasts, once scorned by the proud hoplites, helped seal the fate of mighty Athens.

MARATHON, 490 BC

The first test of hoplite fighting power during the Persian Wars occurred on a narrow Greek plain sandwiched between some hills and the Bay of Marathon. There, a Persian fleet of 600 ships had put ashore an invasion force of about 20,000 men. Undaunted, the Athenians mobilized 10,000 hoplites and marched eastward to repel the invaders.

The Greeks first set up camp on the nearby heights, where the rugged terrain deterred the Persian cavalry. But soon the boldest of the Athenian generals, Miltiades, launched an attack.

Issuing from the hills, the Athenians formed up out of range of the Persian archers. Then, as fast as their armor permitted, they charged straight at the Persian host. This "mere handful" of attackers, so Herodotus reported, seemed to the Persians to be "bereft of their senses, and bent upon their own destruction."

To protect against a flank attack, Miltiades had thinned his center and extended his line. Now, as the furious battle began, the Persians drove back the weak Athenian center. But the phalanxes on the Athenian left and right, eight ranks deep, hammered at the Persian flanks. As a man in the first rank fell, the soldier behind him moved forward to take his place; each subsequent man in the file stepped up to fill the gaps that appeared (below). At length the Athenian phalanxes turned the Persian flanks. Wheeling inward, the Athenians then surrounded their enemy.

The Persian troops who had not been caught fled to their ships and escaped. But according to Herodotus, the Athenians had succeeded in killing 6,400 of their enemy. The Athenians lost 192 men.

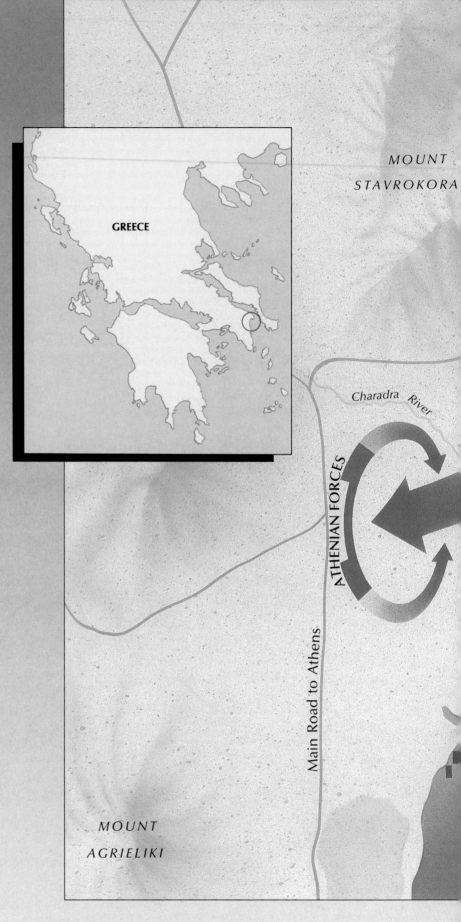

MOUNT STAVROKORA

GREECE

Charadra River

ATHENIAN FORCES

Main Road to Athens

MOUNT AGRIELIKI

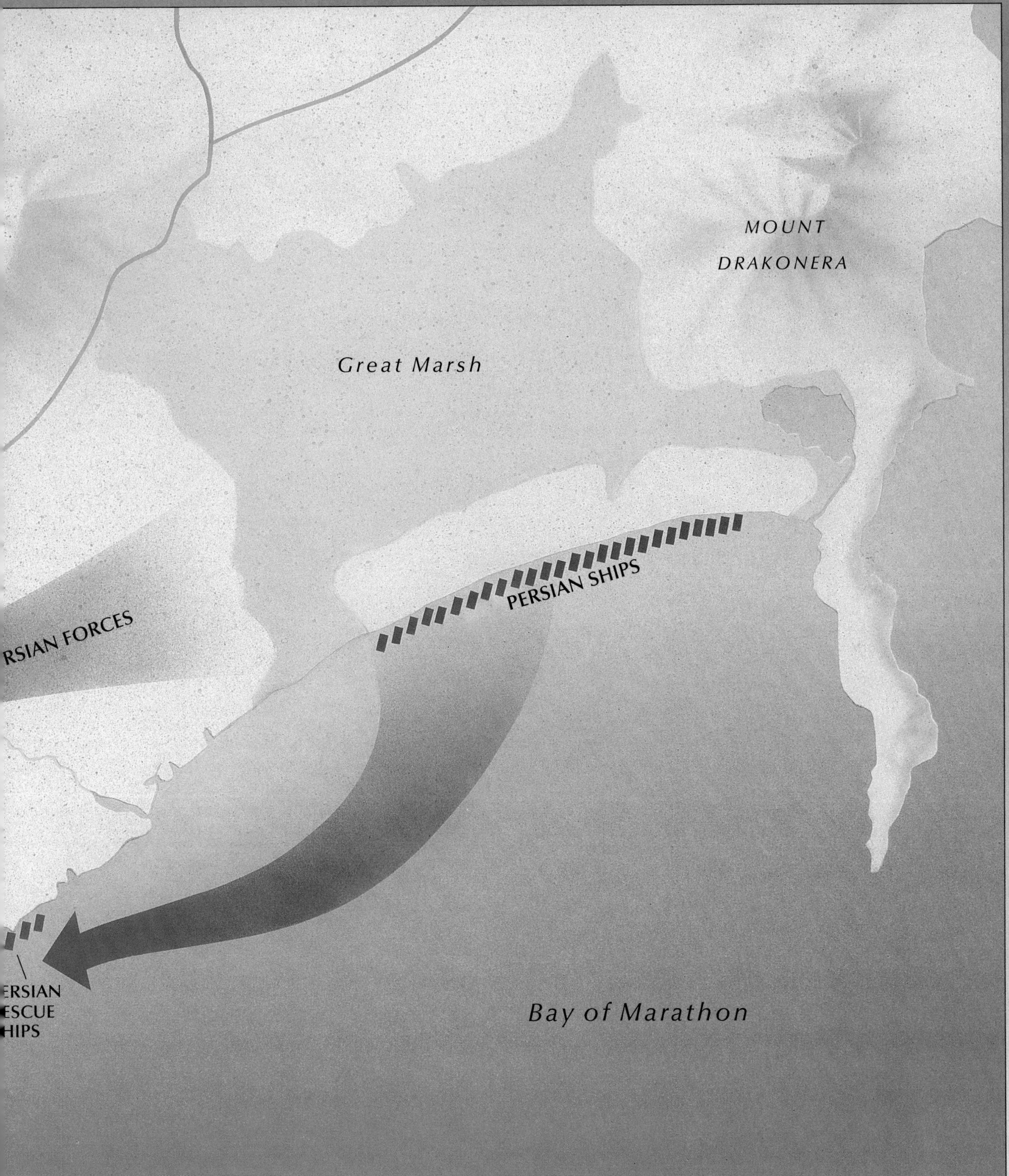

MOUNT DRAKONERA

Great Marsh

PERSIAN SHIPS

RSIAN FORCES

ERSIAN
ESCUE
HIPS

Bay of Marathon

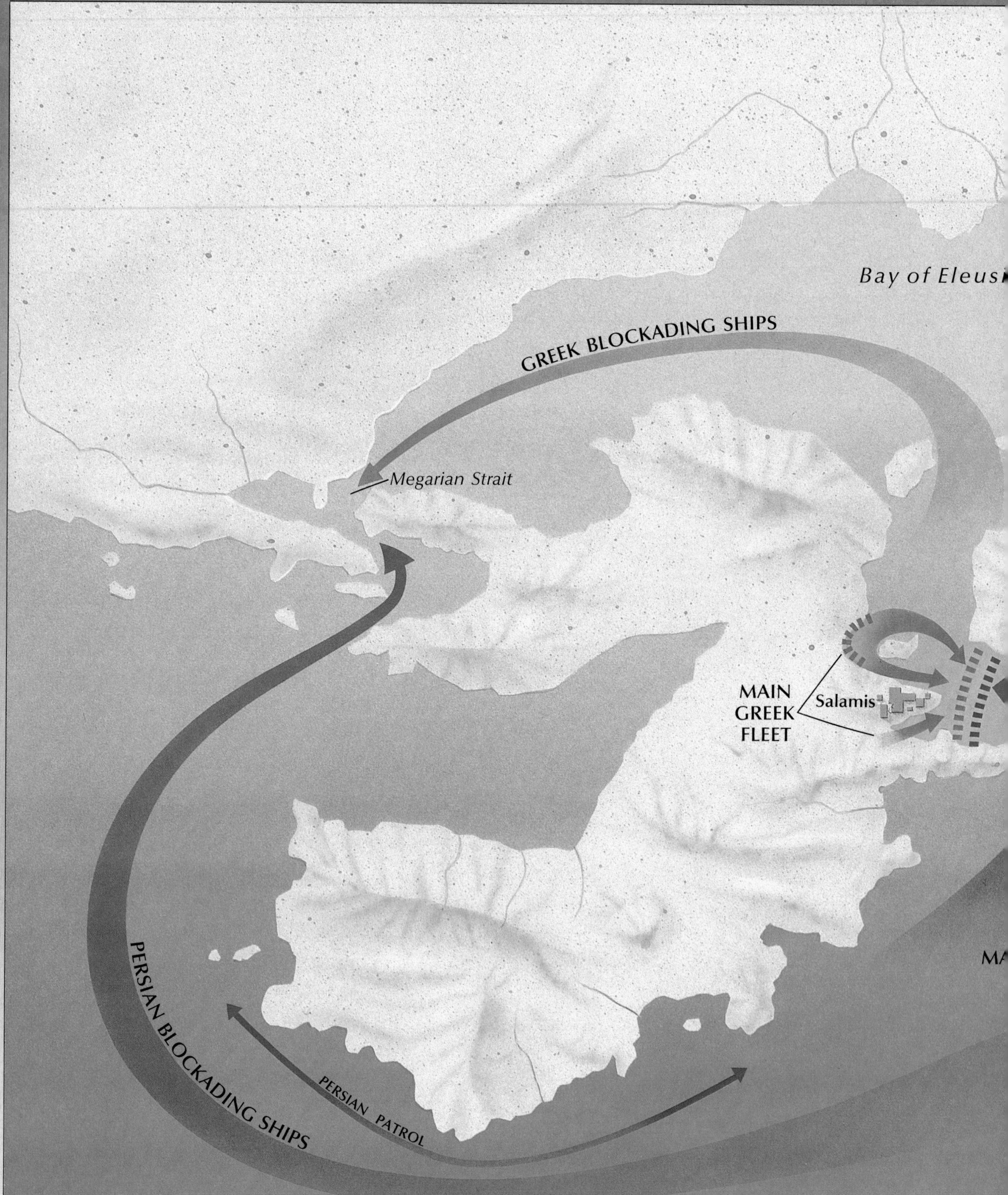

Bay of Eleusi

GREEK BLOCKADING SHIPS

Megarian Strait

MAIN
GREEK
FLEET

Salamis

MA

PERSIAN BLOCKADING SHIPS

PERSIAN PATROL

ATTICA

GREECE

MOUNT AIGALEOS

Piraeus Harbor

PERSIAN FLEET

Saronic Gulf

SALAMIS, 480 BC

The decisive naval battle of the Persian Wars began shortly after dawn on a day in late September of 480 BC when a huge Persian fleet of at least 1,000 ships — mostly triremes — advanced into the channel between the island of Salamis and the mainland of Attica near Athens. Well up the channel lay the Greek fleet of about 380 vessels, apparently trapped.

But the Greek admiral, Themistocles, had laid a trap of his own. He had beached his ships beyond a narrow neck of the channel created by a couple of rocky islets. Forced to thread their way through this bottleneck, the Persians would be unable to advance in wide battle lines. Instead they would have to attack on a constricted front.

As the vanguard of the enemy fleet squeezed through the narrows, Themistocles embarked and surged ahead on the attack. Swooping through the Persian formations, the Greek triremes rammed dozens of enemy vessels, splintering their hull timbers; or sideswiped them to sheer off the oars *(below)*. With Persian ships dead in the water, the Greeks sent troops over their sides to cut up the crews. Soon the Salamis Channel was choked with Persian hulks and dying, floundering men.

The slaughter continued as later waves of Persian vessels advanced blindly into the turmoil — and a secondary Greek assault from the Salamis harbor struck the Persian flank. When at last the surviving Persian vessels turned to run, they plowed into the main body of their own fleet, causing more wreckage. By nightfall the Persians had lost more than 200 ships, to the Greeks' 40, and the debacle was so complete that Xerxes sailed for home, never to attack Greece by sea again.

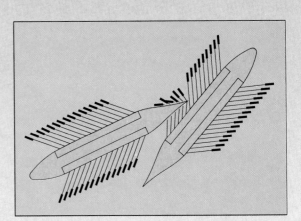

PLATAEA, 479 BC

The largest land battle of the Persian Wars erupted on the banks of the Asopos River, thirty miles northwest of Athens near the town of Plataea. There in 479 BC Mardonius, the Persian general left by Xerxes to police the captive regions of Greece, had encamped a huge force of 100,000 men, including a contingent of northern Greek allies. To meet them marched about 40,000 Greek hoplites — Spartans, Athenians, and troops from other city-states — led by a Spartan general named Pausanias.

For more than a week the main armies faced each other across the Asopos, both wary of a head-on encounter. The Persian cavalry, however, persistently harried the Greeks, destroying a vital supply train and fouling the wells the Greeks depended on for water. Lacking food and water, Pausanias called a nighttime retreat, but his troops fell into confusion. The center withdrew under the cover of darkness; the Spartans and Athenians remained in their positions. Only at dawn did they move separately from their hillside encampments into the open.

Seeing the Greek forces divided, Mardonius hurried his army across the river and attacked, his Persian archers filling the sky with arrows. His Greek allies assaulted the 8,000 Athenians, and the bulk of his forces fell on the 11,500 Spartans. For a while the Spartans crouched beneath their shields against the arrow storm, but then they rose to launch a disciplined counterattack in phalanx. The Persians were forced to cast aside their bows and grapple with the Spartans' spears. Stunned, the Persians gave ground. In the meantime, the Athenians had dealt the Greek allies a decisive blow.

Mardonius's army took flight back across the river, covered by the Persian horsemen. The Greeks caught Mardonius and killed him, then annihilated his elite guard. Finally, they destroyed the Persian camp. Although initially caught off balance, the Athenians and the Spartans — no more than 19,500 hoplites — had destroyed the Persian army as a fighting force.

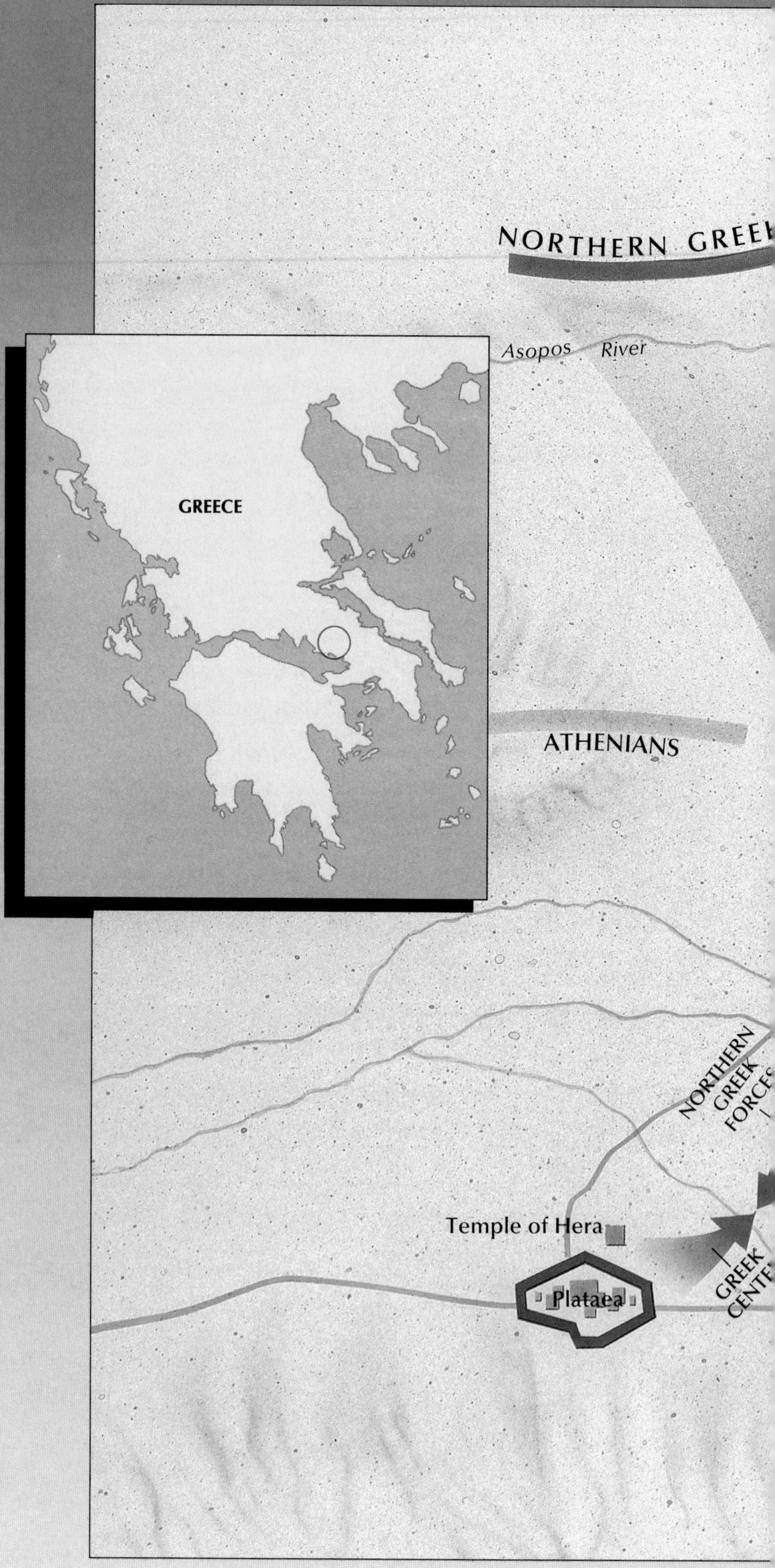

NORTHERN GREEK

Asopos River

GREECE

ATHENIANS

NORTHERN GREEK FORCES

Temple of Hera

Plataea

GREEK CENTER

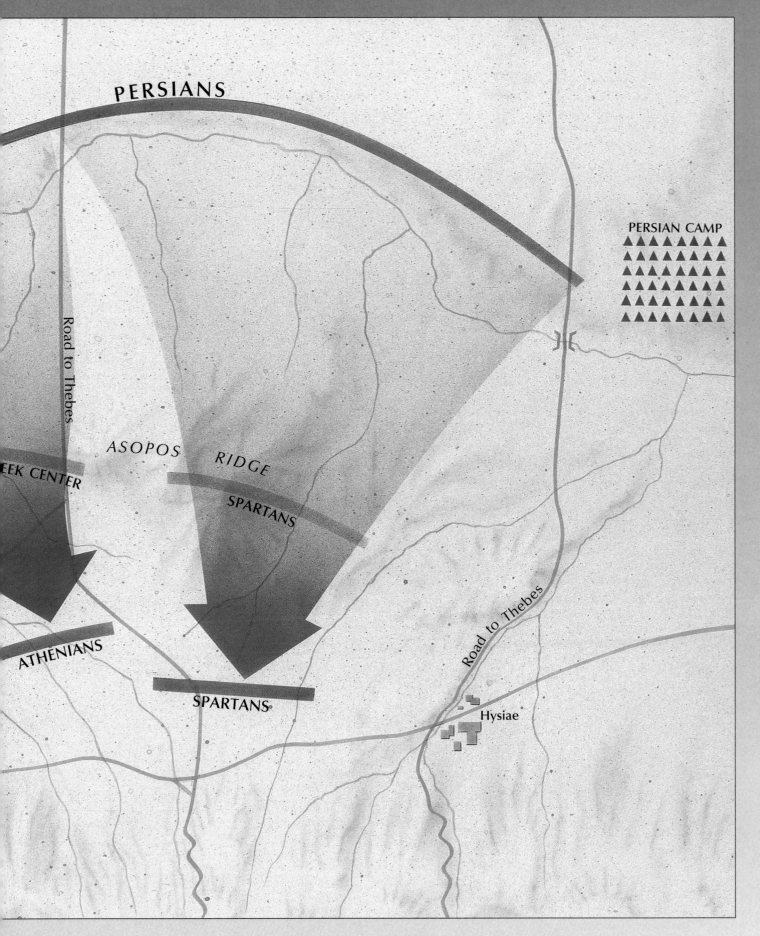

PERSIANS

PERSIAN CAMP
▲ ▲ ▲ ▲ ▲ ▲ ▲
▲ ▲ ▲ ▲ ▲ ▲ ▲
▲ ▲ ▲ ▲ ▲ ▲ ▲
▲ ▲ ▲ ▲ ▲ ▲ ▲
▲ ▲ ▲ ▲ ▲ ▲ ▲
▲ ▲ ▲ ▲ ▲ ▲ ▲

Road to Thebes

ASOPOS RIDGE

EEK CENTER

SPARTANS

ATHENIANS

Road to Thebes

SPARTANS

Hysiae

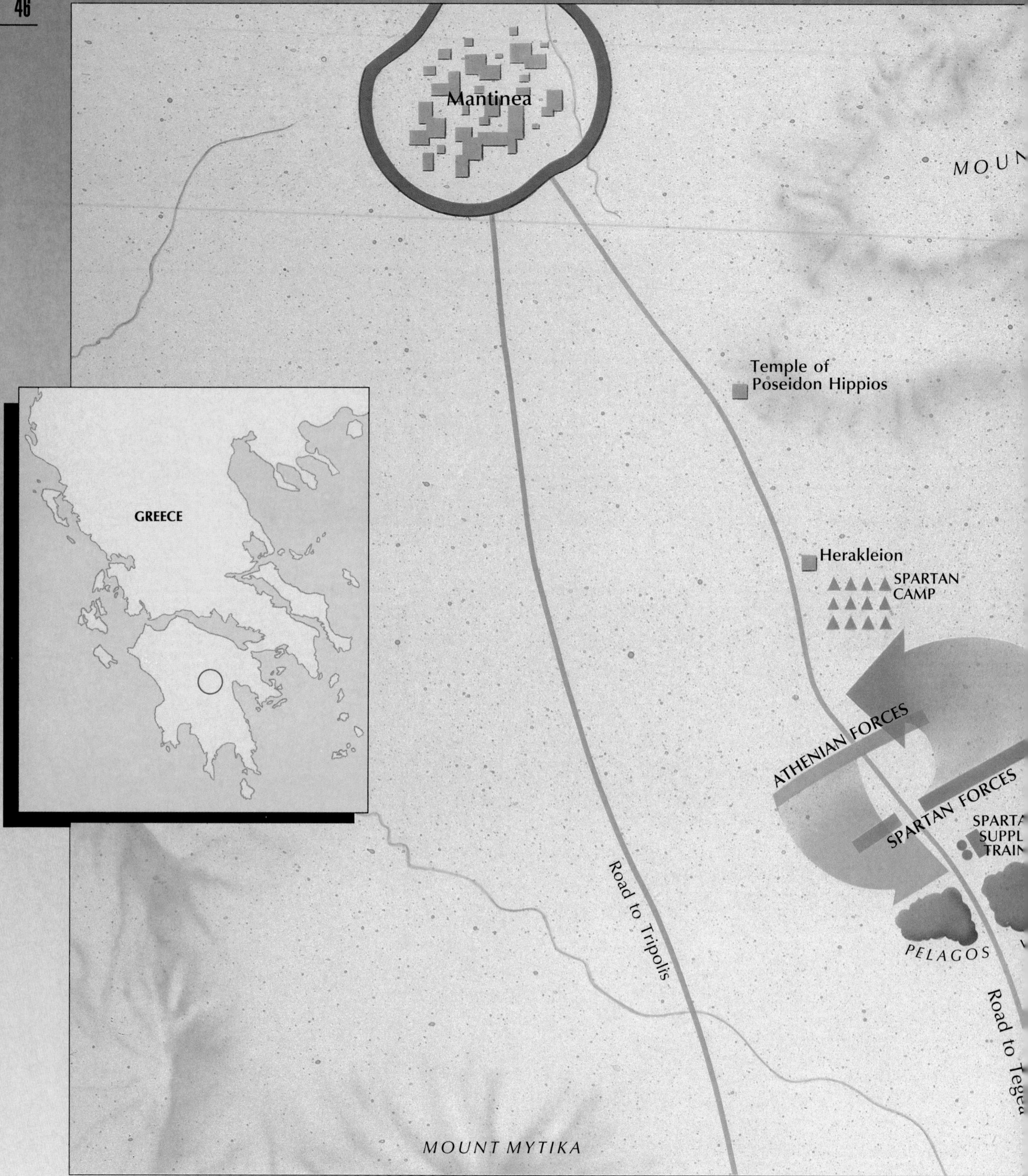

Mantinea

GREECE

Temple of
Poseidon Hippios

MOUN

Herakleion

SPARTAN
CAMP

ATHENIAN FORCES

SPARTAN FORCES

SPARTA
SUPPL
TRAIN

PELAGOS

Road to Tripolis

Road to Tegea

MOUNT MYTIKA

MOUNT STRAVOMYTI

MANTINEA

In the summer of 418 BC, the Athenians managed to muster an army large enough to challenge Sparta, which had dominated the land fighting in the Peloponnesian War. Assembling in Mantinea, a friendly city-state, the Athenian coalition troops collided violently with the Spartan army.

Initially, the 9,000-man Athenian force took a safe position on the lower slopes of Mount Alesion, facing 10,500 Spartan hoplites. But then the Spartans withdrew to the south, vanishing beyond the hills. Fearing that the Spartans were escaping, the Athenian leaders marched their men down into a dusty plain, intending to follow.

The next day, however, the Spartans suddenly returned and, seeing the Athenian force drawn up, swiftly deployed for battle, massing in a formidable front about 1,400 shields wide and eight ranks deep. The Athenians nevertheless attacked — and nearly crushed their enemies. Hoplite formations engaged in battle tended to edge to the right because each soldier naturally sought to protect his own exposed right side behind his the shield of his neighbor. Taking advantage of a Spartan drift to the right, some Athenian troops and the Mantinean allies fell upon the exposed Spartan left, destroying it.

But the victorious attackers failed to follow up their success. Instead, they broke ranks and ran to capture the Spartan baggage train in the rear.

The tightly disciplined Spartans profited by the reprieve. Seeing the threat to their own left evaporate, they hammered in turn at the Athenian left, making a huge wheeling movement across the plain. As towers of choking dust rolled up, the Athenians first faltered, then fell back, and finally fled. The Spartan army did not pursue the beaten foe far; nonetheless, they killed about 1,000 Athenians. Spartan dead totaled no more than 300. Never again did Athens or its allies challenge Sparta on land.

SYRACUSE, 416-413 BC

In laying siege to Syracuse, a rich prize on the island of Sicily, the Athenians attempted to build a great wall around the city. The wall was a formidable bulwark: a double rampart of stone and wood roofed over to give the defenders a fighting platform and punctuated by towerlike strongpoints *(below)*. Soon it stretched from Syracuse's harbor up onto the Epipolae Plateau, a height that commanded the city. No Syracusan column would have been able to shatter such a wall and break out, and no relieving column sent by Syracuse's allies would have been able to break in and lift the siege.

But the Athenian general, Nicias, failed to move swiftly enough to extend the rampart across the plateau and down to the sea to surround the city. Exploiting this failure, the general Gylippus, sent by Sparta to help the Syracusans, marched a relief column of irregular troops across the unwalled section of the plateau and into the city. There he reorganized Syracuse's army, and soon led it in an attack that destroyed Fort Labdalum, the Athenians' main supply base. Then Gylippus craftily built a wall of his own, which cut across the end of the Athenian rampart and made its completion impossible.

Their initiative lost, the Athenians at Syracuse suffered a string of defeats. A naval battle destroyed the Athenian fleet. In a confused night battle, the Athenians killed more of their own men than they did the enemy. When at last the Athenians decided to abandon the siege and retreat, Gylippus hounded them with cavalry and light troops called peltasts. In September 413, the remnants of Nicias's army surrendered; he had lost about 45,000 men in the war. "This was by far the greatest reverse that ever befell an Hellenic army," reported the historian Thucydides, adding that the men had "suffered evils too great for tears."

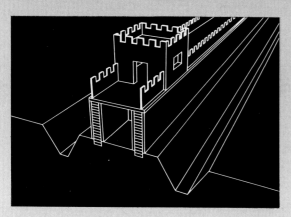

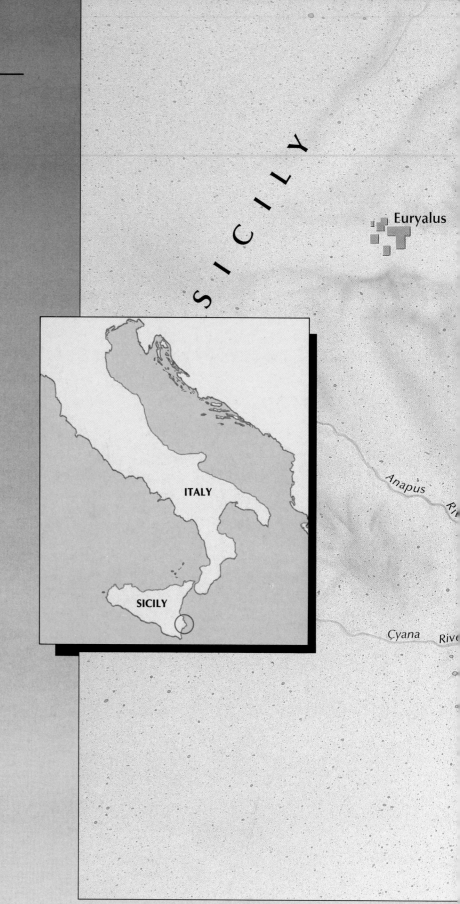

Euryalus

SICILY

ITALY

SICILY

Anapus River

Cyana River

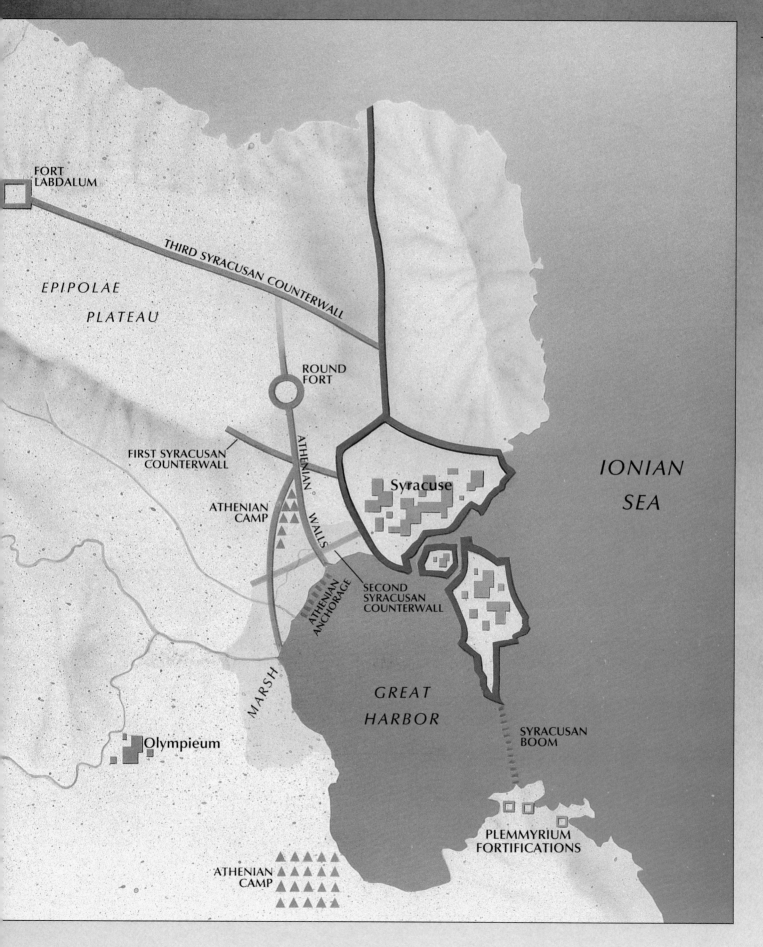

FORT
LABDALUM

EPIPOLAE

PLATEAU

THIRD SYRACUSAN COUNTERWALL

ROUND
FORT

FIRST SYRACUSAN
COUNTERWALL

ATHENIAN
CAMP

ATHENIAN WALLS

Syracuse

IONIAN

SEA

ATHENIAN
ANCHORAGE

SECOND
SYRACUSAN
COUNTERWALL

MARSH

GREAT

HARBOR

Olympieum

SYRACUSAN
BOOM

PLEMMYRIUM
FORTIFICATIONS

ATHENIAN
CAMP

THE HELLENIC UNFOLDING

One day in the mid-sixth century BC, a wandering Greek sage appeared at the court of Croesus, said to be the richest man on earth. The Lydian despot received the visitor hospitably, and even showed him the royal treasure chambers.

"Now tell me," the monarch demanded, "you have journeyed far and seen much. Who is the most fortunate man you have ever met?"

"Why, Tellus of Athens," the visitor replied.

Croesus was taken aback. Who was this Tellus to be more fortunate than Croesus himself? And so the sage explained. Tellus had been a free citizen of Athens, a well-governed Greek city-state. His sons were brave and virtuous, and they had given him many fine grandchildren. Then, after a long and productive life, Tellus had died in heroic battle for his fellow Athenians, who remembered him with honor and gratitude. What more could any man want?

What indeed? The visiting sage, who by tradition was the great Athenian lawgiver, Solon, undoubtedly felt a special bond to his countryman. But his message was meant to be universal. Honor and virtue count more than material wealth: Better to be a private Greek citizen than the most powerful monarch. For wealth and power can vanish overnight — as Croesus would soon discover — and the sum of a man's good fortune can never be known until his days have ended.

Such were the currents of belief that distinguished the several hundred independent Greek states, or poleis, scattered around the Aegean world. In geographic terms, these states were decidedly unimpressive. The Greeks — or Hellenes as they called themselves — scratched a livelihood with much toil from the mostly dry, stony soil of the region. No Greek polis was much larger than a middling Asian town, and most were tiny. The island of Kea, for example, encompassed scarcely fifty square miles yet was divided into four separate states. Moreover, the Greeks were notoriously contentious, constantly bickering and marching into battle over bits of territory or obscure points of prestige.

Yet they were unlike any other people of their age. No other society had such a keen awareness of individual worth or such a belief in what humans could accomplish. Passionate, proud, self-reliant, the Greeks were infused with a vitality of spirit that defied all odds. At the same time, they could be the most rational of people. "All things were chaos until Mind came to set them in order," wrote a sixth-century philosopher from Ionia. His observation permeated every aspect of Greek life.

Greek legend was replete with heroes who overcame their enemies through superior wit, such as the wily Odysseus, whose hollow wooden horse carried soldiers through Troy's impregnable gates. But the Hellenic intelligence reached much further than mere cleverness. The Greeks exhibited a wide-ranging, clear-minded curiosity about all creation: the gods, nature, and particularly themselves. "Wonders are many," wrote the playwright Sophocles, "and none is more wonderful than man."

Such was the rare combination of traits — individual pride, abundant energy, mental agility — that made up the unique Aegean psyche. In the next two centuries, it would carry the Greeks to unprecedented heights, producing the most remarkable civilization the world had yet witnessed. Athenian statesmen would transform the art of political organization. Greek generals would win extraordinary victories. Greek poets, architects, painters, and sculptors would open up new avenues into the human soul. And Greek inquiry into science and philosophy would change the very structure of human thought.

None of this was evident in the first years of the sixth century BC. The Aegean lands had only begun to recover from half a millennium of darkness following the collapse of the Mycenaean empire. Yet the spark of civilization had never quite died; the inhabitants slowly reestablished themselves in independent farming communities that then gave rise to new city-states. Commerce revived, and a taste for fine craftsmanship again took hold. The long-forgotten art of writing was rediscovered, and philosophic examination was kindled, particularly in the Greek communities of Ionia, on the coast of Asia Minor.

By 600 BC, the Aegean was firmly in the hands of Greek-speaking city-states of varying size and affluence. Hellenic colonies had sprung up as far west as Spain, south along the Mediterranean coast of Africa, and north past the Hellespont to the shores of

By 600 BC, the islands and peninsulas of the Aegean Sea were abounding with Greek-speaking settlements linked by trade and culture. The scope of this Hellenic civilization was vast — Greek colonies had been established as far west as Sicily and present-day Marseilles — but many of its most important city-states were situated in a relatively compact area around the Gulf of Corinth. Chief among these mainland powers were Athens, in Attica, and Sparta, on the Peloponnesus. Traditional rivals, the two states united around 490 BC to lead the Greeks against the oncoming Persians, only to renew their feud with a vengeance before the century was over.

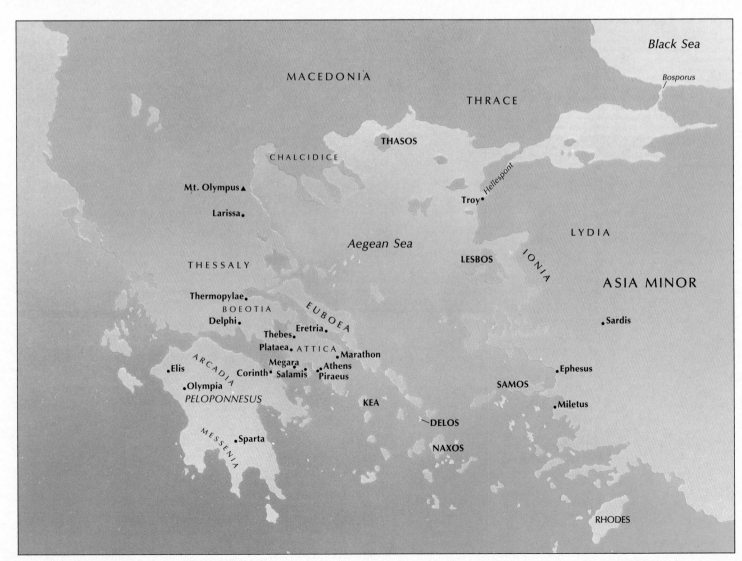

the Black Sea. While each community was fiercely jealous of its independence, all shared a common pride of heritage. The strongest bond was language. All Greeks loved the sound of their Hellenic tongue and would sit for hours raptly attentive to the cadences of a poet, or revel in endless debate in the village marketplace. Their language was an instrument of great flexibility and precision, capable of expressing the most sweeping abstractions, and also of imparting the finest shadings of meaning and emotion.

Another unifying element was the legacy of the eighth-century Ionian poet Homer. Greek youths everywhere were instructed in the *Iliad* and the *Odyssey,* with their tales of adventure and heroism, and their wonderfully human portraits of the Olympian gods and goddesses. These works came to serve as both epic and bible, providing each generation with a vivid ideal of manly prowess set in a framework of religious belief. ''My father, anxious that I become a virtuous man, made me learn all Homer's poems,'' wrote one Athenian.

The gods and goddesses in Homer's pantheon dwelled atop Mount Olympus in Macedonia. Twelve in all, they resembled nothing so much as an ordinary Greek family elevated to divine status and accorded certain powers over humans and nature. At the head sat the sky deity Zeus, king of the gods and defender of human liberty. Hera, his queen, reigned as patroness of women and marriage, while various celestial siblings and offspring had responsibility for other sectors. All Greeks acknowledged the Olympians' supremacy — though in a manner that must have struck other cultures as oddly irreverent. While the Babylonians might prostrate themselves before Marduk, the Egyptians before Osiris or Hathor, the Greeks worshiped standing upright, as befitted their sense of self-esteem. They believed that gods and humans were of the same race, that both drew their breath from Mother Earth. In addition to the Olympians, numerous other deities influenced the Greeks. Each household paid homage to a special set of family gods and heroes, and each city raised a temple to its own divine patron, often a pre-Hellenic nature spirit that had taken on Olympian garb. Athens held a major festival every four years honoring Pallas Athena, goddess of wisdom and the city's legendary founder.

Certain religious fetes drew participants from all over the Hellenic world and, characteristically, the festivals took the form of competitions. Most famous were the Olympian games, which had been founded in 776 BC at Elis on the Peloponnesian peninsula and were held every four years thereafter for the next twelve centuries. There were footraces, chariot races, boxing and wrestling matches, archery contests, and javelin throws, along with processions and sacrifices in honor of Zeus, to whom the games were dedicated. The games brought great honor to the contestants. The winner of an event, crowned with laurel leaves, would return in triumph to his polis, where a special gate might be cut through the city walls to give him entrance. Sometimes he was granted the privilege of dining without charge for the rest of his life in the town hall, along with his city's leading public officers. An Olympian victory was said to bring higher acclaim to a city than victory in battle; so important were the games that in Olympian years, armed conflict between rival states was suspended.

Within the common Greek heritage, each region or city tended to develop its own strongly marked character. The terrain itself engendered differences. Thessaly, with its extensive plains and fertile soil, was rural and conservative in outlook. The natives of Thebes, in the cattle country of Boeotia, were known for their love of tradition and their hard-headed business sense — though to their neighbors, the nimble-witted Atheni-

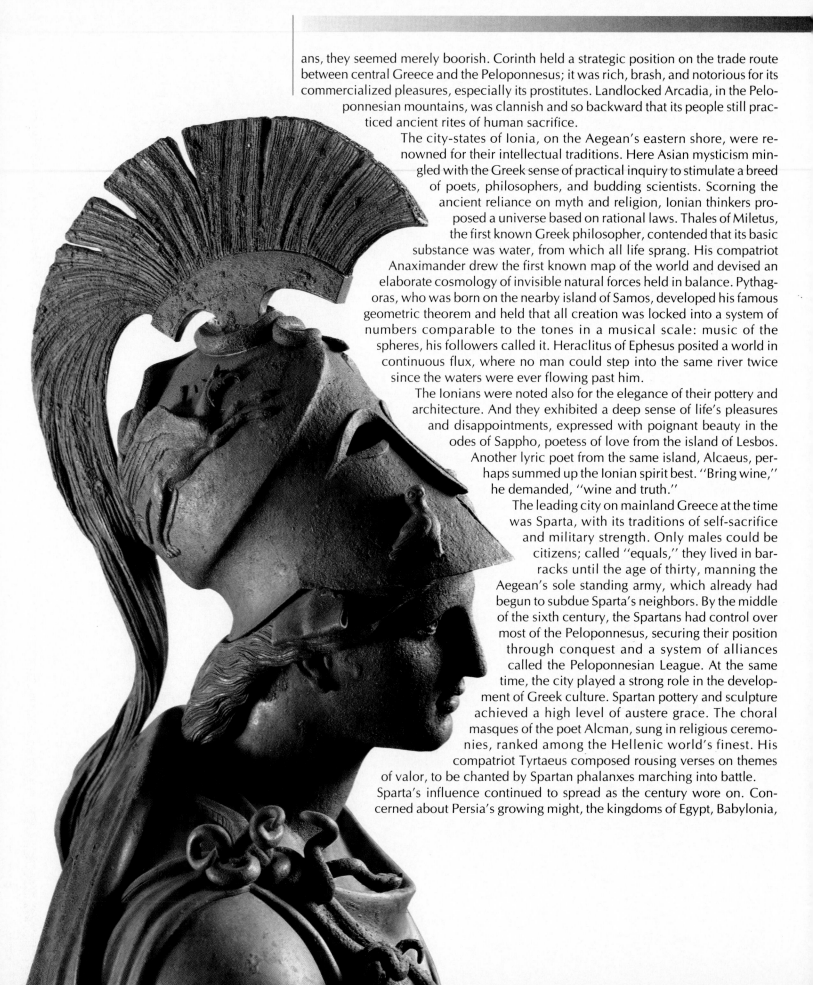

ans, they seemed merely boorish. Corinth held a strategic position on the trade route between central Greece and the Peloponnesus; it was rich, brash, and notorious for its commercialized pleasures, especially its prostitutes. Landlocked Arcadia, in the Peloponnesian mountains, was clannish and so backward that its people still practiced ancient rites of human sacrifice.

The city-states of Ionia, on the Aegean's eastern shore, were renowned for their intellectual traditions. Here Asian mysticism mingled with the Greek sense of practical inquiry to stimulate a breed of poets, philosophers, and budding scientists. Scorning the ancient reliance on myth and religion, Ionian thinkers proposed a universe based on rational laws. Thales of Miletus, the first known Greek philosopher, contended that its basic substance was water, from which all life sprang. His compatriot Anaximander drew the first known map of the world and devised an elaborate cosmology of invisible natural forces held in balance. Pythagoras, who was born on the nearby island of Samos, developed his famous geometric theorem and held that all creation was locked into a system of numbers comparable to the tones in a musical scale: music of the spheres, his followers called it. Heraclitus of Ephesus posited a world in continuous flux, where no man could step into the same river twice since the waters were ever flowing past him.

The Ionians were noted also for the elegance of their pottery and architecture. And they exhibited a deep sense of life's pleasures and disappointments, expressed with poignant beauty in the odes of Sappho, poetess of love from the island of Lesbos. Another lyric poet from the same island, Alcaeus, perhaps summed up the Ionian spirit best. "Bring wine," he demanded, "wine and truth."

The leading city on mainland Greece at the time was Sparta, with its traditions of self-sacrifice and military strength. Only males could be citizens; called "equals," they lived in barracks until the age of thirty, manning the Aegean's sole standing army, which already had begun to subdue Sparta's neighbors. By the middle of the sixth century, the Spartans had control over most of the Peloponnesus, securing their position through conquest and a system of alliances called the Peloponnesian League. At the same time, the city played a strong role in the development of Greek culture. Spartan pottery and sculpture achieved a high level of austere grace. The choral masques of the poet Alcman, sung in religious ceremonies, ranked among the Hellenic world's finest. His compatriot Tyrtaeus composed rousing verses on themes of valor, to be chanted by Spartan phalanxes marching into battle. Sparta's influence continued to spread as the century wore on. Concerned about Persia's growing might, the kingdoms of Egypt, Babylonia, and Lydia all entered into alliances with the powerful Greek city-state. Looking to its own eastern defenses, Sparta began to depose the rulers of potentially dangerous island-states and to install governors favorable to its interests. Samos fell, then Naxos and Thasos. Most of the rulers toppled by the Spartans were unpopular autocrats, and Sparta gradually came to be seen as a champion of liberty against the rule of tyrants.

Tyranny — in the sense of power vested in a single, absolute ruler — was a relatively new form of government in Greece and not in all cases an evil one. Most Aegean cities in earlier centuries had been ruled by groups of landed aristocrats, oligarchs who would meet in council to discuss policy, draw up laws, dispense justice, and settle differences among themselves. The system had evolved from the old tribal confederations of Homeric times, and it still prevailed in Sparta and in many other states. But growing internal pressures were beginning to destabilize a number of city-states. The aristocrats naturally tended to run the government to their own advantage, with the result that they waxed ever richer and more powerful at the expense of lesser folk. In Sparta, for example, where equals numbered fewer than 10 percent of the population, most inhabitants were either serfs, called helots; petty tradespeople; or small farmers with no political rights. Only the disciplined strength of the Spartan warriors served to suppress their aspirations. Yet populations were increasing, and the growing mass of commoners without prospects inevitably led to chaos.

In city after city, ambitious men seized the opportunity to ride the crest of discontent, evict the oligarchs, and install themselves as sole rulers, or tyrants. Usually an aristocrat himself, the tyrant often found it expedient to court the commoners with land

The goddess Athena, portrayed at left with a plumed helmet and a mantle writhing with snakes, was revered by the Greeks as the benefactor of all resourceful individuals. Among those she watched over was the mythic hero Odysseus, whose thirst for adventure was surpassed only by his talent for survival. At right, in a vase painting based on Homer's *Odyssey,* the homeward-bound Odysseus, having stopped the ears of his crewmen with wax, stands lashed to the mast of his galley so that he can hear the haunting song of the birdlike sirens without being lured to his doom. On returning safely to his native shore, Homer's hero raised a prayer of thanks to his patron, "great Athena, Zeus's daughter, who gives the winning fighter his reward!"

grants and public works. And while some tyrants were brutal and repressive, many others sought to rule fairly and wisely. Overall, the tyrants imposed a sorely needed political stability on their domains. Nonetheless, all tyrannies were dictatorships, and many upper-class Greeks saw them as an affront to their cherished privileges.

If the usual response to social unrest was tyranny, one city — Athens — stepped out boldly in another direction. Athens was the central city of Attica, a mountainous tract of 1,000 square miles jutting into the Aegean northeast of Corinth. The region suffered from all the social ills of its neighbors — an entrenched aristocracy, a growing populace of angry commoners, extremes of wealth and poverty. But the Athenians were endowed with a strength of character notable even among the strong-minded Greeks. Perhaps this was because of Attica's poverty of resources — a land so largely barren, with only a few coastal pockets suitable for growing wheat, that it could barely feed its inhabitants. Perhaps it was a result of Athens's unique geographic position, poised between the conservative bastions of mainland Greece and the more progressive influences of Ionia. Whatever the reason, the Athenians approached life's problems with a resilient energy and an innovative restlessness that epitomized the Greek spirit. "They prefer hardship and activity to peace and comfort," a Corinthian said. "They are by nature incapable of either living quietly themselves, or of allowing anyone else to do so."

Over the next two centuries, this Athenian energy would lift the city from obscurity into the front rank of Greek states, to rival Sparta for leadership of the Hellenic world. The contest would be joined on the playing fields of Olympia and on the battlefield, against a backdrop of looming menace from the Persian empire to the east. In the process, Athens would create a new form of government and set off a cultural explosion that reverberates to this day throughout the Western world.

The city faced severe problems as the sixth century opened. The worst was a deepening rift between the various classes of society. Since ancient times the state had been controlled by a few noble families, who claimed descent from the region's original tribal clans. Because the right to hold office required noble birth, commoners became second-class citizens, denied participation in government. At the same time, an increasingly large group of the poorest inhabitants enjoyed no political rights whatsoever. Some had come as immigrants from other states; some were slaves. While a few noncitizens might grow rich through trade or manufacture, most lived in desperate poverty. A tenant farmer had to hand over a great part of his crop to the landlord; what remained was scarcely enough to fend off starvation. Many Athenians were forced to borrow to feed themselves and their families. As collateral they would pledge their personal freedom. When a debt came due, and a debtor could not pay, he became the creditor's slave, an intolerable disgrace for any free-born Athenian.

The statesman who addressed this problem was none other than Solon — the traveling sage who had so proudly informed Croesus of the meaning of Athenian liberty. Solon was a man of wide accomplishment: poet, general, masterful politician. In 600 BC, he had led Athenian armies to victory against the neighboring Megarians, recapturing the key coastal island of Salamis. Six years later he was named chief archon, the state's highest official. From this exalted position, he drew up a new constitution and launched a program of social reform. All debts were canceled or reduced; all debtor-slaves freed. The Athenian civil code, laid down a generation earlier by the magistrate Dracon, had been harsh in the extreme: A person could be put to death for stealing a

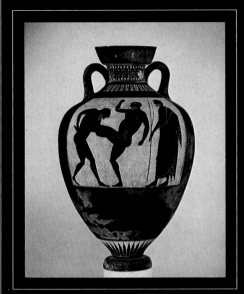

Fiercely competitive, the Greeks delighted in athletic contests and hailed victors with a pomp that in other lands was reserved for royalty. A winner at the Olympian games, held near Elis on the Peloponnesus, was escorted from the arena to the nearby temple of Zeus by a throng of spectators. At the shrine, he would stand before the image of the god to receive his wreath — a garland of olive leaves, attached to a slim headband. Those who wore the garland tasted immortality: Poets sang their praises, sculptors captured their form. So rich was the adulation that the playwright Euripides protested: "Crowns should be given to the good and wise, to him who guides his city best."

Glory was not all that accrued to the prize athlete. The Athenian leader Solon was said to have offered 500 drachmas — a small fortune in those days — to anyone from his polis who won an Olympian crown. And at the city's Panathenaic games, victors received up to 100 amphorae painted with scenes of the event *(above)* and filled with olive oil.

REWARDS OF THE PLAYING FIELD

HURLING THE JAVELIN

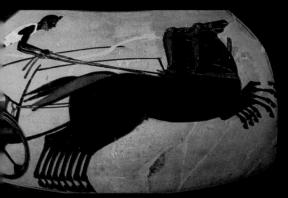

A CHARIOTEER AT THE REINS

THE FOOTRACE

RIDERS DOWN THE STRETCH

1 BATHING FACILITIES
2 TEMPLE OF HERA
3 ALTAR OF HERA
4 THE TREASURIES
5 GREAT ALTAR OF ZEUS
6 STADIUM
7 TEMPLE OF ZEUS
8 HIPPODROME

PANCRATIUM — WRESTLING AND BOXING COMBINED

GRIPPING THE DISCUS

STANDING HIGH JUMP, WITH HAND WEIGHTS FOR IMPETUS

AN ATHLETE IN TRAINING

The first Olympian festival, held in 776 BC, consisted of a single contest — a footrace of one stade, or nearly 200 meters, conducted in an open field near an altar to Zeus. Within a few centuries, the games expanded to include the array shown here, and the Olympian grounds grew to an imposing complex *(lower left)* where tens of thousands gathered every four years to cheer on their favorites. One of the most popular events was the brutal pancratium *(top)*, in which contestants were allowed to kick and throttle their opponents. The militant Spartans were particularly fond of such shows of strength, and their champions not only carried off the lion's share of the prizes in the early years of the games but reportedly inaugurated the custom of competing naked, their bodies oiled. Spartan dominance was soon challenged, however, as the gymnasiums of Athens and other rising city-states turned out formidable contenders.

By and large, such competition served as a peaceable outlet for the bitter rivalries among the Hellenic powers. Yet even the truce observed in Olympian seasons was sometimes threatened. In 420 BC, during the Peloponnesian War, Sparta was banned from the Olympian games for hostile acts, and the contests went forward as they would in a later age — under armed guard.

cabbage. Solon lightened the penalties and introduced new provisions for the care of widows and orphans. Legal disputes, once solely the purview of a patrician council known as the Areopagus, might now be referred to a court of appeals or to people's tribunals, where the judges were selected by lot from the citizenry.

Further adjustments dramatically changed the balance of power within the political system. Solon threw open the franchise to all classes of free men; public office could now be held by any Athenian male who met a certain basic income requirement. In practice this requirement barred the lowest and most populous group, but any male citizen, no matter how poor, could now sit in the Assembly, the state's main legislative body. Once he was enfranchised, his vote carried equal weight with that of the grandest aristocrat. Thus Athens took its first steps along the path that would lead to democracy.

For all his reforms, Solon was no radical. "Sit in the middle of the ship and steer a straight course," the oracle at Delphi had told him, and he firmly embraced this advice. To curb any outlandish impulses in the Assembly, he devised a Council of Four Hundred, elected from the wealthy citizens, which set the body's agenda and drafted all new resolutions. The major administrative officials continued to be the archons, nominated from the richest class but elected by popular vote in the Assembly. Retired archons went on to serve on the Areopagus, which acted as a sort of supreme court and retained final veto power over any law. This way, the wealthy noblemen who served as archons and comprised the Areopagus and the Council of the Four Hundred would be balanced against the masses in the Assembly.

Perhaps as significant as Solon's political changes were his efforts to revitalize the Athenian economy. With its limited agricultural means, Attica clearly could not produce enough food for its increasing population. Solon's solution was to push the state into commerce. Olive oil from the groves that flourished on the stony hillsides became an important export, as did wine in later years. Solon revised the system of weights and measures, bringing it into line with the standards commonly used in the great entrepôts of Corinth and of the eastern Aegean. He urged all fathers to teach their sons a craft, and he offered citizenship to any foreign artisans who chose to work in Athens. The city already had a small pottery industry, and Solon encouraged it; fine red-and-black Attic vases soon became a major trade item.

Having thus laid the foundations for a prosperous, well-managed state, Solon retired from office. His great works did not outlast him. No sooner had Solon departed Athens for a life of travel than the old clan and class rivalries began to reassert themselves. The noble families still retained most of the wealth and, as it soon turned out, a disproportionate share of political power. Personal jealousies flared in the councils of state, and on occasion they erupted into armed conflict.

The antagonisms came to a head in midcentury. A number of quarreling factions — rich versus poor and clan versus clan — had split the body politic. With government at a standstill, in stepped an ambitious nobleman named Peisistratus, who represented the disaffected from all walks of life, urban poor as well as hill-country peasants. Peisistratus devised an ingenious ruse to seize power. Slashing himself on the body and gashing the mules that pulled his carriage, he rushed into the Athens marketplace, dripping blood and crying that he had been attacked by political enemies. The Assembly immediately voted to give him a bodyguard — with which he swiftly stormed the Acropolis, expelled the government, and declared himself ruler. There followed a confused period of coup and countercoup until

Peisistratus recruited a force of mercenaries and secured power permanently.

Having won control by force, Peisistratus spent the next twenty years exercising it with impressive energy and skill. A tyrant in the classic sense, he nonetheless transformed Athens into the leading city of the Hellenic world. Like most populists, Peisistratus did much to benefit the poor. He extended loans to small farmers, confirmed the rights of artisans, and promoted industry and exports. Through a massive public works program — which included a much-needed aqueduct to bring water to the capital — he created employment for hundreds of laborers. He also planted garrisons along the approaches to the Hellespont, to protect the main route into the Aegean for ships carrying grain from the wheat-producing plains of southern Russia or timber from Macedonia.

Athens became a center of art and culture. As the Ionian cities to the east fell under the shadow of Persia, shiploads of talented refugees arrived seeking the tyrant's patronage. Poets, philosophers, sculptors, and architects began to lend a newfound grace to Athenian life. State celebrations at Athens became gala outpourings of cultural genius. Recitations of Homer, whose oldest surviving manuscript had been brought from Ionia, enlivened the Panathenaic Festival, which celebrated Attic solidarity. At the Festival of Dionysus, god of wine and creativity, a new art form — tragic drama — emerged, and a prize was awarded to the most accomplished playwright.

On the tyrant's death in 527 BC, control of the state passed to his sons, and under them the regime began to crumble. One son was slain by assassins in 514 BC; his panicky brother, Hippias, reacted with a reign of terror that turned the populace against him. As the situation deteriorated, various Athenian nobles who had gone into exile saw their opportunity and appealed to Sparta for aid. Thus, in 510, the Spartan king Cleomones led his phalanx into Athens, besieged the Acropolis, and deposed the last of the Peisistratids.

But there was no peace among the fractious nobles until another great Athenian statesman emerged. Cleisthenes was an aristocrat, scion of a noble family, who had cast his lot with the common folk. How he achieved power and accomplished his reforms is unclear. It is likely that he, as a respected leader, presented his points to the Assembly, which approved them. In any event, his first step was to reaffirm the old constitution of Solon, but with several important differences. Instead of having Athenians register as citizens by clan, they would now enroll according to their place of residence, or deme. A deme might include members of several different clans and individuals from all walks of life. By thus substituting geography for genealogy, Cleisthenes channeled a citizen's loyalty from his tribe to his community and placed him on an equal footing with his neighbors.

Next, in order to balance the interests of various regions and classes, Cleisthenes divided Attica into ten electoral districts, each containing a cross-section of demes from different parts of the state. Citizens voted by district, marched to battle in district regiments, backed district athletes, and cheered on district poets at the playwrighting contests.

In national politics, all male citizens were expected to attend the Assembly, still the main legislative body. The sessions, held every ten days or so on a rocky hillside near the Acropolis, were enormous. It took fully 6,000 citizens to make up a quorum. Anyone was permitted to air his views, and when important issues were slated for discussion everyone tried to show up, with farmers from the rural districts trudging long, dusty miles into Athens to cast their votes. For each

year the Assembly elected new archons — the chief administrators — and whatever proposals it passed became the law of the land.

Unwieldy though it may have been, the system worked surprisingly well. A steering committee, the Council of Five Hundred, set the agenda for each Assembly meeting, much as the aristocratic Four Hundred had in Solon's day. But the new council was decidedly more democratic: Members were selected by lot from slates proposed by the new demes. Terms were set at a single year, and no one could serve more than twice.

Various checks and balances were installed to monitor each official's performance, and if any public servant proved inept or — worse — tyrannical or corrupt, the penalties were severe. In extreme cases, the Assembly could call for a vote of ostracism. The citizens voted by writing the name of the accused on clay fragments, or *ostraca;* a majority of such ballots would send the man into exile for ten years. All of this presented the strongest possible contrast to the Persians, who, although they shared in the glory and wealth of an expanding empire, lived under the autocratic rule of a monarch so remote that even most nobles were rarely allowed near him.

The reforms gave Athenian citizens a renewed sense of civic pride and purpose — and just in time. For the Persians were on the march, their seemingly invincible armies sweeping westward across Lydia in 547 BC and across Egypt in 526; to the north, both Thrace and Macedonia were in thrall by 512 BC.

Most mainland Greeks, intent on their own affairs, had at first paid little attention. But nearly half the Greek-speaking world had already fallen into Persian hands, for in capturing Lydia the Persians also acquired the Greek cities of the Ionian coast, which had been in the Lydian sphere of influence. Pro-Persian tyrants were installed as governors in each state, and while they generally ruled with a light hand, the taxes they levied for Persian royal coffers galled the Greek upper class. These aristocrats incited rebellion and called for help from their fellow Greeks to the west.

Sparta, unwilling to commit its forces so far afield, prudently declined. But Athens sent twenty shiploads of soldiers, and the city of Eretria on the island of Euboea dispatched five vessels. The responses were more gestures than serious campaigns. After helping to assault and burn Sardis, the Lydian capital, the western armies sailed home, leaving the Ionians to struggle on alone. The outcome was a foregone conclusion. Persia's disciplined forces swept in and pounded the Ionians into submission. The city of Miletus, at the fore of the revolt, received special punishment. Its houses were burned, its temples sacked, its citizens either massacred, enslaved, or deported. What was more, the Persian ruler, Darius, decided that he would have to chastise the western Greeks for meddling in Ionia.

Darius first sent envoys to the principal Greek states, demanding gifts of earth and water, symbolic of surrender. Some complied, but Athens, Sparta, and Eretria scornfully refused. Thus, in the early summer of 490 BC, a powerful force of Persian cavalry and infantry, numbering about 20,000, embarked for Greece. A quick and decisive victory was expected. With the fleet sailed Athens's onetime ruler Hippias, son of Peisistratus, who was to be reinstalled as tyrant. The Persians landed on Euboea's southern tip and marched up the island to Eretria, ravaging the countryside as they went. The city itself had strong defenses but fell within seven days and was savagely plundered. By August the Persians were ready to deal with Attica.

The Athenians listened to reports of the Persian advance with foreboding, especially when they learned that the enemy had crossed to the plain of Marathon on

Attica's east coast, only twenty-six miles from the city. The Athenian generals sent a messenger to Sparta for help, then pondered their strategy. Should they keep their forces in Athens to defend the city? Or should they send them ahead to meet the Persians in the field? A vote was taken in the Assembly, and the decision was overwhelming: fight at Marathon.

The Athenian army marched forth — a mere 10,000 foot soldiers unsupported by either cavalry or archers. The sight that greeted them at Marathon was daunting. The plain was swarming with Persian troops, the infantry encamped in loose battle array while massed squadrons of cavalry paced about. Another strategy session ensued: to attack despite the odds? Or to stand fast, hoping that the Spartans would arrive in time to help withstand the Persian onslaught? Amazingly, the Greeks had no supreme commander to make the decision for them. Ten different generals, each in charge of his own regiment, acted in committee to determine such matters by majority vote. Further, during actual engagements, the command rotated from day to day among the ten. Now the vote was evenly split, with five for attack and five for delay.

As so often happened, a leader emerged to fill the vacuum. Miltiades, a veteran of earlier Persian campaigns in the north who was impatient to engage the enemy, appealed to the archons in Athens and won approval to attack. By great good fortune, the opportunity arose on his day in command. On the night of August 11, a Persian defector slipped into the Greek camp with news that the Persian cavalry had for some reason temporarily withdrawn. This removed the gravest danger to the Athenian foot soldiers. At dawn the Greek phalanxes charged, rushing forward at a trot that became in the last few yards a flat-out run. The astonished Persians fell back, but soon rallied and broke through the center of the Greek line.

It was a trap. The wily Miltiades had purposely left the Greek center weak in order to strengthen his flanks with double rows of men. Now the flanks spun around, falling upon the Persians and slaughtering them in vast numbers until the remnants fled back to their ships. It was an astonishing triumph of valor and wit over brute strength.

According to legend, the news was sped back to Athens by a messenger who ran the entire twenty-six miles, cried "We have won," and dropped dead. The city was jubilant, and all the more so because the victory had been won without the Spartans. Those tardy allies arrived the next day, explaining that the call for help had unfortunately reached them during a festival of Apollo. They had delayed their departure until the ceremonies ended. No one questioned this reasoning; honor to the gods outweighed any obligation to another Greek state. Nevertheless, the Spartans marched on to Marathon to view the battlefield and pay homage to the Athenian dead. They also carefully studied the Persian corpses. The Persians' spears were shorter than the Greek ones, the Spartans noted, and their wicker shields and padded cloth tunics were less effective than the bronze Greek armor. The mighty Persian war machine might be vulnerable after all.

Darius set about planning a larger expedition against Greece, but never saw it materialize. In 486, the King of Kings fell ill and died at the age of sixty-four, having wielded Persia's scepter for thirty-five years with skill and integrity. Plans for the Greek campaign passed on to his

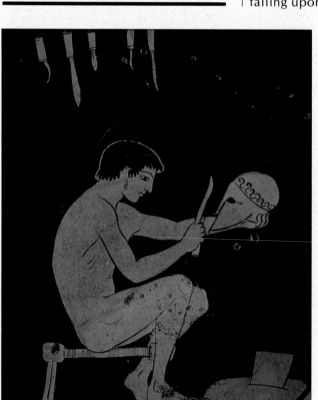

In a scene painted around 480 BC, a young Attic metalworker uses a tool from the rack above his head to put the finishing touches on a bronze helmet. The approach of the Persians spurred such production, with much of the work in Athens being done in shops located near the sanctuary of Hephaistos, the patron god of smiths. Greek colonization had spread this kind of skill throughout the Aegean world, however. The same narrow eye sockets and overlapping nose guard portrayed in the helmet below — trademarks of the so-called Corinthian style — are found in the one at right, buried along with its owner about 500 BC in Thrace, north of the Hellespont.

The triremes used by the Athenians to dominate the Aegean in the fifth century were sleek vessels that traveled under sail to their destinations and were powered by oars during battle. Although each galley carried a small complement of soldiers — ten shield-bearing hoplites and four archers — the object was not so much to board enemy ships as to disable them with the trireme's metal-tipped ram, driven home by some 170 rowers. Pressed together on three levels *(inset)*, the crew took its stroke from a piper, whose pulsating notes rose above the din of battle. Athens had an ample reserve of seawise men to draw on. "The majority," said one observer, "are able to pull an oar when first they set foot aboard a warship."

son Xerxes, an able administrator but a man more at home with the luxuries of the royal palaces than with the hard life of the battlefield. Yet Xerxes was at war from the moment he donned the crown. He had to move quickly to suppress a revolt in Egypt. To prevent further rebellion there, he imposed a repressive occupation — thus reversing the tolerant policies of Cyrus and Darius and earning the Egyptians' lasting enmity. Then Babylon rebelled and received the same harsh treatment. According to one account, Xerxes tore down the city's walls, razed its temples, and ordered the huge golden idol of Marduk melted down and shipped back to Persepolis as ingots. All the while the Greek campaign, urged on him by ambitious advisers, tugged at the back of Xerxes' mind. So in 481 BC, he began assembling, from forty-six different satrapies and states under Persian sway, the greatest armed force that had ever been marshaled on the face of the earth: a quarter of a million men who were to attack in concert with thousands of warships and supply vessels.

The Greeks meanwhile began to prepare in their own haphazard fashion. Though a seafaring people, they were surprisingly lacking in naval strength. Battle to them had

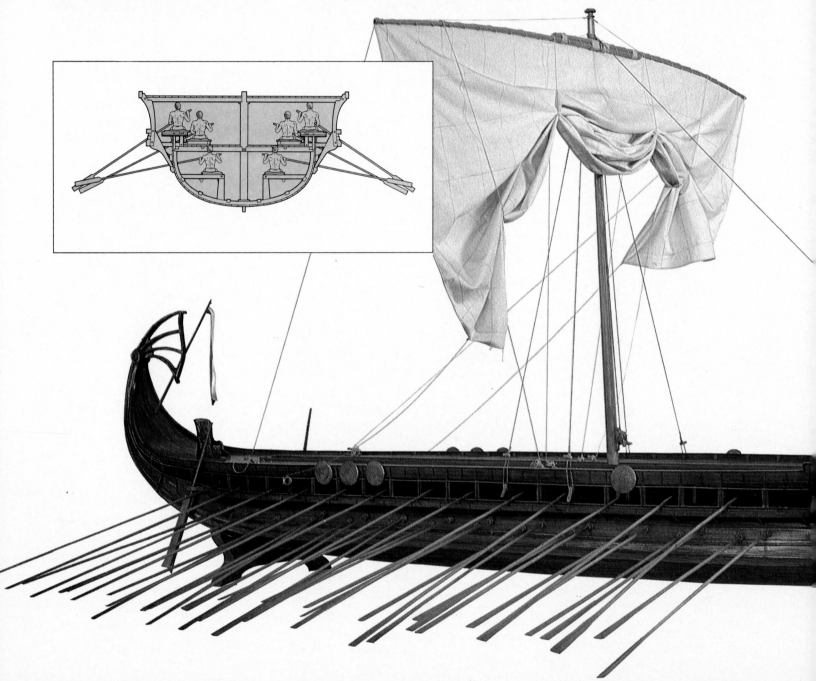

always meant engagement on land, phalanx to phalanx, with ships useful mainly as transport. But now Athens began to build a fighting navy.

The decision was reached in a typically Athenian manner: equal parts pragmatism and foresight, greedy self-interest and high civic pride. A rich vein of ore had been struck at the state silver mines at Laurium, greatly enhancing the city's wealth. The Assembly met to debate how this boon should be spent, with many arguing that it should be distributed among all citizens. A politician named Themistocles had other views. An obscure nobleman whose powerful personality had carried him to high office, Themistocles understood that Greek freedom was at stake, and he also harbored dreams of an Athenian future based on sea power. "I cannot tune a harp," he once said, "but I can take a modest city in hand and raise it to greatness." Themistocles addressed the Assembly at length and persuaded the members to spend the silver on a fleet of 200 warships.

Sparta, as the strongest land power, took the lead in marshaling other Greek states. Most of its neighbors already belonged to the Peloponnesian League, and in the spring of 480 BC Sparta called them together. Some thirty states responded, entering a new and larger compact called the Hellenic League. However, many remained aloof, expecting the Persians to win and hoping they would be generous victors. Indeed, the omens boded ill for the Greeks as word came that Xerxes' immense army was on the march. When Sparta requested counsel from the oracle at Delphi, the sibyl declared that Zeus favored the Persians. Athens got an even more graphic warning from Delphi. The city would be overwhelmed, its towers leveled, its streets flowing with blood. "Fly, fly to the ends of creation," the oracle chanted. "Wait not the tramp of the horse, nor the footmen moving mightily over the land, but turn your back to the foe and retire ye." The sibyl added a typically enigmatic note: "Safe shall the wooden wall continue for thee and thy children."

As always, the Greeks seemed unable to agree on a coherent strategy. At first, Sparta argued for a defense at the Isthmus of Corinth, between Attica and the Peloponnesus. But this meant abandoning all northern and central Greece. The league then decided to make a stand in north Thessaly — until it was pointed out that such a plan would leave the phalanxes open to attack from the rear. So a compromise was drawn: The defenders would make a stand in the mountains along Thessaly's southern border.

As the Greeks argued, Xerxes was moving his juggernaut from Asia into Europe. It was no easy maneuver. The 250,000 soldiers — Persians, Medes, Bactrians, Indians, Ethiopians, even some Ionian Greeks — had to trek en masse through alien country with all their arms and baggage, while an armada of support ships carrying provisions sailed parallel to them, along the coast.

The first obstacle was the Hellespont, a narrow channel three-quarters of a mile wide that divided the two continents. Xerxes' engineers constructed a pair of pontoon bridges, each consisting of 300 boats lashed together with cables and paved with stout planking. But now the gods chose to tax the Persians. A storm blew up and smashed the bridges just as they were completed. In a fury, Xerxes ordered the Hellespont chastised with 300 lashes, branded with hot irons, and symbolically fettered by a pair of shackles thrown into the water. For good measure, he had the engineers beheaded. A second pair of bridges held, and in the spring of 480 BC, the Persian army started across. The procession of foot soldiers, archers, and cavalry, some mounted on camels, took seven days and seven nights to complete the crossing.

The imperial army, always attended by its fleet, slowly worked its way through

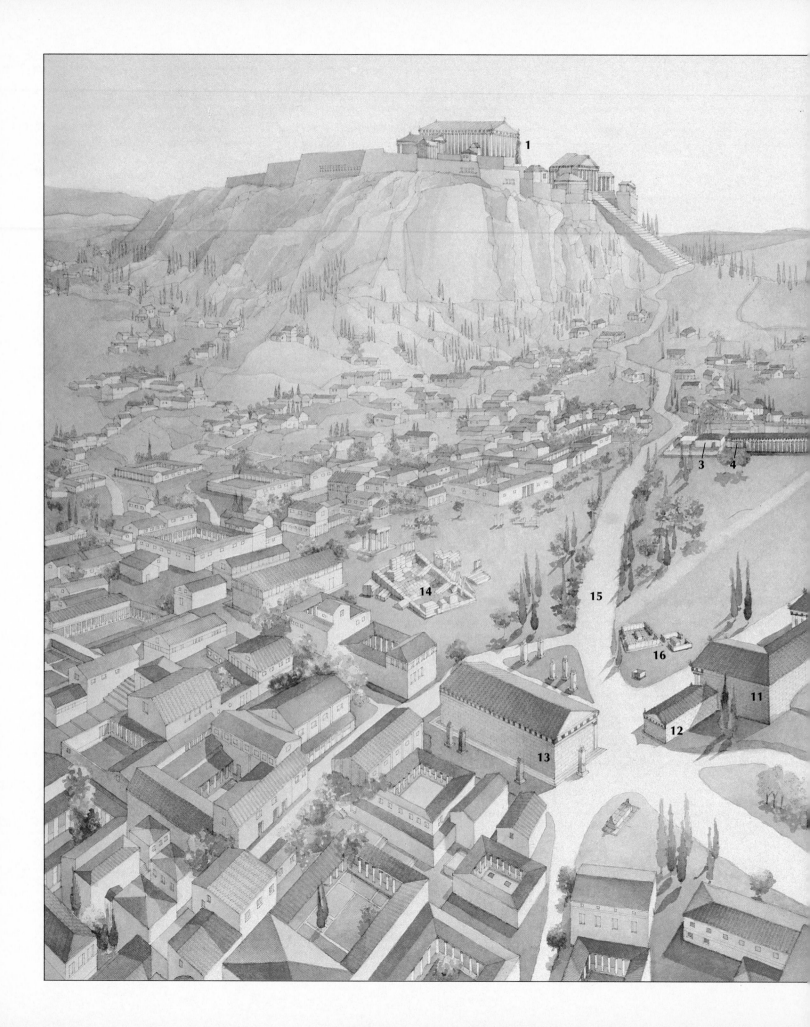

Athens reached the height of its glory in the second half of the fifth century, when the statesman Pericles erected the majestic Parthenon (1) atop the Acropolis to house a colossal ivory-and-gold effigy of the city's divine guardian, Athena. Below the acropolis sprawled the agora, the civic center of Athens. A traveler wending his way from the Parthenon to the heart of the agora might stop for a drink at the southeast fountainhouse (4). Linked to a distant spring by an aqueduct of baked-clay pipes, this well was a favorite gathering place for women of the city, who would pause and converse before returning home with their brimming jars. Continuing on, the traveler would pass the Heliaia (6), where law cases were heard by hundreds of jurors selected by lot. A short distance beyond stood the circular Tholos (8). There a contingent of citizen-senators, who conducted public business by day in the adjacent Bouleuterion (9), would pass the night, ready to respond to any emergency. Near the end of the same street stood a stoa, or colonnaded gallery (13), where the traveler could admire an epic depiction on wooden panels of the victory at Marathon — a battle that preserved the community the poet Pindar called the "Fortress of Hellas, glorious Athens, city of God."

1 PARTHENON

2 PNYX (PUBLIC ASSEMBLY)

3 MINT

4 FOUNTAIN HOUSE

5 SOUTH STOA I

6 HELIAIA (LAW COURT)

7 STRATEGEION (GENERAL'S HEADQUARTERS)

8 THOLOS

9 BOULEUTERION

10 TEMPLE OF HEPHAISTOS

11 STOA OF ZEUS

12 ROYAL STOA

13 PAINTED STOA

14 UNFINISHED LAW COURT

15 PANATHENAIC WAY

16 ALTAR OF THE TWELVE GODS

Thrace and Macedonia, then down the coast of Thessaly. The Greeks had finally resolved to make their stand at Thermopylae, a slim ribbon of land where the central mountains dropped steeply to within fifty feet of the shoreline. The enemy would have to traverse this strip, so constricting that a body of determined men might halt them. An advance force of 7,000 Greeks under King Leonidas of Sparta took up positions in the pass. Leonidas resolved to hold Thermopylae until the main Greek army could enter the fray. Meanwhile the combined Greek navy, 270 warships commanded by the Spartan general Eurybiades, lay in the narrows off the coast, awaiting the Persian fleet.

Xerxes reached Thermopylae in early August, confident that the sheer immensity of his force would put the Greeks to flight. When they held fast, he sent in a regiment of Medes to clear them out. The Greeks cut down the Medes in such appalling numbers that Xerxes was forced to order a retreat. A second attack failed utterly, as did a third. Yet just when it seemed that the Persians were stymied, fortune came to them in the form of an avaricious farmer, who offered to lead them through the mountains in return for a reward. That night a force of Persian infantry made the ascent, and the next morning they were closing in to attack the Greeks from behind.

In the nick of time, Leonidas learned of the danger and ordered the main body of his troops to withdraw. Like a true Spartan, he himself chose death over retreat. With 300 countrymen, he battled through the morning; when their weapons were gone, the Greeks of Thermopylae fought with fists and feet until every last man had fallen. By then Leonidas and his 300 had held the enemy long enough to ensure the safe withdrawal of the rest of the Greek army.

Xerxes marched into Attica, pillaging and burning as he went. All the dark prophecies seemed about to be fulfilled. The citizens of Athens evacuated to the nearby island sanctuary of Salamis. And suddenly the enigmatic pronouncement of the Delphian sibyl came clear. The city's "wooden wall" was the fleet of ships that Themistocles had persuaded his countrymen to build.

Greek warships had already met the Persian fleet in several fierce but inconclusive engagements in the waters off Thermopylae. A strong north wind had blown up, dashing 400 Persian vessels against the rocks and inflicting more damage than the fighting itself. Then, with the retreat on land, the Greek fleet had withdrawn to the south. It had now reassembled in the bay of Salamis, where Themistocles set to work devising a battle plan. He knew that the 300 Phoenician warships that formed the core of the Persian navy were larger and more maneuverable than the smaller, sturdier Greek triremes. In addition to the Phoenician vessels, the Persian fleet included 200-odd Egyptian galleys, some 150 Cypriot ships, and hundreds of vessels from Ionia, the Levant, and other parts of the Persian empire — all carrying detachments of warriors for boarding the enemy. In all, the Persian fleet numbered some 1,200 warships, compared with 380 in the Greek force. And the Greek sailors were not as experienced as those on Persian vessels. But the channel between Salamis and the coast of Attica was narrow, Themistocles knew, only wide enough for fifty ships to advance in line abreast. If the Greeks could lure the enemy into this natural funnel, the Persian advantage in numbers and maneuverability would be worthless.

And so it happened. The Persian fleet, each vessel in full battle array with its banks of oarsmen and its fighting force of spearmen and archers, rounded the tip of Attica and sailed toward the channel. The Persian army had already overrun the nearby mainland, and Xerxes, certain of victory, had set up his throne on the beach where he could watch the battle in comfort.

There was confusion as the Persians crowded together in the narrow passage. Suddenly a trumpet sounded from the heights of Salamis, and the Greek ships surged forward in disciplined ranks. The triremes smashed into the Persian vessels, crushing their hulls and driving them into one another. Greek warriors leaped onto the battered enemy ships, swords flailing. The sands at Xerxes' feet became a litter of shattered timbers and broken bodies. In the aftermath of this catastrophe, Xerxes collected his remaining ships and laid a course for home. His campaign was finished for the year. But he left a sizable army to winter over, commanded by his brother-in-law, Mardonius.

The final act was played out the following year, in August of 479 BC, at Plataea in southern Boeotia. There 40,000 Greek heavy infantry met 100,000 troops of Mardonius. Before going into battle, each Greek swore a solemn oath: "I shall fight to the death, I shall put freedom before life." For three weeks the armies skirmished inconclusively. Then Mardonius, mistaking a shift in the Greek line for retreat, ordered a full assault. The Greeks counterattacked vigorously, their longer spears and heavier body armor telling on the enemy. Mardonius, mounted on a white charger, was knocked to earth and slain. The Persian army, now leaderless, broke and ran.

The Battle of Plataea took place on August 27, 479 BC. About the same time, perhaps on that very day, across the sea on the Ionian coast of Mycale, the Greek navy scored a major triumph over the surviving Persian fleet.

It was the most disastrous reversal of Persian fortune since the birth of the empire. Never again would Persia's military forces intervene directly in Europe. Xerxes retired to his capitals and the delights of his harem. From time to time he would rouse himself to push forward his father's construction projects, adding palaces and monumental halls to the Persian ceremonial capital, Persepolis. But he accomplished little else. Ensconced among his eunuchs and concubines, shielded behind the protocol of court life, the Great King allowed his horizons to narrow to a tiny circle of court gossip and intrigue. Even there he failed. In 465 BC, a group of conspirators, led by the royal chamberlain and the commander of the palace guard, had him murdered in his bed.

In the succession of Persian kings that followed — at least in the view of Greek writers who would be the chief source of information about the empire in this period — none displayed the energy or brilliance of Cyrus or Darius. Under Xerxes' son, Artaxerxes I, money, not troops, became the principal instrument of Persian imperial policy. He used the coin of the realm to meddle in Greek affairs, paying first one polis and then another to stir up trouble and thereby restore Persian hegemony in Ionia. The coins, gold darics, bore an image of Darius holding a bow and quiver of arrows; the Greeks referred to them derisively as "Persian archers."

Intrigue and assassination would continue to bloody the Persian royal house till the end of its existence. The empire moved into steady decline. "Soft countries breed soft men," Cyrus had once observed, and as the Persian dynasty gained in luxury and pomp it began to forfeit its ability to govern. What the emperors lacked in leadership they made up in avarice. Taxes became oppressive. Interest rates soared. Discontent grew rife in the satrapies. Despite the efforts of the last two kings to strengthen their realm, the Achaemenid regime would be ready to topple by the time a man whose spirit matched that of Cyrus — Alexander the Great — marched through the empire's heart in the fourth century BC.

In its brief ascendancy, the Persian empire had become the mightiest power on earth

A young Athenian recites verse from a papyrus held by his teacher.

alpha	A	a
beta	B	b
gamma	Γ	g
delta	Δ	d
epsilon	E	e
zeta	Z	z
eta	H	e
theta	Θ	th
iota	I	i
kappa	K	c, k
lambda	Λ	l
mu	M	m
nu	N	n
xi	Ξ	x
omicron	O	o
pi	Π	p
rho	P	r, rh
sigma	Σ	s
tau	T	t
upsilon	Y	y, u
phi	Φ	ph
chi	X	ch
psi	Ψ	ps
omega	Ω	o

The twenty-four characters of the classical Greek alphabet appear at left with their English transliterations. Several regional variants of Greek script developed from Phoenician writing, but this Ionian version, used in Athens, became standard. Students mastered the letters by scrawling epigrams with a stylus on wax tablets. More important texts were penned on imported Egyptian papyrus or carved in stone like the document at right, a treaty between Athens and the island of Samos. Atop the stone a helmeted Athena clasps the hand of the goddess Hera, patron of Samos.

AN ALPHABETIC LEGACY

Among the gifts bequeathed by the Greeks to Western culture was their alphabet, which would provide the foundation for all European scripts. The Greeks evolved this alphabet from a similar set of phonetic, or sound-based, characters employed by the seafaring Phoenicians as early as 1000 BC. But while the Phoenician alphabet was composed solely of consonants — leaving it to the speaker to fill in the vowel sounds as required — the Greeks developed seven distinct vowels. They were thus equipped to represent the spoken language in print with unrivaled precision.

The clarity and economy of the Greek writing system made it widely accessible. In lands such as Egypt and China, whose scripts consisted of hundreds or even thousands of abstruse symbols, reading and writing remained largely affairs for scribes and scholars. In fifth-century Athens, by contrast, most male citizens were literate. And although Athenian girls were not sent to school, many young women learned to read at home, prompting objections from some quarters. "He who teaches letters to his wife is ill-advised," grumbled a misogynist in a play by Menander. Such complaints were of little avail, however. With the evolution of a concise alphabet, the power of the written word could no longer be neatly confined to one segment of society.

and had set a new standard of enlightened, efficient rule. In bringing so many lands and peoples together under a central administration, the Persians had established a new order of government and engendered an economic and cultural ferment that carried civilization to a level of brilliance it had never experienced before. All future empires — and future societies — of both the Middle East and the Western world would be in their debt.

After the Greek triumphs over Xerxes in 480 and 479 BC, Sparta remained Greece's foremost land power, although Athens now found itself elevated to a new position of influence and respect. The Greek generals gathered after Salamis to decide who had fought most brilliantly; each one voted first for himself and then for Themistocles. "Next to the gods, the Athenians repelled the invaders," declared a Greek historian a generation later.

Preeminent at sea, Athens quickly moved to form a confederation of maritime states, a compact something like the old Peloponnesian League. At Delos in 477 BC, Athens joined with the city-states of Ionia and those of the Aegean islands to launch the Delian League. To seal their alliance, the members symbolically hurled iron weights into the sea, the idea being that the league would endure until the iron floated to the surface.

The league's stated objective was to keep the Persians at bay in the Aegean and to free the Ionian states still under Persian control. Every state had a vote at league meetings, and each willingly contributed ships or money to the common cause. Athens offered its entire fleet of 200 triremes. In the first dozen years of the league's existence, its forces soundly rebuffed the Persians in several engagements along the coast of Asia Minor.

As the Persian menace receded, however, the league's member states grew restive. Assessments ran high, and the dominance of Athens became increasingly vexatious. Already the island of Naxos had tried to withdraw and had been severely punished by the Athenian navy. Then, in 465 BC, Thasos attempted to drop out. Athens again sent in its ships and took the island by storm, forcing Thasos to tear down its walls, surrender its fleet, and relinquish all its possessions on the adjacent coast. The island became an Athenian vassal.

The Athenians maintained that such actions were necessary in the name of league solidarity. And by securing the sea lanes and enforcing the peace, the league had in truth brought a new prosperity to the entire region. Trade flourished and industry expanded. Athenian outposts in the Hellespont and around the Black Sea ensured a steady supply of grain and fish from Russia and the Black Sea.

Yet as Athens tightened its grip, the other states paid a heavy price for security. Athenian garrisons loomed throughout the Aegean, and Athenian officials began to meddle in the internal affairs of member states. The league's treasury was moved from Delos to Athens in 454 BC — for safekeeping, the Athenians insisted. Legal disputes among members were adjudicated by Athenian courts. Athenian coinage and the Athenian system of weights and measures were imposed everywhere.

ΣΧΟΛΗ	schole	school
ΓΕΩΜΕΤΡΙΑ	geometria	geometry
ΦΥΣΙΚΑ	physika	physics
ΦΙΛΟΣΟΦΙΑ	philosophia	philosophy
ΑΣΤΡΟΝΟΜΙΑ	astronomia	astronomy
ΑΣΤΗΡ	aster	star
ΓΑΛΑΞΙΑ	galaxia	galaxy
ΚΩΜΗΤΗΣ	kometes	comet
ΜΕΤΕΩΡΟΝ	meteoron	meteor
ΑΤΟΜΟΝ	atomon	atom
ΜΟΥΣΙΚΗ	mousike	music
ΜΕΛΩΙΔΙΑ	meloidia	melody
΄ΑΡΜΟΝΙΑ	harmonia	harmony
ΣΥΜΦΩΝΙΑ	symphonia	symphony
ΧΟΡΟΣ	choros	chorus
ΘΕΑΤΡΟΝ	theatron	theater
ΔΡΑΜΑ	drama	drama
ΚΩΜΩΙΔΙΑ	komoidia	comedy
ΤΡΑΓΩΙΔΙΑ	tragoidia	tragedy
ΠΟΙΗΤΗΣ	poietes	poet
ΧΑΡΑΚΤΗΡ	charakter	character
΄ΗΡΩΣ	heros	hero
ΚΡΙΤΙΚΟΣ	kritikos	critic
΄ΙΣΤΟΡΙΑ	historia	history
ΠΟΛΙΤΙΚΑ	politika	politics
ΜΗΤΡΟΠΟΛΙΣ	metropolis	metropolis
ΔΗΜΟΚΡΑΤΙΑ	demokratia	democracy
ΑΡΙΣΤΟΚΡΑΤΙΑ	aristokratia	aristocracy
ΜΟΝΑΡΧΙΑ	monarchia	monarchy
ΑΘΛΗΤΗΣ	athletes	athlete
ΓΥΜΝΑΣΙΟΝ	gymnasion	gymnasium
ΣΤΑΔΙΟΝ	stadion	stadium

Featured above are a few of the many classical Greek words that have made their way into the modern lexicon. Drawn from the sciences, the arts, politics, and ordinary conversation, the words show the influence of the ancient Greeks on the history of human thought.

The statesman Solon, who was elected archon of Athens in 594 BC, laid the framework there for a democratic society. "The laws I passed were alike for low-born and for high-born," he proclaimed. "My aim was straightforward justice for each."

The homely Socrates was likened to a satyr, and his sharp wit won him many enemies in Athens. Yet he blazed a trail for Western philosophy, prompting his followers to subject their every assumption to the test of reason.

Pericles, who helped forge an Athenian empire in the fifth century while promoting social reforms within the city, dealt frankly with its citizens. "He was never compelled to flatter them," Thucydides observed.

I n his celebrated eulogy for Athenians slain in the Peloponnesian War, Pericles summed up the genius of the city he governed: "I say that Athens is the school of Greece and that the individual Athenian in his own person seems to have the power of adapting himself to the most varied forms of action with the utmost versatility and grace." This was no idle boast. The city had its narrow-minded men, but it remained a haven for artists and scholars through the most turbulent times, and its leading lights were indeed uncommonly versatile. Pericles himself, in the fashion of the lawgiver and poet Solon, was a man of letters who used his own funds to produce *The Persians,* the first play of the dramatist Aeschylus. The historian Thucydides served his city as a general, commanding troops in the Peloponnesian War even as he dissected that struggle in prose. And the philosopher Socrates fought in at least three campaigns, enduring winter marches with the same fortitude that he would later show in meeting a sentence of death on charges of impiety. Others paid a price for their part in civic life — both Thucydides and the statesman Themistocles were exiled. But they trusted in posterity, and it redeemed them.

THE INTELLECTS OF ATHENS

Ostracized after an ill-fated campaign during the Peloponnesian War, Thucydides made the best of his plight, examining the conflict in a treatise that set an enduring standard for the objective study of history.

A pioneer of medical science, Hippocrates left his native island of Kos to study in Athens. He attacked the superstitions that shrouded the treatment of disease, arguing in one tract that epileptic seizures were caused not by the gods but by a hereditary brain disorder.

The playwright Aeschylus sought in the tragic plight of his characters to confirm the justice of the divine order. "Zeus, who guided men to think," he wrote, "has laid it down that wisdom comes alone through suffering."

Themistocles, whose far-sighted policies saved Athens at Salamis, was later accused of consorting with the enemy and lived out his days in exile among the very Persians he had helped to defeat.

From a confederation of equals, the Delian League had evolved into an Athenian maritime empire, with a population of two million and more than 170 tributary states pouring tax money into Athenian coffers.

As Athens's star had ascended, that of Sparta had fallen. In 464 BC, Sparta was hit by a series of devastating earthquakes brought on, it was thought, by a sacrilege against the god Poseidon. Sparta's most important province, Messenia, rose in revolt about this time, setting off an exhausting conflict that continued for nearly a decade before the Spartans finally quelled the rebels. Soon after, several states withdrew from the Peloponnesian League, and the small communities of Elis joined together in a democracy along Athenian lines. Sparta, champion of oligarchy, seemed to be fading on all fronts.

Athens, meanwhile, was reaching heights of splendor. One-sixth of the revenues from the Delian League was set aside for the goddess Athena, and it was used to adorn the capital with magnificent temples, theaters, gymnasiums, and other public buildings. Art and drama flourished, and in this fertile society Athenian democracy was extended to virtually the entire free, native-born male population. The major change was the removal of all economic barriers to public office. The property qualifications for officials were reduced to a token sum, breaking the grip of the wealthier classes on the post of archon and other key positions. The Areopagus, still dominated by the wealthy, was reduced to a more or less advisory chamber, with some minor judicial and religious functions. For the first time, citizens were paid for performing public duties — the funds coming ultimately from league revenues. Now an urban craftsman or day laborer no longer had to suffer a reduction in income for the time he spent as a juror or on the Council of Five Hundred. Attendance at these forums became a form of subsidy for lower-class families. The civil courts, largely staffed by older citizens, resembled a kind of old-age pension system. Only the army, where each hoplite was expected to furnish his own arms, remained a preserve of the relatively well-to-do. Athens' all-powerful fleet, on the other hand, was a democratic stronghold, with its tens of thousands of oarsmen recruited from the urban lower class and paid from Delian League funds.

The Athenians kept a tight rein on their leaders. All terms were limited to one year. Virtually all officials, including the archons, were selected by lot rather than by vote, so all male citizens had an equal chance at office. The sole exceptions were key posts in which special skills were obviously necessary: the state architect, certain financial officers, and the committee of generals charged with defense.

These men were nominated by districts and elected by the Assembly. Naturally, they wielded major influence. A popular general might be reelected for many years running; with a strong following in the Assembly, he could mold state policy and see that it was carried out to his liking. Even so, his actions were subject to constant public scrutiny. Any misstep might cost him reelection or, in extreme cases, the supreme civil penalty of ostracism. Most of Athens's great war heroes had tasted the bitter bread of exile at one time or another, even Miltiades and Themistocles.

The Assembly needed good advice and leadership, and found it in a young landowner named Pericles. Coming from a noble but traditionally liberal family — the constitutional reformer Cleisthenes was his great uncle — Pericles himself had helped the movement that, in 461 BC, reduced the power of the Areopagus. And it was Pericles who later introduced the policy of state pay for public service. He had commanded a squadron of Athenian ships in a brief war with Sparta and Thebes in 457 BC, and had emerged a lifelong advocate for a large, aggressive navy. Year after year, throughout the 440s and 430s, the Assembly, which trusted his wisdom and honesty, elected him to the board of generals. Because of the Assembly's confidence in Pericles, his power was far greater than his elected position as a general warranted. He was the foremost political leader of his day, and under his guidance Athens reached its apogee.

One of Pericles' first priorities was to rebuild the public areas of Athens, large sections of which still bore the ravages of Persian occupation. Enlisting the finest architects of the day and tapping the resources of the Delian League, Pericles erected court buildings, colonnaded marketplaces, theaters for the city's drama festivals, and gymnasiums where Athenian youths could harden their bodies and stretch their minds in philosophical debate. On the Acropolis, he built a complex of temples that ranked among the wonders of the ancient world. The greatest of these was the Parthenon, which dominated the hill's highest crest. Designed by the architects Ictimus and Callicrates, and dedicated to the goddess Athena, it took fourteen years to construct and embellish. The project so drained Delian League funds that even a few Athenians complained. Athens was becoming, said one, "like some vain woman, hung round with precious stones and figures and temples, which cost a world of money."

In certain respects that might have been true. But the magnificent Parthenon was the epitome of restraint and proportion, with a kind of strength tempered by grace that caught the very essence of the Athenian spirit. The sculptor Phidias carved its marble friezes and created its gilded, forty-foot-high statue of Athena in a style of dignified naturalism that has never been surpassed. Centuries later the Roman historian Plutarch, a Greek-born citizen of what was then the world's greatest city, Rome, would stand enraptured before the Parthenon and the other Periclean temples. "Each one," he said, "possesses a beauty that seemed vulnerable the moment it was born and at the same time a youthful vigor that makes it appear to this day as if it were newly built."

In the exalted setting of Periclean Athens, theater reached new heights of intensity and meaning. The tragic drama of the Greeks had originated not as entertainment but as a solemn religious and social rite. So it continued. A chorus of dancers and singers, accompanied by flute and drum, would chant lyrics celebrating high moral truths and humankind's relationship to the gods. Gradually the form expanded to include dialogue between actors — initially, only two actors — and plots taken from myth or history. The dramas were staged during the city's annual Festival of Dionysus. The audience would troop into the huge open-air theater on the south slope of the Acropolis and sit in rapt attention through several full days of dramatic presentations and award ceremonies.

Numerous dramatists wrote plays for the festivals, but three — Aeschylus, Sophocles, and Euripides — towered above the rest. Aeschylus, the most traditional of the three, had fought as a soldier at both Marathon and Sala-

His boots deposited beneath the couch, one of the guests at a festive symposium savors the tune of a young piper in the scene below, painted on a drinking bowl like the one that the guest holds in his hand. The Greek symposium — a fraternal conclave held in a comfortably appointed *andron,* or men's room — generally lasted long into the night, with the wine and the conversation flowing freely. At its best, it was an occasion for lively philosophical debate; at worst, it degenerated into a bawdy drinking bout, critics noted, with the last round bringing "madness and hurling of furniture."

mis, and he drew on the experience for his play *The Persians,* staged in 472 BC with the youthful Pericles as producer. Aeschylus's later themes came mostly from myth and legend — dark, brooding epics full of passion and blood, in which the ill-starred deeds of mortals are set in stark relief against the majesty and power of the Olympian gods.

Sophocles — aristocrat, general, intimate of Pericles — took a more measured view of relationships among humans and gods. His main concern was character and how a superabundance of any trait — pride, for example — could upset the natural balance of things, causing ruin. Wonderfully productive, with 123 plays to his credit, Sophocles worked out his dramas with unfailing nobility and grace. He was also an innovative craftsman who increased the scope and flexibility of the tragic form in a number of ways, among them the addition of a third actor.

Euripides wrote later in the Periclean age, at a time when traditional beliefs were coming under fire from all directions. His plays reflected this uncertainty. They depicted a world in which the gods were losing their grip on Greek minds and attention was turning toward purely human concerns, fraught with doubts and complexities. ''He paints men as they are,'' said Sophocles, who much admired the younger playwright. ''I paint men as they ought to be.'' Euripides' works reveal an unequaled depth of insight into the passions and motivations of his fellow Greeks.

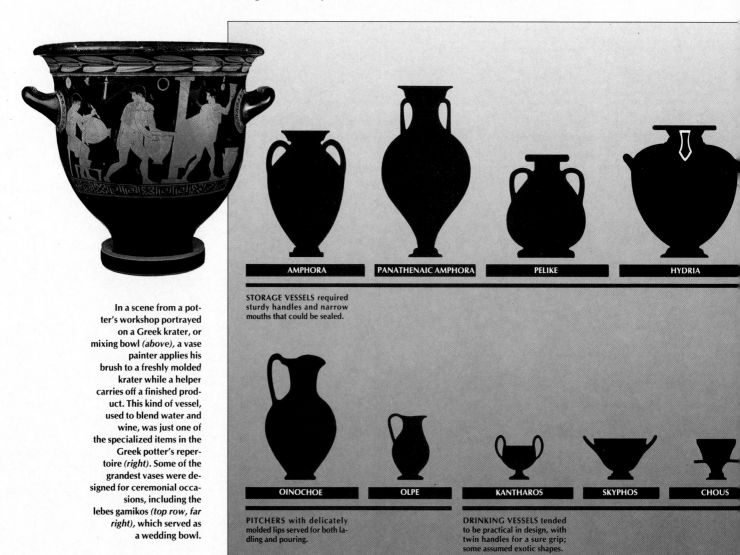

In a scene from a potter's workshop portrayed on a Greek krater, or mixing bowl *(above),* a vase painter applies his brush to a freshly molded krater while a helper carries off a finished product. This kind of vessel, used to blend water and wine, was just one of the specialized items in the Greek potter's repertoire *(right).* Some of the grandest vases were designed for ceremonial occasions, including the lebes gamikos *(top row, far right),* which served as a wedding bowl.

AMPHORA **PANATHENAIC AMPHORA** **PELIKE** **HYDRIA**

STORAGE VESSELS required sturdy handles and narrow mouths that could be sealed.

OINOCHOE **OLPE** **KANTHAROS** **SKYPHOS** **CHOUS**

PITCHERS with delicately molded lips served for both ladling and pouring.

DRINKING VESSELS tended to be practical in design, with twin handles for a sure grip; some assumed exotic shapes.

Another flourishing theatrical form was comedy, also performed at the Festival of Dionysus. Despite its religious venue, Attic comedy could be irreverent. Its supreme practitioner, Aristophanes, poked outrageous fun at statesmen, generals, poets, philosophers — anyone of consequence in fifth-century Athens. Aristophanes' humor was marvelously inventive and often bracingly earthy. One play, *Lysistrata,* staged during a war with Sparta proposed a simple end to the conflict: The women of Athens declared a domestic strike, refusing to sleep with their husbands until the men laid down their weapons. There was much ribald wordplay on the proper place to sheath a sword.

In the exuberant heyday of Pericles' rule, Athens became a cultural crossroads for artists and thinkers from all over the Greek world, including Herodotus of Halicarnassus, tireless traveler and author of the world's earliest surviving volume of history. Herodotus read aloud parts of his book *Histories,* an account of the Persian Wars, to eager Athenian audiences before it was published — that is, copied by scribes onto papyrus scrolls. Another who thrived in Athens's bubbling intellectual stew was Anaxagoras of Clazomenae, who thought the world and everything in it was an organized system of tiny particles activated by an abstract process similar to thought. Anaxagoras was challenged by a Sicilian, Empedocles, who proposed four basic elements — earth, air, fire, and water — which were suffused by the competing forces of love and strife.

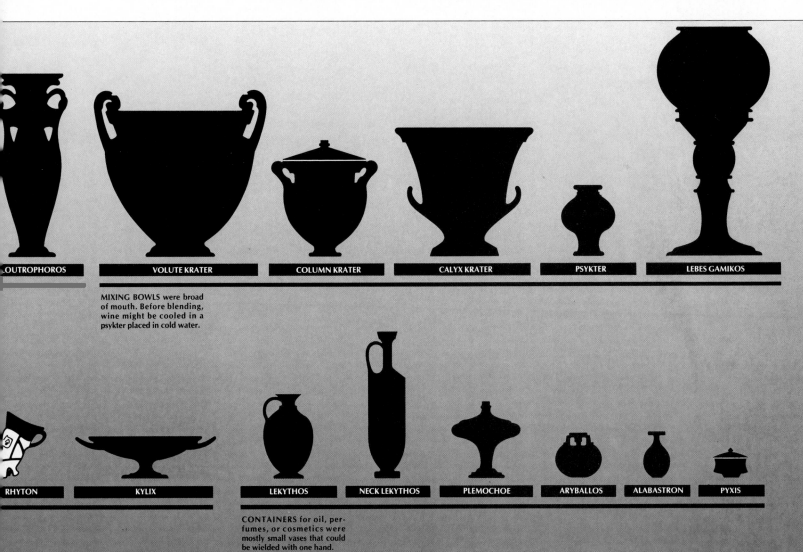

OUTROPHOROS   VOLUTE KRATER   COLUMN KRATER   CALYX KRATER   PSYKTER   LEBES GAMIKOS

MIXING BOWLS were broad of mouth. Before blending, wine might be cooled in a psykter placed in cold water.

RHYTON   KYLIX   LEKYTHOS   NECK LEKYTHOS   PLEMOCHOE   ARYBALLOS   ALABASTRON   PYXIS

CONTAINERS for oil, perfumes, or cosmetics were mostly small vases that could be wielded with one hand.

The most radical view of all filtered down from Thrace, where Democritus of Abdera held that nothing existed but the particles themselves — he called them atoms — and that all else was illusion. His was the ultimate materialism.

Many ordinary Athenians perhaps paid little heed to these recondite ruminations, but they gloried in their polis's fame and status. Attica's population had risen to 300,000, making it the largest state in Greece. It was also the only state to have a cash reserve left over after paying annual expenses. Trade goods poured in through the port of Piraeus: timber from Macedonia and Thrace, flax from Egypt, copper from Cyprus, and iron from Asia Minor. Athens was the largest importer of grain in the ancient world, with shipments arriving through the Hellespont from the Black Sea at the rate of half a million bushels a year.

Despite their city's prosperity, most Athenians led frugal lives. Private houses tended to be modest mud-brick structures with courtyards but no windows; only the well-off had furniture. In the benign Greek climate, most people spent their days out-of-doors — farmers in their fields, vineyards, and olive groves, artisans turning out pottery or hammering bronze and iron in open courtyards. In their leisure hours, Athenians gathered in the marketplace, or agora, with its open-air booths and food stalls, and its handsome marble colonnades. There they joined in gossip and debate, mulling over the peccadilloes and politics of the day. The typical Greek diet was plain — a crust of bread dipped in wine to start the day, the same at lunch, then an evening meal of bread and goat cheese, a vegetable such as beans or cabbage, perhaps some fish, followed by fruit and nuts. Most people ate meat, usually either goat or sheep, only on feast days.

Nor could much difference be discerned between rich and poor in their style of dress. Men and women alike wore loose-fitting garments that hung from the shoulder — either a cloaklike *peplos,* or a sewn tunic called a *chiton.* The usual fabric was wool, woven at home, though a wealthy person might don a cool linen tunic in the warm months. There was no attempt at sartorial display. "Our love of what is beautiful does not lead to extravagance," Pericles himself once explained. "Our love of things of the mind does not make us soft. We regard wealth as something to be used, not as something to boast about."

As in all Greek cities, Athenian society was aggressively masculine. Only men could be citizens, and only upper-class male children were given a formal education. At an early age, the boys were sent each day to a schoolmaster who drilled them in reading, basic arithmetic, and music. They would then go to a gymnasium, where they would be trained in wrestling, boxing, and throwing the discus and the javelin. To the Athenian aristocrats, perfection of body was as important as development of the mind, and education was partly a toughening process. Aristophanes spoke of children marching in ranks to their music lesson through a snowstorm with "never a cloak between them." At the age of eighteen, an Athenian youth was deemed a man. He took vows of citizenship, served in the army or navy, and cast his vote in the Assembly.

Wealthy women were expected to remain at home from birth to death. The exigencies of life might force some lower-class wives to operate market stalls or to work in fields. Women enjoyed few of the rights of Athenian democracy, but many women wielded a degree of quiet influence nonetheless. Pericles' concubine, Aspasia, is said to have helped him write his speeches. And it was amazing to all that every morning, when the great statesman left home, he could be seen kissing Aspasia good-bye.

Slaves of course had no legal rights whatsoever. At the time of Pericles, fully one-fourth of the population lived in servitude, their ranks swelled by prisoners taken in

Early each spring, the citizens of Athens assembled to honor the god Dionysus, portrayed here with a grapevine in one hand and a drinking bowl in the other. As the patron of wine and delirium, Dionysus had long been the object of ecstatic fertility cults, whose rites once included human sacrifice. At the Athenian festival, bulls were offered up instead, and in the theater of Dionysus, the raptures of drama supplanted the frenzy of the cultists. Yet the intoxicating power of the god was not forgotten. "These blessings he gave," wrote the playwright Euripides: "Laughter to the flute and the loosing of cares, when the shining wine is spilled at the feast of the gods."

Athens's overseas conquests. Few slaves were used in agriculture. Many worked as domestics in the wealthier households: A large estate might own dozens of slaves. Others worked for artisans and merchants. Indeed, much of the manual labor in Athens was performed by slaves, who provided manpower for shipyards, marble quarries, and silver mines. Although life could be harsh under the foreman's lash, some house slaves and those with special skills fared well enough. A few managed to accumulate enough money to buy their freedom.

As the century progressed, the splendor of the Athenian state seemed to grow with each passing year. "Our city is an education to all Greece," the aging Pericles declared in 431 BC. Yet dark forces were building that would lead to its sudden and catastrophic decline. Like the protagonist in a Sophoclean tragedy, Athens became the victim of its own overreaching ambitions.

The city's increasingly aggressive stance had already led to an expensive land war in central Greece against Sparta and its allies. The conflict had ended with a peace treaty in 445 BC, but Sparta continued to look with alarm on its rival's expansionism. By 440, the Athenian empire virtually encircled the Aegean, extending from the island of Rhodes in the east, up through the Hellespont and beyond, along the coast of Thrace and Chalcidice, with alliances in Thessaly, Euboea, Boeotia, and even in the Spartan bastion of the Peloponnesus. Sparta, intent on keeping a stable balance of power among the Greek states, saw the scales tipping dangerously.

Tensions came to a head in 433 BC, when Athens invoked a trade embargo against Megara, a Spartan ally. The Spartans and their allies strapped on their armor and marched against Attica. So began the Peloponnesian War, an epic and calamitous struggle that continued on and off for the better part of three decades, and came to embroil virtually the entire Hellenic world.

The first year of the war went well enough for the Athenians. Pericles, his army outnumbered by nearly two to one, abandoned the rural areas and retreated into the city. The invaders laid waste to the vineyards and olive groves, but they had no siege craft and had to fight on the plains; they could not seriously threaten the walled city. Moreover, the nearby port of Piraeus was still secure, and the vital shipments of grain continued to arrive. But then, in the second year, catastrophe overtook the Athenians. A great plague broke out in the crowded city, perhaps carried by ship from Egypt. Suddenly masses of people were afflicted with raging fever and insatiable thirst. Sores covered their bodies, and they began to die by the hundreds, then the thousands. In the demoralized city, the fabric of society was torn asunder and lawlessness prevailed; few thought that they would live to be called to account for their actions.

Before the epidemic finally ran its course, anywhere from one-fourth to one-third of the city's inhabitants perished, including Pericles. The Spartans and their allies fled Attica in fear of becoming infected by the plague, thus giving the Athenians a chance to repair their fortunes. The Athenian navy was still capable of continuing the war, and its triremes assaulted the Peloponnesian coast, harassing Spartan allies. A stalemate ensued, Athens in command of the sea, Sparta preeminent on land. At last, in 421, a temporary truce was declared.

Through these early years of the war, except for the plague time, the Athenians somehow managed to maintain their usual urbane existence. Theatrical contests continued, with Euripides mounting his provocative tragedies and Aristophanes aiming his humorous barbs at the city's leaders. An Athenian general, shorn of his command after a defeat in Macedonia, sat down to chronicle the hostilities. Thucydides' *History of the Peloponnesian War* remains a masterpiece of detailed, insightful analysis. New currents of thought continued to arrive from Ionia, conveyed by visiting philosophers known as Sophists, who set up schools in the city. The Sophists purported to teach discourse and rhetoric — important skills in a democracy. But they did more. Amid the turmoil and disruption of a stalemated war, intellectuals were questioning many ancient beliefs, notably the supremacy of the gods. The Sophists offered a new view, a kind of skeptical humanism summed up by Protagoras of Ceus: "Man is the measure of all things." With this dictum, humankind was elevated to a central position in the universe.

At the same time, Athens produced its own philosopher. He was Socrates, a man of powerful mind and body, who had fought bravely as a foot soldier against the Spartans. His intellectual goal was to define, through ceaseless questioning, what was good in the soul. Each new idea, every accepted belief, the very foundations of human thought — all these he subjected to the closest scrutiny. Such challenging discourse attracted a large following among young, upper-class men. No less an authority than the Delphian oracle pronounced Socrates "the wisest man in Greece." Among Socrates' targets was the democratic system of Athens, which he felt had allowed the city to fall into war through a series of irresponsible actions. It was a bias he had no trouble imparting to his aristocratic disciples. Two of them, Critias and Alcibiades, went on to play highly controversial roles after the Peloponnesian War broke out anew.

The war came to a head with a naval expedition against Syracuse, in Sicily, by which the ever-adventurous Athenians hoped to expand their empire toward the west. A fleet of ninety-four warships and support vessels, carrying 7,500 foot soldiers, set out from Athens in midsummer of 415 BC. One of the generals in command, Nicias, had grave doubts about the venture; another general, Alcibiades, was its most enthusiastic backer.

Alcibiades was a remarkable figure. Young, rich, talented, strikingly handsome, he was blessed with a roguish charm that was difficult to resist. He also had a way of making enemies; his roistering nocturnal escapades were famous throughout Athens. At the same time, he was politically ambitious, and an ardent spokesman for continuing the city's overseas expansion.

Yet no sooner had the great fleet arrived in Sicily than the campaign came to a standstill. Alcibiades was the cause. Conservative elements in Athens accused him of mocking a state-protected religious cult, and he was recalled to stand trial on the rare charge of impiety. With its strongest general gone, the expedition had no clear plan of operation. Nicias merely cruised along the Italian coast while the summer faded into autumn. Then he put into port at Catana, on the east coast of Sicily. Meanwhile Alcibiades, rather than face a hostile Athenian court, defected to Sparta, where he traitorously urged the Spartan king to invade Attica.

The following summer the Athenians made a futile attempt to build a siege wall around Syracuse. The defenders, using the time to good purpose, built up their army and their own small fleet. Some reinforcements commanded by a Spartan arrived to bolster their forces. On the Athenian side, more ships and men were sent at Nicias's request, doubling the size of his armada.

Finally, in August of 413 BC, Nicias decided to attack but made a grave tactical error: He allowed the Athenian fleet to be trapped in Syracuse's harbor. The enemy demolished the triremes. Ashore, meanwhile, the Athenian army was routed by the

Syracusans. It was the worst defeat in the history of Athens. Nearly two-thirds of its entire navy lay wrecked on the Sicilian shore; 45,000 men, many of them levied from subject states, had been lost.

The debacle at Syracuse was the turning point of the war. The vassal states of the Delian League, seeing their opportunity, became rebellious. A revolution flared in Athens itself, led by a party of antidemocratic landowners whose fortunes had suffered severely from relentless military assessments. For the first time in nearly a century, democracy was suspended and power was handed over to a council of oligarchs. Among them was Critias, another of Socrates' disciples.

But democracy was not quite dead. It survived in what remained of the Athenian navy, which had come to think of itself as the true state. Among the navy's officers in the eastern Aegean was — amazingly — the irrepressible Alcibiades, who had fled Sparta after being caught in a liaison with the king's wife. The sailors, always among his staunchest supporters, had accepted his return and put him in a position of leadership. Now Athens had two governments: an oligarchy at home, a democracy at sea. But soon word spread through the army that the oligarchs were plotting to surrender the city to Sparta, and in 410 BC the hoplites overthrew the government without bloodshed, reinstating the democrats.

All this while, Sparta had been building a navy of its own, and now it was able to challenge Athens at sea. In 405 BC, the Spartan fleet, led by an able and energetic commander named Lysander, met the Athenians in the Hellespont and defeated them. Lysander then swept down on Athens and laid siege to the city. The Athenians held out through the autumn and winter of the next year. But their vital grain shipments from the Black Sea area had been cut off at the Hellespont. Starved into submission, they surrendered in 404 BC.

Some of Athens's enemies demanded that the vanquished capital be sacked and burned, and its citizens sold into slavery. But Sparta decreed that Athens be allowed to stand. The memory of Athenian heroism against the Persians, nearly a century earlier, still resonated, and because of it the Spartans withheld their wrath. Athens did suffer one final ignominy, however. The Spartans set up what amounted to a puppet oligarchy, with Critias eventually emerging as virtual tyrant. He launched a reign of terror such as the city had not experienced since the repressions of Peisistratus's sons. Eventually Critias was overthrown and democracy restored yet again, but not until 1,500 citizens had been put to death.

For the weary, disheartened Athenians, the golden age had ended. But they could still cling to their cherished democracy, and, although they could not know it, great days were still to come in the fields of art, philosophy, and science. The world had not yet heard, for instance, the names Plato or Aristotle.

THE FLOWERING VOICE OF POETRY

From the dry evidence of public records, it would seem that Greek drama burst into being around the spring of 534 BC, when the first tragedies were staged by official decree at the Festival of Dionysus in Athens. But Greek tragedy was more than a public entertainment devised by a government to amuse a populace, and more than a ritual honoring Dionysus the god. It was the flowering of an art whose roots stretched back past memory into the Bronze Age and beyond. Both in content and in form, it was the full expression of the consciousness of an entire people.

The content of tragedy was myth, the vast collection of stories contained in the epics and hymns of Homer and his successors and engraved in the heart and mind of every Greek. In the familiar and ancient tales of the *Iliad* and the *Odyssey* lived every kind of character; the adventures and dilemmas of the characters mirrored every kind of human situation. And the greatest of the tragic poets — Aeschylus, Sophocles, Euripides — interpreted the characters and situations for their audiences to reveal to them the human condition. How do mortal men and women stand in relation to the immortal gods? What choices about the patterns of existence do humans have? What are the consequences of choice? How might people understand the ambiguity of the world and live with the fact that it is both evil and good, both kind and cruel? The tragic poets explored all of these questions in their plays.

But the tragic poets were not the first to explore the myths. They were the heirs of generations of Greek lyric poets, who had forged the language into verse forms of unparalleled beauty and versatility. *(Some of their work appears on the next two pages.)*

The forms were as familiar as the myths to the Greeks: The poetry was always sung for audiences, not written down for solitary readers. The verse itself was musical, with the distinctive rhythms that were specific to particular kinds of poems.

The poets might sing at symposiums and other private gatherings, but they achieved fame and fortune in poetic contests held at religious festivals. There, robed and garlanded, they competed in rhapsody, which was the unaccompanied intoning of verse, usually epic; in kitharody, or solo singing of verse to a lyre's accompaniment; and in choral lyric, for which they trained singers and dancers.

These contests were held all around Greece — in Delos, in Sparta, in Olympia — but not, until the early sixth century BC, in Athens. Poets were brought there by Peisistratus and his sons; rhapsodic contests were instituted there at the Great Panathenaic festival. And there, within the next generations, against the background of political upheaval and the Persian Wars, the great synthesis that was tragedy occurred.

Tradition credits the synthesis to the poet Thespis of Icaria, who conceived the idea of an actor to serve as counterpoint to his choruses. The actor was masked, a startling innovation: The actor was not a man singing his own verse, but a man impersonating another and speaking in another's voice.

Thespis won the tragedy prize at the first of the Festival of Dionysus contests, but only fragments of his poetry survive. The sweep of Greek tragedy can be seen in the works of his successors *(some of which is shown on pages 88-95).* These poets competed against others in contests not only in Athens but at festivals held all over Greece. They added actors to Thespis's one. And in their respective plays, they orchestrated the separate rhythms and forms of the lyric poets — the rhapsodies, the kitharodies, the choruses — into single works, harmonies that sang the passions of the human heart.

Songs of Early Poets

Elegies, satires, love songs for solo singers; hymns, paeans, processionals for choruses — all of these the lyric poets of Greece bequeathed to the dramatists of Athens. Each kind of verse had its own distinct form. All shared the rich legacy of myth.

Not much of the lyricists' verse is preserved — just enough to show the variety of their styles and characters. Among the poets, Sappho, born in Lesbos in the seventh century BC, was unique both because she was a woman and because of her delicate genius: Plato is said to have called her the tenth muse. Sappho was famed for her love songs and for the joy in the natural world that appears in such poems as her song for the evening star, given here.

Alcaeus of Lesbos knew and loved her; enough words of their poems have survived to show that she refused him. Alcaeus's own poems reflect a life of war and politics — and a robust appreciation of life's pleasures, especially drinking, as the excerpt opposite reveals.

Simonides of Kea, born about 550 BC, was a widely traveled court poet, patronized by the tyrants of Athens, Thessaly, and Syracuse. He was a master, admired for the range and perfection of his songs, for the elegance of his funeral epigrams (one for a soothsayer killed at Thermopylae is given here) and for the depth he gave to mythic themes. His lament for Danaë, shown here, is an example. It concerns the woman who bore a child — the hero Perseus — to Zeus. Her father imprisoned her with the infant in a chest and cast them into the sea. By a miracle, they reached shore.

Younger than Simonides, Pindar of Thebes was as extensively patronized and achieved even greater fame. Lofty, idealistic, and profoundly religious, he celebrated in his odes the Greeks' victories in the Persian Wars and the victories of athletes at Olympia. The introduction to his first Olympian Ode, in honor of Hieron, a victor in the horse races, is given here.

Evening Star

You are the herdsman of evening
Hesperus, you herd
homeward whatever
Dawn's light dispersed

You herd sheep — herd
goats — herd children
home to their mothers

Sappho

First Olympian Ode

Water is preeminent and gold, like a fire
burning in the night, outshines
all possessions that magnify men's pride.
But if, my soul, you yearn
to celebrate great games,
look no further for another star
shining through the deserted ether
brighter than the sun, or for a contest
mightier than Olympia — where the song
has taken its coronal
design of glory, plaited
in the minds of poets
as they come, calling on Zeus' name,
to the rich radiant hall of Hieron
who wields the scepter of justice in Sicily,
reaping the prime of every distinction.
And he delights in the flare of music,
the brightness of song circling
his table from man to man.

Pindar

WINTER SCENE

Zeus rains upon us, and from the sky comes down
enormous winter. Rivers have turned to ice. . . .

Dash down the winter. Throw a log on the fire
and mix the flattering wine (do not water it
too much) and bind on round our foreheads
soft ceremonial wreaths of spun fleece.

We must not let our spirits give way to grief.
By being sorry we get no further on,
my Bukchis. Best of all defenses
is to mix plenty of wine, and drink it.

Alcaeus

EPITAPH

This is the grave of that Megístias, whom once the Persians
and Medes killed when they crossed Spercheíos River; a seer
who saw clearly the spirits of death advancing upon him,
yet could not bring himself to desert the Spartiate kings.

Simonides

DANAË AND PERSEUS

. . . when in the wrought chest
the wind blowing over
and the sea heaving
struck her with fear, her cheeks not dry,
she put her arm over Perseus and spoke: My child
such trouble I have.
And you sleep, your heart is placid;
you dream in the joyless wood;
in the night nailed in bronze,
in the blue dark you lie still and shine.
The salt water that towers above your head
as the wave goes by you
heed not, nor the wind's voice; you press
your bright face to the red blanket.
If this danger were danger to you,
your small ear would attend my words.
But I tell you: Sleep, my baby, and let the sea sleep, let
our trouble sleep; let some change appear

Zeus father, from you.
This bold word and beyond justice
I speak, I pray you, forgive it me.

Simonides

TRAGEDIANS

Among the scores of tragic poets, the greatest were said to be three. Aeschylus, the oldest, was born a decade or so before 500 BC. Son of an aristocrat, he was a soldier who fought at Marathon. He produced more than seventy plays; seven survive. Genial, brilliantly educated Sophocles, born around 497, was an Athenian who served in battle with Pericles in the Samian War. Seven of his 130 plays have been preserved. Euripides, born about 480, was an austere philosopher, reclusive and less idealistic than his colleagues. He wrote some ninety plays. Eighteen remain.

Almost all of these tragedies were first presented as trilogies followed by satyr plays — wild mimes honoring the god Dionysus — in the theater of Dionysus Eleuthereus by the Acropolis in Athens. The enormous stone shell of the amphitheater could seat 15,000; its semicircular shape created acoustics famed for centuries. Within it was the round orchestra or dancing floor, with the altar of Dionysus at the center, and the skene, or stage, behind. This was a platform surmounted by a rectangular wooden building whose facade concealed dressing and prop rooms and whose three doors provided exits and entrances.

A play began at first light, when an actor, in his linen-and-plaster mask, long tunic and cloak, and high shoes, gave the prologue. Then the lines of the chorus swept in singing. Second and third actors entered to speak the dialogues, which alternated with the commentary songs of the chorus, until the play rose to its end, and chorus and actors together sang the kommoses, or final laments.

The music has been lost, but the words of the poets still reverberate, as the passages on this and the following pages show.

THE PERSIANS

The Persians, presented in 472 BC with the young Pericles as leader of the chorus, was a departure in that it dealt with a contemporary subject. It described the Greek defeat of Xerxes as a Persian tragedy, brought about by overreaching. In this messenger's speech to the Persian court (an earlier section of which explains the naval strategy), Aeschylus describes the defeat at Salamis in much more vivid detail than that found in the accounts of historians.

. . . And when the light of the sun had perished
and night came on, the masters of the oar
and men at arms went down into the ships;
then line to line the longships passed the word,
and every one sailed in commanded line.
All that night long the captains of the ships
ordered the sea people at their stations.
The night went by, and still the Greek fleet
gave order for no secret sailing out.
But when the white horses of the daylight
took over the whole earth, clear to be seen,
the first noise was the Greeks shouting with joy,
like singing, like triumph, and then again
echoes rebounded from the island rocks.
The barbarians were afraid, our strategy
was lost, and there was no Greek panic in
that solemn battle-song they chanted then,
but battle-hunger, courage of spirit;
the trumpet's note set everything ablaze.
Suddenly by command their foaming oars
beat, beat in the deep of the salt water,
and all at once they were clear to be seen.
First the right wing in perfect order leading,
then the whole fleet followed out after them,
and one great voice was shouting in our ears:
"Sons of the Greeks, go forward, and set free
your fathers' country and set free your sons,
your wives, the holy places of your gods,
the monuments of your own ancestors,
now is the one battle for everything."
Our Persian voices answered roaring out,
and there was no time left before the clash.
Ships smashed their bronze beaks into ships,
it was a Greek ship in the first assault
that cut away the whole towering stem
from a Phoenician, and another rammed
timber into another. Still at first
the great flood of the Persian shipping held,
but multitudes of ships crammed up together,
no help could come from one to the other,
they smashed one another with brazen beaks,
and the whole rowing fleet shattered itself.
So then the Greek fleet with a certain skill
ran inwards from a circle around us,
and the bottoms of ships were overturned,
there was no seawater in eyesight,
only wreckage and bodies of dead men,
and beaches and rocks all full of dead.
Whatever ships were left out of our fleet
rowed away in no order in panic.
The Greeks with broken oars and bits of wreck
smashed and shattered the men in the water
like tunny, like gaffed fish. One great scream
filled up all the sea's surface with lament,
until the eye of darkness took it all.

Aeschylus

THE TROJAN WOMEN

...You ships' prows, that the fugitive
oars swept back to blessed Ilium
over the sea's blue water
by the placid harbors of Hellas
to the flute's grim beat
and the swing of the shrill boat whistles;
you made the crossing, made fast ashore . . .
alas, by the coasts of Troy;
it was you ships, that carried the fatal bride
of Menelaus . . .
Now she has killed
the sire of the fifty sons,
Priam; me; unhappy Hecuba,
she drove on this reef of ruin . . .
Come then, sad wives of the Trojans
whose spears were bronze,
their daughters, brides of disaster,
let us mourn the smoke of Ilium.
And I, as among winged birds
the mother, lead out
the clashing cry, the song; not that song
wherein once long ago,
when I held the scepter of Priam,
my feet were queens of the choir and led
the proud dance to the gods of Phrygia.

Euripides

The siege of Troy and its consequences loomed large in the imagination of all Greeks, especially the tragedians. Euripides' *Trojan Women,* produced in 416 BC, is set in Troy after its fall.

The play is a long lament on the horrors of war — for the warriors who have died and the women who must go as captives of foreign chieftains. In this passage, Hecuba, the Trojan queen, mourns the terrors of the Greek invaders and the cruel fate that she and her children must suffer.

ANTIGONE

. . . Danaë suffered too.
She went from the light to the brass-built room,
chamber and tomb together. Like you, poor child,
she was of great descent, and more, she held and kept
the seed of the golden rain which was Zeus.
Fate has terrible power.
You cannot escape it by wealth or war.
No fort will keep it out, no ships outrun it.

Remember the angry king,
son of Dryas, who raged at the god and paid,
pent in a rock-walled prison. His bursting wrath
slowly went down. As the terror of madness went,
he learned of his frenzied attack on the god.
Fool, he had tried to stop
the dancing women possessed of god,
the fire of Dionysus, the songs and flutes.

Where the dark rocks divide
sea from sea in Thrace
is Salmydessus whose savage god
beheld the terrible blinding wounds
dealt to Phineus' sons by their father's wife.
Dark the eyes that looked to avenge their mother.
Sharp with her shuttle she struck, and blooded her hands.

Wasting they wept their fate,
settled when they were born
to Cleopatra, unhappy queen.
She was a princess too, of an ancient house,
reared in the cave of the wild north wind, her father.
Half a goddess but, child, she suffered like you.

Sophocles

Produced in 441 BC, the play *Antigone* relates the tragic fate of the daughter of Oedipus of Thebes, condemned for honoring her rebellious brother's corpse. Here the chorus mourns for Antigone with glances at tragic myths familiar to the Greeks: of Danaë *(page 87);* of Lycurgus, who raged at the god Dionysus, was driven mad, and killed his son Dryas; of Phineus, whose second wife caused the blinding of his first wife Cleopatra's sons.

AESCHYLUS:
ANCIENT VENGEANCE

Aeschylus's great trilogy, *The Oresteia*, explores the age-old tale of the house of Atreus on the intimate scale of human love and hate, and on the broader measure of history. The background to the story is this: Atreus, king of Mycenae (or Argos) slaughtered the children of his brother Thyestes; only a son, Aegisthus, survived. Later, Atreus's sons Agamemnon and Menelaus married the sisters Clytemnestra and Helen. When Helen left Menelaus for Paris of Troy, the brothers mounted the expedition that began the Trojan War, Agamemnon sacrificing his daughter for fair winds on the journey. In *Agamemnon*, which begins the trilogy, the king returns victorious from Troy. But in his absence Clytemnestra has taken Aegisthus as a lover and with him rules the kingdom; to avenge her daughter and keep power, she murders Agamemnon. In *The Libation Bearers*, Orestes, son of Clytemnestra and Agamemnon, returns to Mycenae from hiding and, to avenge his father, murders Clytemnestra and her lover. Savage goddesses called the Eumenides, or Furies, pursue him, demanding his blood for his mother's. The final play, *The Eumenides*, resolves the issue: Younger gods, led by Athena — with a jury of mortals — judge Orestes, deciding that vengeance is satisfied and that the killing must end. They transform the Eumenides, taking them into the hierarchy of new gods as protectors of Athens.

With this tangle of relationships, Aeschylus illuminated larger issues. In ages when private acts guided public policy, the result was death and destruction; so the chorus sings of Helen in the passage from *Agamemnon* printed here. The custom of vengeance traps nations for generation after generation; a chorus of war captives laments the fact in this passage from *The Libation Bearers*. Yet, with a new order of civilization, these patterns can be altered, and *The Eumenides* closes with a quiet song of peace.

AGAMEMNON

. . .She took to Ilium her dowry, death.
She stepped forth lightly between the gates
daring beyond all daring. And the prophets
about the great house wept aloud and spoke:
"Alas, alas for the house and for the champions,
alas for the bed signed with their love together.
Here now is silence, scorned, unreproachful.
The agony of his loss is clear before us.
Longing for her who lies beyond the sea
he shall see a phantom queen in his household.
Her images in their beauty
are bitterness to her lord now
where in the emptiness of eyes
all passion has faded."

Shining in dreams the sorrowful
memories pass; they bring him
vain delight only.
It is vain, to dream and to see splendors,
and the image slipping from the arms' embrace
escapes, not to return again,
on wings drifting down the ways of sleep.

Such have the sorrows been in the house by the hearthside;
such have there been, and yet there are worse than these.
In all Hellas, for those who swarmed to the host
the heartbreaking misery
shows in the house of each.
Many are they who are touched at the heart by these things.
Those they sent forth they knew;
now, in place of the young men
urns and ashes are carried home
to the houses of the fighters.

The god of war, money changer of dead bodies,
held the balance of his spear in the fighting,
and from the corpse-fires at Ilium
sent to their dearest the dust
heavy and bitter with tears shed
packing smooth the urns with
ashes that once were men.
They praise them through their tears, how this man
knew well the craft of battle, how another
went down splendid in the slaughter:
and all for some strange woman.
Thus they mutter in secrecy,
and the slow anger creeps below their grief
at Atreus' sons and their quarrels.
There by the walls of Ilium
the young men in their beauty keep
graves deep in the alien soil
they hated and they conquered. . . .

THE EUMENIDES

. . .Home, home, o high, o aspiring
Daughters of Night, aged children, in blithe processional.
Bless them, all here, with silence.

In the primeval dark of earth-hollows
held in high veneration with rights sacrificial
bless them, all people, with silence.

Gracious be, wish what the land wishes,
follow, grave goddesses, flushed in the flamesprung
torchlight gay on your journey.
Singing all follow our footsteps.

There shall be peace forever between these people
of Pallas and their guests. Zeus the all seeing
met with Destiny to confirm it.
Singing all follow our footsteps.

THE LIBATION BEARERS

. . .Terror, the dream diviner of
this house, belled clear, shuddered the skin, blew wrath
from sleep, a cry in night's obscure watches,
a voice of fear deep in the house,
dropping deadweight in women's inner chambers.
And they who read the dream meanings
and spoke under guarantee of God
told how under earth
dead men held a grudge still
and smoldered at their murderers.

On such grace without grace, evil's turning aside
(Earth, Earth, kind mother!)
bent the godless woman
sends me forth. But terror
is on me for this word let fall.
What can wash off the blood once spilled upon the ground?
O hearth soaked in sorrow,
o wreckage of a fallen house.
Sunless and where men fear to walk
the mists huddle upon this house
where the high lords have perished.

The pride not to be warred with, fought with, not to be beaten down
of old, sounded in all men's
ears, in all hearts sounded,
has shrunk away. A man
goes in fear. High fortune,
this in man's eyes is god and more than god is this.
But, as a beam balances, so
sudden disasters wait, to strike
some in the brightness, some in gloom
of half dark in their elder time.
Desperate night holds others.

Through too much glut of blood drunk by our fostering ground
the vengeful gore is caked and hard, will not drain through.
The deep-run ruin carries away
the man of guilt. Swarming infection boils within.

For one who handles the bridal close, there is no cure.
All the world's waters running in a single drift
may try to wash blood from the hand
of the stained man; they only bring new blood guilt on.

But as for me: gods have forced on my city
resisted fate. From our fathers' houses
they led us here, to take the lot of slaves.
And mine it is to wrench my will, and consent
to their commands, right or wrong,
to beat down my edged hate.
And yet under veils I weep
the vanities that have killed
my lord; and freeze with sorrow in the secret heart.

SOPHOCLES: EXPLORING EVIL

In his Theban trilogy, Sophocles produced a study in ambiguity. The plays show that a person may be both innocent and guilty, and may with the right intentions do what is evil. Courage and acceptance seem the only responses to a cruelly irrational universe.

The opening play, *Oedipus the King*, unfolds a horror. Oedipus, a hero so wise that he solved the riddle of the Sphinx, has married the widowed queen of Thebes and so become its king. When the play begins, Thebes is cursed: It shelters a patricide who married his own mother, outraging the gods. Oedipus is that man. Acting in ignorance, unaware of his parentage, he still had acted. He had once killed a stranger — his father — and the woman he had married was his mother. Step by terrible step, he is led to the truth; the blind seer Tiresias, whose speech is printed here, begins his enlightenment. When Oedipus understands what he is, he blinds himself and wanders into exile.

In *Oedipus at Colonus*, the king, shunned by everyone except his daughter, Antigone, ends his wanderings at a hill outside the city of Athens. His — and humankind's — lot is mourned by the chorus in the verses shown here. Yet Oedipus, cursed, is also blessed: The earth opens at Colonus to take him into death and free him, and the place of death is sanctified.

The play *Antigone* shows once again a man acting as he thinks right, yet doing wrong. Creon, Antigone's uncle and father-in-law, has saved Thebes from revolutionaries, among them Antigone's now-dead brother. As revenge, Creon forbids that the body be buried. Antigone cannot bear the sacrilege, although defiance means death. She buries the body, admitting her deed in the dialogue printed here. She is entombed alive. Creon realizes too late his injustice and is punished. Antigone hangs herself in her tomb; Creon's son kills himself.

OEDIPUS THE KING

. . .If you are king, at least I have the right
no less to speak in my defence against you.
Of that much I am master. I am no slave
of yours, but Loxias', and so I shall not
enroll myself with Creon for my patron.
Since you have taunted me with being blind,
here is my word for you.
You have your eyes but see not where you are
in sin, nor where you live, nor whom you live with.
Do you know who your parents are? Unknowing
you are an enemy to kith and kin
in death, beneath the earth, and in this life.
A deadly footed, double striking curse,
from father and mother both, shall drive you forth
out of this land, with darkness on your eyes,
that now have such straight vision. Shall there be
a place will not be harbour to your cries,
a corner of Cithaeron will not ring
in echo to your cries, soon, soon, —
when you shall learn the secret of your marriage,
which steered you to a haven in this house, —
haven no haven, after lucky voyage?
And of the multitude of other evils
establishing a grim equality
between you and your children, you know nothing.

OEDIPUS AT COLONUS

. . .Though he has watched a decent age pass by,
A man will sometimes still desire the world.
I swear I see no wisdom in that man.
The endless hours pile up a drift of pain
More unrelieved each day; and as for pleasure,
When he is sunken in excessive age,
You will not see his pleasure anywhere.
The last attendant is the same for all,
Old men and young alike, as in its season
Man's heritage of underworld appears:
There being then no epithalamion,
No music and no dance. Death is the finish.

Not to be born surpasses thought and speech.
The second best is to have seen the light
And then to go back quickly whence we came.
The feathery follies of his youth once over,
What trouble is beyond the range of man?
What heavy burden will he not endure?
Jealousy, faction, quarreling, and battle —
The bloodiness of war, the grief of war.
And in the end he comes to strengthless age,
Abhorred by all men, without company,
Unfriended in that uttermost twilight
Where he must live with every bitter thing.

This is the truth, not for me only,
But for this blind and ruined man.
Think of some shore in the north the
Concussive waves make stream
This way and that in the gales of winter:
It is like that with him:
The wild wrack breaking over him
From head to foot, and coming on forever;
Now from the plunging down of the sun,
Now from the sunrise quarter,
Now from where the noonday gleams,
Now from the night and the north.

ANTIGONE

Creon
You — tell me not at length but in a word.
You knew the order not to do this thing?

Antigone
I knew, of course I knew. The word was plain.

Creon
And still you dared to overstep these laws?

Antigone
For me it was not Zeus who made that order.
Nor did that Justice who lives with the gods below
mark out such laws to hold among mankind.
Nor did I think your orders were so strong
that you, a mortal man, could over-run
the gods' unwritten and unfailing laws.
Not now, nor yesterday's, they always live,
and no one knows their origin in time.
So not through fear of any man's proud spirit
would I be likely to neglect these laws,
draw on myself the gods' sure punishment.
I knew that I must die; how could I not?
even without your warning. If I die
before my time, I say it is a gain.
Who lives in sorrows many as are mine
how shall he not be glad to gain his death?
And so, for me to meet this fate, no grief.
But if I left that corpse, my mother's son,
dead and unburied I'd have cause to grieve
as now I grieve not.
And if you think my acts are foolishness
the foolishness may be in a fool's eye.

Chorus
The girl is bitter. She's her father's child.
She cannot yield to trouble; nor could he.

Creon
These rigid spirits are the first to fall.
The strongest iron, hardened in the fire,
most often ends in scraps and shatterings.
Small curbs bring raging horses back to terms.
Slave to his neighbor, who can think of pride?
This girl was expert in her insolence
when she broke bounds beyond established law.
Once she had done it, insolence the second,
to boast her doing, and to laugh in it.
I am no man and she the man instead
if she can have this conquest without pain.
She is my sister's child, but were she child
of closer kin than any at my hearth,
she and her sister should not so escape
their death and doom. I charge Ismene too.
She shared the planning of this burial.
Call her outside. I saw her in the house,
maddened, no longer mistress of herself.
The sly intent betrays itself sometimes
before the secret plotters work their wrong.
I hate it too when someone caught in crime
then wants to make it seem a lovely thing.

Antigone
Do you want more than my arrest and death?

Creon
No more than that. For that is all I need.

EURIPIDES:
DENIAL OF THE GOD

Euripides wrote tragedies on Iphigenia, Agamemnon's daughter; on the murderous Medea; and on Hippolytus, Theseus's son, who was falsely accused of trying to seduce his stepmother. Perhaps his most brilliant and terrifying work, however, concerned the god who was patron of his own art. That play was *The Bacchae,* written at the end of Euripides' life, when he had retired from weakening, strife-torn Athens to the wilds of Macedonia.

The god Dionysus was a primitive spirit of fertility and divine creativity, who gave humanity the gift of wine. He was worshiped in often-secret, bloody, and orgiastic rites throughout Greece. Those who accepted him, believers said, became a part of him and partook of divine inspiration. Those who refused to worship him were driven to madness.

In Euripides' play, the young god Dionysus appears with his chorus of pious and joyful believers in Thebes to receive its worship and to prove his own divinity: He was said to have been conceived by Zeus with a Theban princess. But Pentheus, king of Thebes, a rigid and excitable man, denies the god and in fact commits the sacrilege of putting him in chains. Then Dionysus fills the women of Thebes with madness and sends them — led by Pentheus's mother — into the mountains to revel as his Bacchae, or followers. And he drives Pentheus insane, luring him to the high fields, where the women are. There Pentheus meets a terrible end at the hands of his demented mother, who has been driven to bestial frenzy. For reasons of decorum, such violence was not shown in tragedy: The scene on the mountain is described by a messenger, whose speech is given here.

THE BACCHAE

. . .There were three of us in all: Pentheus and I, attending my master, and that stranger who volunteered his services as guide. Leaving behind us the last outlying farms of Thebes, we forded the Asopus and struck into the barren scrubland of Cithaeron.

There in a grassy glen we halted, unmoving, silent, without a word, so we might see but not be seen. From that vantage, in a hollow cut from the sheer rock of the cliffs, a place where water ran and the pines grew dense with shade, we saw the Maenads sitting, their hands busily moving at their happy tasks. Some wound the stalks of their tattered wands with tendrils of fresh ivy; others, frisking like fillies newly freed from the painted bridles, chanted in Bacchic songs, responsively.

But Pentheus — unhappy man — could not quite s the companies of women. "Stranger," he said, "from where I stand, I cannot see these counterfeite Maenads. But if I climbed that towering fir that overhangs the banks, then I could see their shameles orgies better."

And now the stranger worked a miracle. Reaching for the highest branch of a great fir, he bent it down, down, down to the dark earth, till it was curved the way a taut bow bends or like a rim of wood when forced about the circle of a wheel. Like that he forced that mountain fir down to the ground. No mortal could have done it. Then he seated Pentheus at the highest tip and with his hands let the trunk rise straightly up, slowly and gently, lest it throw its rider. And the tree rose, towering to heaven, with my master huddled at the top. And now the Maenads saw hi more clearly than he saw them. But barely had they seen, when the stranger vanished and there came a

great voice out of heaven — Dionysus', it must have
been — crying: "Women, I bring you the man who has
mocked at you and me and at our holy mysteries.
Take vengeance upon him." And as he spoke
a flash of awful fire bound earth and heaven.
The high air hushed, and along the forest glen
the leaves hung still; you could hear no cry of beasts.
The Bacchae heard that voice but missed its words,
and leaping up, they stared, peering everywhere.
Again that voice. And now they knew his cry,
the clear command of god. And breaking loose
like startled doves, through grove and torrent,
over jagged rocks, they flew, their feet maddened
by the breath of god. And when they saw my master
perching in his tree, they climbed a great stone
that towered opposite his perch and showered him
with stones and javelins of fir, while the others
hurled their wands. And yet they missed their target,
poor Pentheus in his perch, barely out of reach
of their eager hands, treed, unable to escape.
Finally they splintered branches from the oaks
and with those bars of wood tried to lever up the tree
by prying at the roots. But every effort failed.
Then Agave cried out: "Maenads, make a circle
about the trunk and grip it with your hands.
Unless we take this climbing beast, he will reveal
the secrets of the god." With that, thousands of
hands tore the fir tree from the earth, and down, down
from his high perch fell Pentheus, tumbling
to the ground, sobbing and screaming as he fell,
for he knew his end was near. His own mother,
like a priestess with her victim, fell upon him
first. But snatching off his wig and snood
so she would recognize his face, he touched her cheeks,
screaming, "No, no, Mother! I am Pentheus,
your own son, the child you bore to Echion!
Pity me, spare me, Mother! I have done a wrong,
but do not kill your own son for my offense."
But she was foaming at the mouth, and her crazed
eyes rolling with frenzy. She was mad, stark mad,

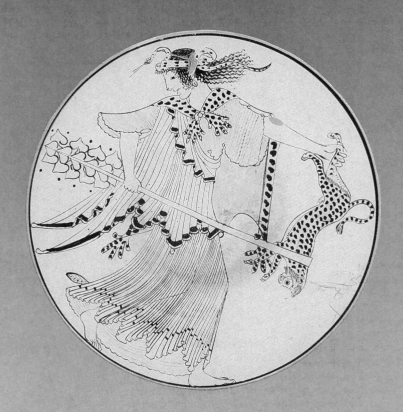

possessed by Bacchus. Ignoring his cries of pity,
she seized his left arm at the wrist; then, planting
her foot upon his chest, she pulled, wrenching away
the arm at the shoulder — not by her own strength,
for the god had put inhuman power in her hands.
Ino, meanwhile, on the other side, was scratching off
his flesh. Then Autonoë and the whole horde
of Bacchae swarmed upon him. Shouts everywhere,
he screaming with what little breath was left,
they shrieking in triumph. One tore off an arm,
another a foot still warm in its shoe. His ribs
were clawed clean of flesh and every hand
was smeared with blood as they played ball with
scraps of Pentheus' body.

   The pitiful remains lie scattered,
one piece among the sharp rocks, others
lying lost among the leaves in the depths
of the forest. His mother, picking up his head,
impaled it on her wand. She seems to think it is
some mountain lion's head which she carries in
triumph through the thick of Cithaeron. Leaving her
sisters at the Maenad dances, she is coming here,
gloating over her grisly prize. She calls upon Bacchus:
he is her "fellow-huntsman," "comrade of the
chase, crowned with victory." But all the victory
she carries home is her own grief.

   Now, before Agave returns, let me leave
this scene of sorrow. Humility,
a sense of reverence before the sons of heaven —
of all the prizes that a mortal man might win,
these, I say, are wisest; these are best.

DAWN OF THE ROMANS

3 Midway through the first millennium before Christ, two new peoples rose to importance in Europe. One group, the Romans, occupied an embryonic city-state on the Tiber River in the central part of the Italian peninsula. The other group, the Celts, inhabited a great many small, rural enclaves strewn over territory stretching 1,600 miles from central Europe to the Iberian Peninsula.

It would be difficult to imagine two cultures of sharper contrast. The Romans and Celts differed not only in language, religion, and way of life but also in their essential interests and temperaments. The Romans were sober, disciplined, and orderly, with a predilection for written law and a passion for political organization. The Celts were high-spirited warriors — headhunters no less — who loved drinking and brawling. In one regard, however, they were very much alike. Both developed a taste for imposing their will upon others by force of arms. Thus, although initially they were hundreds of miles and worlds apart, they were embarked upon a collision course that would lead to repeated conflict — and the eventual ascendancy of one and eclipse of the other.

Rome was rooted, ethnically as well as geographically, in that region of the western coastal plain of central Italy known as Latium. Bounded on the north by the Tiber River, on the east by the Apennine Mountains, and on the south by the Volscian Hills, this region covered only about 700 square miles. And its inhabitants, the Latins, were merely one group among dozens of diverse peoples who inhabited the Italian peninsula during the first millennium BC. These Latins were a meld of a group of newcomers with an indigenous society that had inhabited the area for centuries. The newcomers were Indo-Europeans who originated on the Eurasian steppes, from the same basic Aryan rootstock as the people who had become Persians, Aryan Indians, and Greeks. They had migrated first to central Europe and then, late in the second millennium BC, down into Italy, where they merged with a resident population of unknown origin.

The land of the Latins was far different from the parched region of sparse vegetation that it would be 3,000 years later. The soil then was well watered and rich in ash from volcanic activity; there were more than fifty craters within twenty-five miles of where Rome would be built, some of them still smoking in 1000 BC. The hills were thick with pine and fir trees, and oak, beech, and laurel covered the plains. Gradually the Latins cleared sections of forest to grow millet, wheat, and figs. Later, they would learn from the Greeks to cultivate grapes for wine and olives for oil. Their pigs foraged the forest floor for roots and nuts while their oxen and sheep grazed grassy meadows. Because the loose volcanic soil was easily eroded, they constructed dams and extensive drainage systems to prevent their hillside fields from washing away.

A group of Latin sheepherders took up residence about 1000 BC or so on a hill on the east bank of the Tiber, some fifteen miles from the river's mouth. The steep and densely wooded eminence, the Palatine Hill, was naturally moated by marshes and afforded some protection from enemies. It was the most impregnable of the seven hills (actually three separate hills with four adjacent spurs) on which one day would rise the city of Rome. These pioneer Romans built small, round mud huts and buried the ashes of their dead in urns in the marshy ground below — the area that eventually would become the city's great public square, the Forum. They left no written records of those days. They did not adopt writing until the sixth century BC, and the first history of Rome would not appear until late in the third century BC. By then, both Roman and Greek writers were resorting to myth to explain the city's origins.

The story of Romulus and Remus was to become the best known of these legends. Sired by the god of war, Mars, these newborn twins were left on the bank of the Tiber to be washed away by floodwaters but were rescued by a she-wolf who suckled them. According to the story, Romulus eventually established Rome on April 21, 753 BC, after slaying his brother in a fight over which hill the city should be built upon. One later Roman writer, Livy, was so convinced that the city's destiny had been ordained by the gods that he had Romulus announce, ''Go, proclaim to the Romans it is heaven's will that my Rome shall be the capital of the world.'' As tradition said, Rome was not built in a day. The clusters of mud huts on the Palatine Hill grew slowly. By the eighth century BC, some 200 years after the first shepherds settled there, larger buildings made of timber appeared. Small villages also began to dot the neighboring hills.

These hilltop settlements, though similar to farming villages springing up throughout

The great Etruscan bronze statue of a wary, protective she-wolf, cast about 480 BC, became a symbol of Rome. The city's legendary founders, the twins Romulus and Remus, were said to have been suckled and protected by a mother wolf. The wolf's naturalistic head and rib cage reflect the Etruscan artistic tradition, but the stylized curls of the animal's mane were borrowed from earlier Greek and Near Eastern figures of lions; wolves do not have manes. In the fifteenth century AD, figures of the infant twins were added to the bronze figure, probably by the Italian Renaissance sculptor Antonio Pollaiuolo.

Latium, possessed certain advantages. They were far enough from the coast to protect the inhabitants from the many pirates who plied the Mediterranean. The Tiber itself was so swift and treacherous that it was unsuitable for navigation by all but small boats. (Rome eventually had to establish its harbor downstream at Ostia, at the river's mouth.) More important, the hilltop villages commanded routes of communication that bore the peninsula's budding commerce and, in centuries to come, would be tramped by its warring armies. The Tiber Valley itself was already an important conduit for east-west trade. And commerce moving on several routes that ran north and south through the region had to funnel into a narrow ford across the Tiber just south of Rome. One staple of early Italian commerce was the salt found in abundance near the Tiber's mouth. So much of it was transported along a route from there to Rome and on into the interior that the ancient pathway was called the Via Salaria — "Salt Road." Later, the roads built by the Romans to follow these natural conduits would, as the saying had it, "all lead to Rome."

The separate villages grew and began to coalesce. The first tentative steps toward union probably stemmed from their shared religion, a form of nature worship. Early in the seventh century BC, inhabitants from various villages joined in a religious festival called the Septimontium, a reference to the "Seven Mounts," or hills. Less than a century later, by 600 BC, the villages had grown into a single, large, flourishing city with a population of perhaps 80,000 — traders and other workers as well as farmers — centered on the Forum and surrounded by protective earthworks.

During the following century, the growth of the city was profoundly influenced by its neighbors just across the Tiber, the Etruscans — in those days the most powerful and advanced people on the Italian peninsula. The Etruscans inhabited a dozen city-states that shared a common language and culture but not a single government. Their homeland, Etruria, extended across the breadth of the peninsula, from the Arno River south and east to the west bank of the Tiber. The foundations of Etruscan power were farming and the mining and refining of metal ores. But the Etruscans also were skilled traders and seafarers who carried on commerce with other Mediterranean powers. Their trading partners included Carthage, the increasingly important Phoenician colony on the North African coast, and the Greek colony at Cumae, some 300 miles south of Rome on the peninsula's west coast. About 600 BC, Etruscan invaders — probably from the cities of Tarquinii and Caere — took over Latium and started bringing the city on the seven hills into the mainstream of Mediterranean commerce and culture.

The transformation occurred during the following century under two, or perhaps three, Etruscans who ruled successively as kings of Rome with the backing of a handful of powerful Etruscan families that took up residence in the metropolis. To begin with, the conquerors may have given the city its name, Rome, which probably came from the Etruscan language, a non-Indo-European tongue of puzzling origin. Most important, the Etruscans introduced to the Romans the alphabet they had adopted from the Greeks, who in turn had obtained it from the seafaring Phoenicians. Roman religion also borrowed from the Etruscans. Under that aegis, Jupiter, Minerva, and Juno were established as the leading deities in the Roman pantheon, and a large Etruscan-style temple dedicated to the triad was constructed on the Capitoline Hill. The Romans welcomed all the deities they could appropriate — the more the better, especially in time of war. They took them from Greece and overseas as well as from other Italian cultures. From Greece, too, though probably via Etruscan intermediaries, came the anthropomorphic notion that the gods looked and behaved like earthly beings.

In addition, Roman priests adopted from their Etruscan rulers the ancient practices of divination and augury. The purpose was to ascertain the will of the gods, and thus foretell the future, by methods such as inspecting the entrails of animals at sacrifice or observing patterns in the flight of birds. The Romans took these practices so seriously that rulers or generals would seldom launch a battle without first consulting with a priest. But they preferred the Etruscan brand: As late as the first century, Roman *augures* were still being imported from Etruria.

Romans learned new skills from Etruscan potters and metalworkers, who were among the most advanced in Europe. Etruscan engineers dug tunnels to drain marshy farmland and the remaining waterlogged sections of the Forum, beginning work on the Cloaca Maxima, Rome's great network of sewers. They taught the Romans how to pave their roads with cobblestones and how to use the arch in stone construction. They built the first bridge, a wooden structure, across the Tiber. They probably passed on the concept of rectangular layouts of streets, which characterized their own cities.

Not least of all, they introduced Romans to their social customs — for example, how to dress. The long, flowing mantles worn by the Etruscans were the forerunners of the loosely draped Roman togas. In Roman hands, togas became an indicator of status. Only a citizen could wear one, and males wore only white togas — edged in scarlet or royal purple if they were priests, city officials, or mere boys, the latter group being given the privilege as a reminder of the Roman ideal that young males were to be treated with respect. The Etruscans also evidently gave the Roman aristocracy a taste for high living, including lavish parties and celebrations that often featured spirited dancing or contests such as chariot racing. Etruscan nobles also fostered fierce hand-to-hand fights between slaves or prisoners of war that were the gory prototypes of Rome's later gladiatorial contests.

Despite the wide-ranging Etruscan influences, the Romans kept their own special identity. They retained their Latin tongue and most of their own political and social institutions. These institutions included a distinctive two-tier caste system. All Roman citizens were born into one of two classes: the nobles, known as patricians, or the commoners, called plebeians. (Neither women nor slaves qualified as citizens.) Patricians were wealthy and came from the old aristocratic families. Although some plebeians amassed wealth, most were ordinary farmers or tradesmen, artisans or laborers.

Patricians dominated the monarchy. The king, whether Etruscan or Roman by birth, was a patrician. He typically was elected by the Senate, a patrician council comprising leaders from the city's leading families. The selection was then presented for approval to an assembly called the Comitia Curiata. This assembly, or "committee," consisted of the thirty kinship-based groups, or curiae, into which all of the arms-bearing men of Rome, patricians and plebeians alike, had been divided. Each curia conducted its own religious worship and contributed a specific quota of ten cavalrymen and 100 infantrymen to the Roman militia. In the assembly, each curia member had a vote, but decisions hinged upon a majority of the groups rather than of the individual voters. The king consulted with the Senate and the Comitia Curiata. But in theory at least, he ruled with absolute authority. He led the state to war as commander in chief, conducted religious ceremonies as the chief priest, and imposed punishments as the supreme judge.

The concept of absolute authority, known as imperium, characterized society at all levels. In the family, for example, the father ruled like a king. He was the paterfamilias, head of the household, which included not only family members but also slaves. He owned all the property and exercised total control over his children, whom he could sell into slavery or even put to death with impunity. Upon his death, he was succeeded as paterfamilias by the eldest son. If a family head lacked a son, the women of the household came under the guardianship of his nearest male relative.

Though theoretically unlimited, patriarchal power, like the imperium of the king, was typically applied with restraint. One of the limiting factors was ancestral custom, what the Romans called *mos maiorum,* "ways of the fathers." Another was the concept of *pietas,* the proper observance of obligations to the gods, to the family, and — as an extension of the duty Romans felt toward the family — to the state. Ultimately, the impetuous exercise of imperium was checked also by the character trait that Romans admired most — *gravitas.* Literally translated as "dignity," the word also implied something broader — gravity — and thus suggested the sober, dignified, weighty approach to life that marked not only the individual personality but most things Roman.

The power of the paterfamilias extended from the family level to the larger kin group. Each family unit belonged to a gens, or clan, the grouping of families claiming descent from a common ancestor through the male line. There were about sixty patrician clans during Etruscan domination of Rome in the sixth century BC. Each was headed by a wealthy male landowner who sat in the Roman Senate and wielded great influence over the families of his clan and over his plebeian clients, the tenant farmers who worked his land and artisans who depended on his protection.

It was the heads of the clans and other patricians who decided, after about a century of Etruscan domination, to take back the imperium they

By 400 BC, the vigorous and warlike Celts with their iron-based culture dominated much of the European continent, as shown in the larger map below. The center of the Celts' power, and the location of their principal fortified towns, was in present-day Austria, southern Germany, France, and the Low Countries. But they had also penetrated into the Po Valley in northern Italy, into the Iberian Peninsula, and as far as the British Isles. The smaller map shows the Italian peninsula during the same period, when an emerging Rome was challenging the Etruscan city-states for territory while also fighting off several combative tribes such as the Volsci and Aequi.

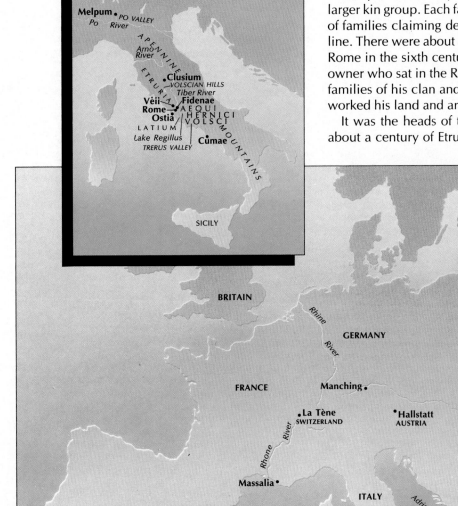

Etruscan temples usually had walls and columns made of sun-dried brick and foundations of tufa, a soft yellow-gray volcanic stone. The roof, tiled with terra-cotta and heavily decorated, was supported by beams and rafters of wood. The interior was laid out simply, with a large, open-air main chamber and, behind it, up to three smaller enclosed rooms.

Etruscans demonstrated their passion for art in the lavish way they decorated their temples. The temple buildings themselves, as seen above, sometimes seemed squat and heavy. But they were embellished with vividly painted terra-cotta sculptures, like those presented here and on the next page, that gave them a spirited air.

Six-foot-tall statues, usually of gods and goddesses adopted from the Greek pantheon, paraded across the temple roofs, faces beaming with the warm, enigmatic smiles that characterized Etruscan statuary. Bands of colorful tiles, often with floral motifs, ran underneath the eaves, and terra-cotta plaques decorated with human or divine faces were ranged along the edges of roofs to protect wooden rafters and beams from the elements. So elaborately decorated were the shrines that the Greeks, who favored simple elegance in their temple design, sniffed at what they considered the Etruscans' vulgar taste.

ORNAMENTED TEMPLES

A bearded satyr attempts to seduce a female mortal in the terracotta statue above, which once decorated a temple at Satricum, a town near Italy's west coast. The smiling face at left belongs to Turms, the Etruscan version of the Greek Hermes, messenger of the gods. The head was part of a full-length statue atop a temple in Veii, an Etruscan metropolis twelve miles from Rome.

Dressed in Etruscan-style tunic and cloak, the sun god Aplu — known as Apollo to the Greeks — stood on a temple ridgepole in Veii. The statue was created in the sixth century BC, possibly by a sculptor named Vulca, the only Etruscan artist so famous in his own time that his name would still be known 2,500 years later.

This damaged but still vivid sculpture of two warriors locked in furious combat — one of them is broken off at the hip — embellished a temple in the city of Falerii during the fifth century BC. About thirty inches high, the terra-cotta was probably wedged into a corner of the pediment over the temple entrance.

A silenus, the legendary chief of satyrs, decorated the eaves of a temple built at Pyrgi about 460 BC. Such plaques were made by pressing clay into a mold, firing it, and then painting the result in bright colors.

had granted their current king, Tarquinius Superbus. Perhaps they had grown tired of the monarchy. Almost certainly they and other Latins were weary of the Etruscans, for a general uprising occurred throughout Latium during the same period. Whatever the case, shortly before the turn of the fifth century BC — tradition pinpoints the year as 509 BC — they rebelled and rid themselves of Tarquinius, the entire institution of the monarchy, and the Etruscan families that had dominated Roman life.

The patricians replaced the monarchy with their own special form of republic. The single king was supplanted by a pair of chief magistrates who came to be known as consuls. The two consuls retained the trappings of imperium installed under the Etruscan monarchy, including the aide who carried the fasces, the bundle of rods with ax blade protruding that nearly twenty-five centuries later would become the symbol of Mussolini's Italian Fascists. The consuls also retained a good deal of the substance of authority, such as supreme command in foreign affairs. But the patricians curtailed executive power in several important ways. They deprived the consuls of the king's religious authority and of much of his imperium in domestic matters. And whereas the king had enjoyed lifetime tenure in office, consuls were elected for only a year. Indeed, to exercise any power at all, the two men had to pull together, for each could veto the acts of the other. As the name consul implies, they had to consult with each other.

Executive power was so effectively limited that new provisions had to be worked out to avoid paralysis. As the institution finally evolved, the consuls ruled during alternate months; if both were together on the battlefield, they commanded on alternate days. However, during a war or other state crisis, the consuls, conferring with the Senate, could appoint a dictator to rule with absolute authority for up to six months.

Consuls were elected from the membership of the all-patrician Senate by a new kind of assembly that had largely taken over the duties and powers of the old Comitia Curiata, with its kin-group organization. The name of this new body, the Comitia Centuriata — assembly by centuries — referred to the Roman military formation, which ordinarily consisted of approximately 100 soldiers. The new assembly evolved from a system of classification of the male population intended to simplify wartime conscription. All male citizens, from seventeen to sixty years old, were grouped into seven classes based on how much military equipment they could provide in time of war. Patricians and the wealthiest of the plebeians, who could furnish horses, weapons, and armor, ranked at the top; poor plebeians, who could muster only slings and stones, occupied the class next to the bottom. The very bottom class consisted of the poorest men who, because they had no weapons at all, served in noncombatant roles. Each class was responsible for organizing and outfitting a certain number of centuries to be fielded in time of war. The two wealthiest classes, which could provide the most equipment, numbered ninety-eight centuries between them. All of the five lower-ranking classes together — far more populous than the top two classes — formed only ninety-five centuries.

While only about 100 men would actually go into battle as members of a century, many more than that might support the unit and be counted as part of it for voting purposes. Members of the assembly gathered on the Field of Mars outside the city when summoned by a trumpet call. The issue might be the election of new consuls, a declaration of war, or some proposal from the consuls. Although all free men were members of the Comitia Centuriata, votes were cast by centuries, not by individuals.

Because the wealthy classes had the most centuries, the patricians always controlled the vote. And because the roll call began with the top classes, a majority was achieved before the poorer plebeian centuries down the line had a chance to cast their dissenting ballots. If the issue was election of consuls, the patricians topped off their iron-handed control by convening the Senate. It was the job of the Senate to ratify the assembly's selections. The Senate, of course, contained only nobles who had been selected by the consuls, who themselves were former senators.

The patricians monopolized sacred as well as secular offices. Only patricians could become priests, and they controlled the religious Colleges of Pontiffs and Augurs, which were closely intertwined with the secular government. Augurs were necessary, for example, to provide assurance that the signs were auspicious for proceeding with a given matter of government business. In addition, religious rituals performed by priests were a necessary prelude to most public acts. The inability to perform these rituals further excluded plebeians from public life. Many plebeians felt enormous frustration. Their lives were less tolerable under the republic than under the monarchy. The kings, with their lifetime tenure, had been less beholden to the patricians than the new consuls were, and more likely to protect the plebeians from the grossest abuses.

Plebeian grievances extended up and down the ranks. Wealthy plebeians, no matter how vast their fortunes, could not achieve political and social equality even by marrying into the patrician class, for intermarriage was forbidden. But the plight of the farmers, who made up the bulk of Rome's population, was much worse. Typical peasants had to eke out a living on only about an acre and a third of land, which they might supplement by grazing animals on the public commons. The harsh debt laws enacted by the patricians haunted practically every farmer. Falling into debt after a season or two of failed crops was commonplace. Because the farmers could not under Roman law offer a mortgage on land in return for a loan, they frequently pledged their own persons as security. If they defaulted, the creditors could sell them into slavery or even put them to death. Farmers fortunate enough to keep up with their debts might be brought down in any case, along with fellow plebeians in the city, by one of the famines that periodically afflicted Rome because of drought or crops lost to warfare.

The plebeians began to fight back very early in the fifth century BC, not long after the founding of the Roman republic. Their battle for political equality and economic justice came to be known as the Struggle of the Orders. At first, it took the form of isolated incidents of violence, which the patricians quickly avenged. Then the plebeians hit upon the idea of enhancing their bargaining power by withholding their services from the Roman army, which was frequently engaged in battle with the Etruscans to the north or with Rome's southern neighbors in Latium. The plebeians realized that the patricians might be able to run the state without the lower class, but that they could not defend it alone. According to tradition, the plebeians staged the first of five major military strikes in 494 BC. Called out for a campaign, plebeian soldiers instead withdrew from the city — they called the action a *secessio*, or secession — and held a massive protest rally on the Mount of Curses. There, the story goes, they announced a list of demands and started establishing their own assembly, with its own officers, as an alternative to the patrician regime. To protect these officers, they swore an oath to punish by death anyone who so much as touched them with violent intent.

Apparently the patricians respected the threats. The new assembly survived, and less than a generation later, in 471 BC, the government officially recognized the plebeian state within a state. This assembly was simply grafted onto the government alongside the Curiata — which continued to meet, though obsolete for all practical purposes — and the powerful Centuriata. The new assembly was called the Comitia Tributa — Assembly of the People by Tribes — which referred to representation by place of residence. Its officers, known as tribunes, were elected annually by the assembly. There were two tribunes, a number that soon increased to at least ten.

The power of the assembly and its tribunes grew rapidly — thanks to the unrelenting pressure of the plebeians, who continued to wield their new weapon, the military strike. The assembly, for example, began to register influential expressions of popular opinion, which were called plebiscites, and to share legislative duties with the patrician Centuriata. The tribunes, already equipped with the right to prevent such arbitrary exercises of a patrician magistrate's authority as summary arrest, took on an extraordinary new power. Simply by calling out the word *veto* — "I forbid!" — a tribune could stop any act of the patrician consuls and other magistrates or block any measure proposed by a member of the Senate or the Centuriata.

Plebeians meanwhile pressed a case for the reform of Roman law. The law consisted of unwritten ancestral customs that patrician magistrates could pick and choose from by whim. Plebeians wanted the law codified. After continuing agitation, they succeeded about 450 BC, when the government approved the Twelve Tables, a law code inscribed on twelve different clay tablets. The Tables were a mixture of old and new. For example, the new code retained the prohibition against intermarriage between patrician and plebeian (although this ban was repealed only five years later). But it also started loosening the tyrannical hold of the male head of household on his family, by giving wife and children some legal means of escaping his authority. The new code launched the great tradition of Roman law. It inspired the recording of cases, with the result that magistrates could draw from written precedent instead of plucking vague customs from memory. And the Tables proved so enduring that Roman schoolboys were still learning them by heart four centuries later.

The Struggle of the Orders was to continue for two more centuries after the promulgation of the Tables, but despite the military strikes, plebeians and patricians alike took care that their internal differences did not seriously imperil the common good of their state. Together they created a civic pride and patriotism that energized Rome's expansion by conquest. Under the monarchy, the city had seized territory from its neighbors, increasing the area it controlled from perhaps fifty square miles in its earliest days to about 350 square miles. Soon after the launching of the republic in 509 BC, however, the Romans found themselves in a struggle to maintain those territorial gains — and, indeed, their very existence — against enemies on practically every front.

The first military task of the Roman republic was to fend off Etruscans attempting to regain control of the city. About 500 BC, according to tradition, an army under Lars Porsenna from the Etruscan city of Clusium was halted at the Tiber by the bravery of the legendary Horatius Cocles. Fighting alone on the west bank of the Tiber, Horatius held off the invaders while the bridge leading to Rome at his back was being destroyed. Having saved the city, Horatius then leaped into the river and died a martyr. His bravery at the bridge would be celebrated thereafter in poetry and story.

A year or so after beating back the Etruscans, the Romans found themselves at odds with their neighbors in Latium. These Latin cities shared with Rome and one another a common language and religion, and common political institutions. After throwing out

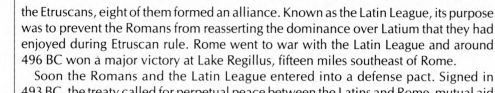

the Etruscans, eight of them formed an alliance. Known as the Latin League, its purpose was to prevent the Romans from reasserting the dominance over Latium that they had enjoyed during Etruscan rule. Rome went to war with the Latin League and around 496 BC won a major victory at Lake Regillus, fifteen miles southeast of Rome.

Soon the Romans and the Latin League entered into a defense pact. Signed in 493 BC, the treaty called for perpetual peace between the Latins and Rome, mutual aid in the event of war, and equal shares of whatever booty might be gained. In the pact, Rome relinquished its claims of hegemony over Latium. The treaty also provided for the sharing of private rights of citizenship, enabling Latins and Romans to conduct business and own property in each others' cities. This provision helped foster social and economic unification in Latium and became a key tool in Rome's later drive to weld together the people of Italy.

bronze Celtic warrior

rare bronze shield

The major military threat to the new alliance came from the Apennine Mountains. Two highland tribes, the Aequi to the east and the Volsci to the south, repeatedly invaded Latium during the fifth century BC. To drive a wedge between the highlanders, the Romans and Latins formed another alliance, this one with the Hernici people, who resided between the Aequi and Volsci. This was an early application of what became a familiar Roman policy — divide and conquer. Beating back the intruders required nearly a century, during which the Latins and Romans established new colonies in the liberated territories. The Romans populated the colonies with landless plebeians so poor that they previously had been unable to arm themselves and were thus ineligible for military service. Giving them land in the new colonies increased the pool of men available for the Roman army. The army grew more proficient as well, learning the art of war in the long campaigns against the Aequi and the Volsci.

By the late fifth century BC, the Romans felt ready for a showdown with their old

This bronze helmet probably belonged to a wealthy warrior; most Celtic soldiers wore leather helmets. The bird of prey on the crest originally had eyes of colored glass and articulated wings that could flap up and down.

Artistry in Weapons

Renowned for his ferocity and courage, the Celtic warrior — depicted in the figure opposite — plunged into battle naked but for a helmet, belt, and a metal collar called a torque. It was a ritual, perhaps of religious significance, to disrobe before fighting.

In battle, Celts hurled javelins and used other spears for thrusting at the enemy. For close-in combat, they depended on swords and daggers of iron — giving them an advantage over foes wielding softer bronze weapons. Most Celtic shields, which protected the body from knee to shoulder, were made of leather-covered wood; some were inlaid with bronze. Helmets were often topped with horns or animal figures that gave the wearer the appearance of great height.

The Celts believed that their fighting gear, including the torques around their necks, possessed magical, lifesaving properties. Confident of their invulnerability, they rushed wildly into battle, blowing trumpets and emitting blood-chilling war cries that inspired terror in their enemies.

rival, the Etruscan city of Veii. Only a dozen miles north of Rome, Veii stood on a steep hill enveloped on three sides by ravines. Its prosperity derived from the salt pans near the mouth of the Tiber and from fertile farmland, much of it either irrigated or reclaimed from swamp by an ingeniously engineered honeycomb of underground drainage tunnels. The rivalry with Rome evidently dated to ancient disputes over control of the salt beds, and Veii kept it alive by maintaining a foothold in Latium on the east bank of the Tiber at Fidenae, just a few miles upstream from Rome. The two cities had gone to war twice during the previous century, with inconclusive results. This time, the vastly improved Roman army laid siege to the precipitous inclines of Veii. By one account the city withstood the siege for a full decade, a determined resistance that led to the creation of Rome's first professional army; the soldiers, accustomed to short summer campaigns, were paid to stay in the siege lines year round. Veii surrendered in 396 BC. The victors promptly annexed the city and its environs, thus nearly doubling Roman territory at one stroke. The patrician rulers of Rome distributed much of the conquered land among the poor to help quiet plebeian agitation. Rome followed up the conquest by seizing the southern approaches to the Etruscan homeland and turning that territory over to its allies in the Latin League for colonization. Magnanimous in victory, Rome was now the leading city in all Latium.

Meanwhile, the once-powerful Etruscans faced a new invasion from the north. These intruders were the Celts, barbarians whom the Romans referred to as Gauls. Marauding bands of Celts marched through the Alps into the Etruscan-dominated Po Valley at the beginning of the fourth century BC, just when the Romans were laying siege to the city of Veii. In fact, Roman tradition insisted that on the very day the Romans seized Veii, the Celts captured the Etruscan town of Melpum, near present-day Milan.

The Celts fascinated the people of the Mediterranean — most of all the Romans, whose legions they would soon encounter. Because the early Celts left no written records, it was the descriptions of Roman and Greek observers that caught and preserved their fierce mien. "Nearly all the Gauls are of a lofty stature," a Roman writer named Ammianus Marcellinus reported centuries later, "fair and of ruddy complexion; terrible from the sternness of their eyes, very quarrelsome, and of great pride and insolence. A whole troop of foreigners would not be able to withstand a single Gaul if he called to his assistance his wife, who is usually very strong and with blue eyes."

These fearsome Celtic women wore their golden hair elaborately plaited and decorated themselves with makeup and ornamentation. The men cultivated luxuriant moustaches and washed their hair with lime to stiffen it into spikes. Some of them, believing nudity was sacred, fought naked. Celts often rode from the battlefield with the severed heads of the enemy slung from their horses' bridles. "The whole race," concluded the Greek historian Strabo, "is war mad and both high spirited and quick for battle, although otherwise simple and not uncouth."

The flamboyant Celts originated in central Europe. They sprang from a mingling of two peoples in their distant ancestry. Modern scholars would call one group the Battle-Ax people, for the distinctive axes, with shaft holes drilled through metal or stone heads, that were often found in their graves. This group moved into central Europe from somewhere east during the third millennium BC. They spoke a language that probably was the ancestral tongue of Indo-European, the family of languages that included both Latin and Celtic. The other group — later to be dubbed the Bell Beaker people for their bell-shaped clay cups — were of unknown origin. They arrived in central Europe a few centuries later, sometime after 2000 BC. Wherever they originated, in their travels they introduced copper metallurgy to various tribes of western Europe. From the fusion of the Battle-Ax and Bell Beaker peoples evolved a series of cultures culminating in the Celts. The last of these intermediate peoples, the Celts' immediate predecessors, became established about 1250 BC. They were skilled in working with bronze, which they turned to advantage in both the scythe and the sword. Because they cremated their dead and placed the ashes in pottery urns in collective burial plots, they came to be known to modern archaeologists as the Urnfield culture.

The societal traits characteristic of the Celts emerged some five and a half centuries later, about 700 BC. One of the earliest important Celtic settlements was situated in the upper Danube Valley near where the northern Austrian village of Hallstatt would later be built. Not far away towered the Salzberg — literally "salt mountain" — which provided a source of wealth for the embryonic community. Celtic miners burrowed through rock and clay and dropped shafts more than 1,000 feet long to extract the salt.

But the key to Celtic culture was iron, a metal new to western Europe, although smiths in the Near East had known it for centuries. The Celts, who may have learned iron technology from traders, mined and heated the ore and forged it into a variety of shapes. Easier to find than the copper and tin that went into bronze, and easier to work, iron yielded a bounty of tools and weapons. Celts hammered out plowshares, bridle bits for horses, and huge swords more than a meter long that were favored by their nobles. They also shaped iron tires for four-wheeled wagons, which in life served farmers and warriors and in death furnished the biers for princely burials in elaborate mortuary chambers covered by round earth mounds.

During the following three centuries, the Celts migrated both east and west across the face of Europe, familiarizing local tribes with the new iron technology at the point of the sword. By 500 BC, the Celts had settled a broad swath of territory from Czechoslovakia in the east across Switzerland and southern Germany to Spain, France, and parts of Britain, soon extending to Ireland.

Because all the Celts spoke variants of the same language and shared a religion and general outlook on the world, they might have been united, under the right circumstances, into one enormous nation. But they seem never to have considered themselves a single people, and, unlike the Romans, who had an intense concern for administration and organization, the Celts cared little for government. They owed their allegiance to the tribe and never forged a state.

Scores of Celtic tribes were scattered about Europe. Each occupied its own region, although that tenancy was sometimes temporary because of the Celt propensity to move on. Another trait — the tendency of tribes to fight one another as fiercely as they clashed with groups outside their culture — largely dictated the shape of Celtic settlements. In the early days, these settlements were rural and usually established on hilltops or plateaus for ease of defense. Farms and other homesteads were clustered around a small, walled, defensive enclave later known as a hill fort. Enclosed by a deep ditch and stone or earthen ramparts braced with timbers, the hill fort contained the crude wooden homes of the chieftain and other prominent members of the community and served as an administrative center. During cattle raids and other attacks, the hill fort became a sanctuary where the settlement's farmers and other workers living outside the walls could take refuge with their families and their herds.

Over the centuries, the hill forts became the hubs of fortified Celtic towns that the

Romans referred to as oppida. These were urban centers with fortifications that protected the homes and workshops of artisans as well as the nobility. One thriving oppidum, Manching, near the Danube in southern Germany, covered 1,130 acres. Its timber-framed wall ran nearly four miles around the town and was held together by an estimated 300 tons of iron nails.

As the oppida grew larger and more elaborate, a stratified class structure emerged. At the top, the tribal chieftain or king was elected for life by the nobles. Below him came an aristocracy ennobled either by birth or accomplishment. It included the wealthy, the most honored warriors, and the powerful Celtic priests known as Druids. Next was a class of freemen, to which belonged well-off farmers, bards whose oral poetry and stories helped perpetuate tribal tradition, and the highest-ranking artisans, such as blacksmiths, whose skill with iron was so revered that overtones of supernatural powers attached to the trade. Lumped together at the bottom was the remainder of the population, a mass of laborers, serfs, and outright slaves who possessed neither property nor much in the way of rights and privileges.

Women, whatever their class, ranked behind men, who exercised patriarchal authority over the household somewhat in the Roman style. Nonetheless, women were occasionally singled out for honor or special privilege. Roman writers remarked admiringly

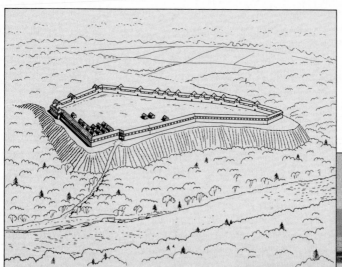

The fortress village of Heuneberg (above), a Celtic settlement in southern Germany, sat atop a steep rise overlooking the upper Danube, a major artery of trade. Here, agricultural products grown in the surrounding region, and wares from the iron, bronze, and pottery works inside the walls, were traded for jewels, fabrics, and utensils from as far away as Sicily. By the fifth century BC, Heuneberg, like most major Celtic towns, was ringed by a formidable rampart. As shown at right, a timber framework faced with stone held in place a filling of earth and rubble twelve feet thick. Two gates punctuated the rampart; both were narrow to make them easier to defend. The wall was bolstered by guard towers and topped by a wooden palisade. The houses of Heuneberg's artisans and traders were built in rows parallel to the wall.

upon their courage and physical strength. Some women — probably those in the nobility — were granted the privilege of taking more than one mate, a practice evidently open to most men. And like male nobles, highborn women went to the grave sumptuously adorned and accompanied by accouterments made of gold and silver.

Girls and boys alike took part in the Celtic system of education known as fosterage. Before the age of seven, children were sent to foster families — usually in a different settlement — who were paid to rear them. A large part of fosterage was teaching the children skills commensurate with their social status. For example, the daughter of a farmer learned to grind grain and make bread; a nobleman's daughter learned more genteel skills, such as sewing and embroidery. The Celts of this era had neither writing nor a well-developed arithmetic to pass on to their children. All boys were taught physical skills; in the case of a nobleman's son, however, the curriculum would emphasize the art of war. For girls, fosterage usually ended at the age of fourteen, when they returned home to be betrothed. A boy typically remained with his foster parents until he was seventeen. Even so, a girl's parents paid about a third more for her education because she was considered more fastidious than a boy and needful of more attention. In addition to getting an education, the fostered children were expected to provide new bonds between their own groups and the groups that reared them.

The economic structure of the tribe was based on agriculture. Farmers raised cattle, horses, pigs, and sheep — the last, a versatile animal, gave them milk and mutton as

well as wool. They also grew wheat, barley, and other grains, which they stored for the winter in six-foot-deep pits lined with basketwork or clay. Farming benefited greatly from Celtic innovations in ironworking. Iron plowshares bit deeper into the earth than wooden ones. Iron scythes hastened the work of the harvest, which was speeded up even more by the invention — at some unknown time before the first century BC — of a horse-powered reaper so fascinating to the Romans that they depicted it in sculpture.

Blacksmiths and other skilled workers supplemented the agricultural economy. So too did a lively commerce between Celtic settlements and two Mediterranean cultures to the south, the Etruscans and the Greeks. At first, pottery and other imports trickled north across the Alps into central Europe from Etruria and from Greek colonies farther south on the Italian peninsula. Then, about 600 BC, Greek sailors established a trading post at Massalia — later called Marseilles — on the French Mediterranean coast. Massalia was situated near the mouth of the Rhone, the largest river linking the Mediterranean with central Europe. The subsequent commerce with the Celtic settlements as far north as Germany transformed a minor trading post into a thriving colony.

Traffic flowed up and down the Rhone Valley. The Celts supplied salted meat, leather, textiles, and other commodities to Massalia for that colony's own consumption and for export. In exchange came Greek pottery, Etruscan bronze vessels, and the import most prized by the hard-drinking Celts — wine. The French many centuries later would have to confess that the first wine drunk in Burgundy came from Greece. Greek wine was transported by ship in large ceramic jars called amphorae. Many of these jars were then off-loaded onto small river boats. But because amphorae were so heavy — weighing as much as 350 pounds when empty — the contents often were decanted into wineskins or wooden casks for transport in horse-drawn wagons. Before adopting coinage in the fourth century BC, the Celts calculated the worth of wine and other purchases in terms of the two commodities they valued most: cattle and slaves. The Celts exported slaves, captured in raids or battle, in exchange for imports. A large jar of wine was said to be worth one slave. Only wealthy Celts could afford Greek wine, which they drank undiluted with water, shocking the Greeks. The common folk imbibed barley-based ale or mead, made by fermenting honey and water.

The commerce with the Greeks and Etruscans affected more than Celtic thirst. Greek merchants introduced the olive tree and the grapevine as well as wine. They also brought along ideas about building better fortifications for the Celtic hill forts and oppida. The Celts began to protect their settlements with walls of sun-dried clay bricks much like those of Greek cities. Actually, the very growth of fortified towns may well have been triggered in the first place by the opening of Greek commerce, which encouraged Celtic chieftains to build urban centers specializing in the production of leather, textiles, and other commodities expressly for export to Massalia.

The Celts also felt the impact of trade in the arena of arts and crafts. The influence of the vivid classical designs that adorned the Greek wine amphorae was so powerful that it led to the maxim "Celtic art owed much to Celtic thirst." Part of that debt was direct. Celtic pottery, bronze vessels, and stone statuary borrowed heavily from Mediterranean models. Mostly, however, the imported designs served as a stimulus that inspired Celts to create their own art, as did the motifs and themes found in such objects arriving from Persia and other lands to the east.

The result was a sudden flowering of the Celtic creative imagination. This outburst of productivity, which began about 450 BC, much later came to be known as the period of La Tène — after the region near Lake Neuchâtel in Switzerland where many early examples of the new art were created. La Tène contrasted in style and abundance with the earlier Hallstatt period, which had centered around the upper Danube, and it signaled the migration westward of powerful and wealthy chieftains whose patronage encouraged Celtic art. Swords and shields, pottery, gold and bronze jewelry, even the safety-pin-like fibulae for fastening together cloaks — all bore the dreamlike, intricate, and highly stylized whorls and spirals and curling tendrils that characterized La Tène. Though incorporating borrowings from the Greeks, Etruscans, and others, this Celtic artistry soared on strikingly distinctive wings of its own.

Many of the elusive motifs of La Tène art stemmed from the powerful aura of religion and superstition that pervaded the everyday existence of the Celts. They were obsessed with magic and the observance of ritual. They found menace and omen at every turn and surrounded themselves with talismanic objects and propitiatory rituals aimed at placating the gods and warding off random everyday evils. A bog reeked of evil and was to be avoided. Fire was sacred: Cattle driven through it were assured long life. A sprig of mistletoe, especially if found growing on the sacred oak tree, possessed the magic to heal humans and even to imbue them with fertility.

No object was venerated more than the human head. In ways that mystified their contemporaries — and, later, modern scholars — the head seemed to embody the essence of Celtic religious feeling. To the Celts, the life of the head survived, soullike, the death of the body. Although they had plenty of opportunity in their gory battles to observe that such was not the case, they seemed to believe a severed head could move, speak, sing, and most important, ward off evil. Artists painted, molded, and sculpted the human head on everything from a bronze flagon for wine to the decorated wickerwork sides of a two-wheeled war chariot. But it was not just artistic representations of human heads that the Celts cherished. They revered the real thing and demonstrated that reverence on the battlefield with behavior revolting to Romans and other Mediterranean peoples. Celtic warriors decapitated the slain enemy and took home their heads. The most prized heads — those of slain enemy heroes, for example — were embalmed in cedar oil. In at least one tribe, it was the custom to select certain skulls and decorate them with gold for use as drinking cups.

If this head fetish struck others as ghoulishly incomprehensible, the Celtic pantheon of gods was almost as bizarre. It comprised several hundred deities, most of them evidently thrown in helter-skelter without the discipline of clear hierarchical order. There were scores of all-purpose gods and goddesses, along with some specialized deities who looked out for blacksmiths, for example, or antlered animals, or even orators. A Roman writer reported seeing a representation of this god of oratory: He was an old man with golden chains that emerged from his mouth and linked him to the ears of a group of eager listeners.

Keeping the chaotic pantheon straight was one of the duties of the Druids. These priests — whose name may have been derived from roots meaning "knowledge of the oak," a reference to their most sacred tree — occupied such a high station in Celtic society that candidates for the role usually were drawn from the nobility. Typically but not exclusively male, Druids officiated at services intended to propitiate the gods and goddesses. Worship usually took place in natural settings, woodland clearings or sites near springs or deep pits that Druids filled with animal bones and other offerings. On occasion, the Druids offered up humans — presumably criminals or prisoners of war — who were sacrificed by burning, drowning, or hanging.

Druids bore other responsibilities. Like Etruscan and Roman priests, they divined the future from the patterns they perceived in the flights of birds or even in birdcalls. They also acted as the tribe's jurists, handing down judgment according to the traditions of the Celts' unwritten laws. All of this required intensive training that sometimes lasted twenty years. Much of the training consisted of memorizing immense amounts of information relating to Celtic religion, law, history, and tradition. This knowledge was largely preserved in the form of verse, which apparently helped inscribe the words in memory.

Why the Celts did not commit such knowledge to writing until more than five centuries after the birth of Christ remains a mystery. Druids and other learned Celts were surely exposed to the Greek alphabet through the voluminous trade emanating from the Greek colony at Massalia after 600 BC. Other peoples such as the Romans and Etruscans quickly adopted writing after such exposure. Perhaps the Druids felt that information falling within the province of the priesthood should not be profaned by reducing it to writing. Or perhaps they realized that the maintenance of the difficult oral tradition, with its years of training, ensured their high status in Celtic society.

Celtic religious occasions often were accompanied by lavish festivals with much eating and drinking. Although the Celts were so conscious of their waistlines that they levied fines for obesity, a typical feast featured enough food to last for several days. The meal might include huge quantities of roast or boiled pork — perhaps a fine boar recently hunted down by a young warrior — accompanied by butter, cheese, honey, and other trimmings. Guests gathered in a Celtic hall, a rude timber or mud-brick structure half sunk into the ground. They sat in a circle on animal pelts or hay placed on the earthen floor, eating from low tables. Seating was arranged according to a strict protocol that gave prominence — and the choice cuts of meat — to those of the highest nobility, bravery, wealth, or storytelling ability. The best cut of all, the "champion's portion," which was usually the haunch of a boar, was awarded to the man whose boastful war stories proved most convincing. The food was washed down with copious quantities of wine or other alcoholic drink. "They use a common cup," said the Greek writer Athenaeus, "drinking a little at a time, not more than a mouthful, but they do it rather frequently."

Feasting Celts were entertained by minstrels who played lyres and by bards who sang of tragic love and fallen heroes. But male celebrants often provided their own diversions. "When they become drunk, they fall into a stupor or into a maniacal rage," the Sicilian writer Diordorus Siculus reported. "At dinner they are wont to be moved by chance remarks to wordy disputes and, after a challenge, to fight in single combat, regarding their lives as naught."

Fighting was a way of life for the Celts, whether it took the form of drunken brawls, cattle raids on neighboring tribes, or outright warfare. Thanks to the advanced technology of their metallurgists, they had the tools for it: well-balanced spears, long iron swords (later replaced by shorter, lighter ones), broad-bladed daggers, and swift two-wheeled war chariots with iron tires that were fitted tightly onto one-piece wooden rims while still hot from the forge. But it was their fierce joy in combat — sometimes drummed to a frenzy by the incantations of the Druids — that drove the Celtic warriors. They were always daring, sometimes reckless, seldom efficiently organized — "every single step the Celts took," according to the Roman Polybius, "being commended to them rather by the heat of passion than by cool calculation." That passion often

Celts thought that human heads or skulls had mysterious powers. They believed a head was the dwelling place of the soul and retained the strength of the person from whom it was severed; hence, they were fond of displaying detached heads, either real ones taken in battle and in ceremonial sacrifice, or effigies such as the stone warrior heads shown here. Trophy heads were placed on poles or nailed to homes or town gates to ward off evil. A Celtic warrior might sling a head from his saddle or around his neck to protect himself and terrify his enemies. Sometimes, skulls were placed in food storage pits, presumably to keep the provisions safe from vermin and rot.

terrified the enemy. The sound of Celts in full-throated battle created such a tumult, said Polybius, "it seemed that not only the trumpets and the soldiers but all the country round had got a voice and caught up the cry."

In appearance, too, Celtic warriors were awe inspiring. Most wore conventional trousers and tunics or leather coats but looked bizarre with their long hair stiffened from washing in lime to keep it out of their eyes. Others wore nothing at all, save for gold armlets and the hollow neck rings known as torques. These were mercenary spearmen (gaesatae in Celtic) who would fight for any tribe that paid them and who followed the Druids' teaching that nudity was sacred and brought divine protection.

Even on a battlefield where hundreds of warriors were massed, the Celts sometimes preferred to engage in single combat. Such tactics began when one or more of the handsome Celtic chariots, drawn by pairs of specially bred ponies in bronze-studded harnesses, raced furiously toward the enemy ranks. Each chariot carried two men, a charioteer and a warrior. As they careered near the foe, the warrior hurled spears and then leaped from his chariot. Drawing his sword, he challenged an enemy warrior to fight. Occasionally in intertribal rivalries, such a single duel settled matters. More often, other warriors — borne by chariot and on foot — joined in to generate full-scale battle.

One of the Celts' most daring and far-reaching campaigns came at the start of the fourth century BC, when tribes from Switzerland and southern Germany pressed across the Alps into northern Italy. Evidently drawn by indications of the declines of Etruria and the allure of rich vineyards and other plunder, a tribe called the Insubres invaded first. They were soon followed by four other tribes. In the wake of each tribe's war bands came a great entourage of women, children, and servants, along with livestock and belongings piled high on four-wheeled carts. The Celts drove the Etruscans out of the Po Valley while the Romans were seizing the southern Etruscan stronghold of Veii. Then, about 390 BC, after attacking the Etruscan city of Clusium, a Celtic horde estimated at 30,000 warriors crossed the Apennines and headed for Rome, some eighty miles down the peninsula. To stop them, a force of Roman conscripts perhaps one-third that size marched up the Tiber Valley about a dozen miles and took up position on the east bank where a little stream called the Allia emptied into the Tiber. The Celts quickly turned the Roman right flank. Many of the Roman defenders panicked and fled at the first sound of the Celtic war cry, reported the later historian of Rome, Livy, "hardly waiting even to see their strange enemy from the ends of the earth."

Triumphant in the Battle of Allia, the Celts poured into Rome and sacked it. They remained for seven months, looting, burning, and terrifying the city. Legend has it that when the Celts, short of food and afflicted with dysentery, decided to return to northern Italy, they heaped one final humiliation upon Rome by forcing the city to pay for its freedom. The ransom was 1,000 pounds of gold as determined by the Celts' own weights. When the Roman magistrate protested that these weights were too heavy, the Celtic chieftain added his own iron sword to the scale and exclaimed, "Woe to the vanquished!"

The Romans neither forgot nor forgave. While Celtic war bands went on to plunder new places — by 275 BC they would penetrate the Balkans and Asia Minor and even attack the sacred Greek city of Delphi — the Romans patiently rebuilt their city and their power. They would face the Celts again on the battlefield, and they would fare far better.

CREATING AN IDEAL BEAUTY

Through networks of trade, the Greeks spread the bounty of their artistic talent and, in return, learned from other cultures how to enrich their own artistry. Even as the Celts of the Rhone Valley were acquiring goods fashioned by the Greeks and adopting some of their techniques, similar exchanges were taking place in other regions visited by Greek merchant ships.

On the north shore of the Black Sea, the Greek colony of Olbia did a brisk business with the tribal Scythians, trading jewelry, painted pots, and elaborately embossed vessels for grain and meat. In the eastern Mediterranean, the Greeks had a thriving emporium at Naucratis, on the Nile, and another at the mouth of the Orontes River in Syria. The contacts with Egypt and the Near East were especially important for Greek artisans, providing not only markets for their wares but also exposure to older cultures. Sojourning in Egypt, Greek sculptors saw how monumental human figures could be hewn out of hard stone. Returning home, they moved beyond the modest efforts in wood and limestone that had occupied their Greek predecessors and began to work with native marble on a grand scale.

Greek artists managed to draw lessons in technique from their tradition-bound counterparts in the East while surrendering nothing of their own originality. In Egypt, the philosopher Plato would later remark, the attachment to precedent was such that "no painter or artist is allowed to innovate on the traditional forms or invent new ones." In Greece, by contrast, experimentation was encouraged. The pursuit of patronage led masters to explore fresh technical angles in their workshops in an effort to surpass the competition. No sooner had sculptors refined the crafting of marble than an alternative emerged — cast bronze, which allowed the human body to be captured in action without the risk of an extended stone limb collapsing under its own weight.

In potters' studios, meanwhile, new modes of decorating vessels were developed that spawned sharp differences in style from city to city — and subtler ones from shop to shop. Artists took to signing their pots, and a few even added sly epigrams like the boast an Attic vase painter directed at one of his colleagues: "As Euphronios never, ever could."

Along with new methods, Greek artists brought to their craft a fresh attentiveness to the world around them, relying on their powers of observation to lend a lifelike quality to the most exalted of themes. The Olympian gods and the human heroes of the Olympian games were portrayed in the same manner, and scenes taken from the rarefied world of Homer were fleshed out with prosaic details from daily life. The goal was not pure realism, for Greek artists of this era had little interest in portraying the physical or emotional peculiarities of their human subjects. They sought rather to embody timeless ideals in a convincing fashion, making vivid paragons of beauty that spoke to the spirit through the senses. As people in far-off lands began to prize such works and to heed their appeal, the Greek concept of artistry — rooted in reality but aspiring to perfection — became the property of the world.

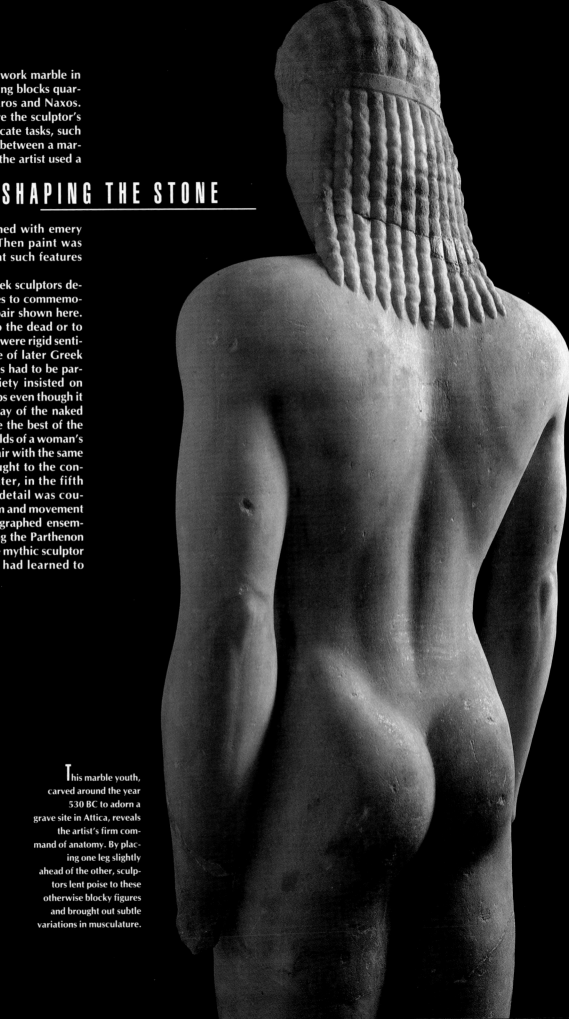

Greek sculptors began to work marble in the seventh century BC, using blocks quarried from the islands of Paros and Naxos. Iron chisels and knives were the sculptor's principal tools, but for delicate tasks, such as hollowing out the space between a marble figure's arm and torso, the artist used a bow drill to bore a series of holes that yielded a clean break when chiseled. Once the stone had been shaped, it was polished with emery or some other abrasive. Then paint was usually applied to highlight such features as the eyes and lips.

SHAPING THE STONE

In the sixth century, Greek sculptors devoted most of their energies to commemorative figures such as the pair shown here. Designed to pay tribute to the dead or to honor the gods, these icons were rigid sentinels, lacking the fluid ease of later Greek statuary. The female figures had to be partially veiled, because society insisted on keeping women under wraps even though it welcomed the public display of the naked male body. Sculptors made the best of the restriction, exploring the folds of a woman's dress or the braids of her hair with the same meticulous care they brought to the contours of a man's body. Later, in the fifth century, this passion for detail was coupled with a sense of freedom and movement to produce vividly choreographed ensembles such as those crowning the Parthenon *(pages 122-123)*. As did the mythic sculptor Pygmalion, Greek artists had learned to breathe life into stone.

This marble youth, carved around the year 530 BC to adorn a grave site in Attica, reveals the artist's firm command of anatomy. By placing one leg slightly ahead of the other, sculptors lent poise to these otherwise blocky figures and brought out subtle variations in musculature.

Commissioned around 500 BC by a wealthy Athenian, this pensive maiden was placed atop a column on the Acropolis to honor the goddess Athena. Although female nudes would not be accepted into the Greek repertoire until the fourth century, the sculptor of this figure used costume and tresses not to hide the form but to embellish it.

These figures with their luxuriously folded gowns — thought to represent the goddesses Hestia *(far left),* Dione, and Aphrodite — were part of a tableau celebrating the birth of Athena that was installed above the Parthenon's east wall. The elements of the tableau were first molded in clay; apprentices then blocked out the figures in marble, and a master sculptor completed the work. Over the years, the statues were ravaged by invaders and weather.

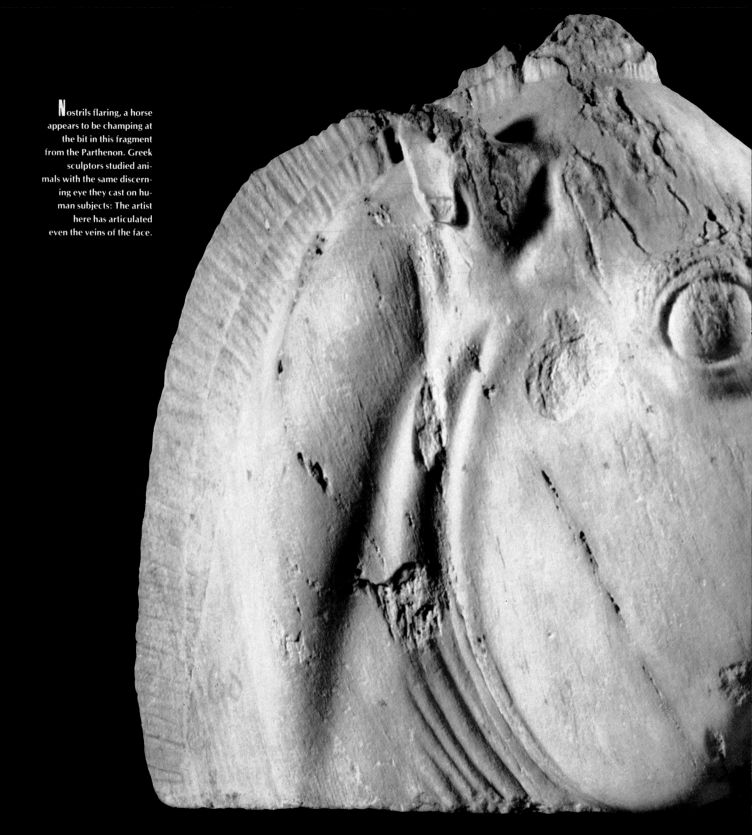

Nostrils flaring, a horse appears to be champing at the bit in this fragment from the Parthenon. Greek sculptors studied animals with the same discerning eye they cast on human subjects: The artist here has articulated even the veins of the face.

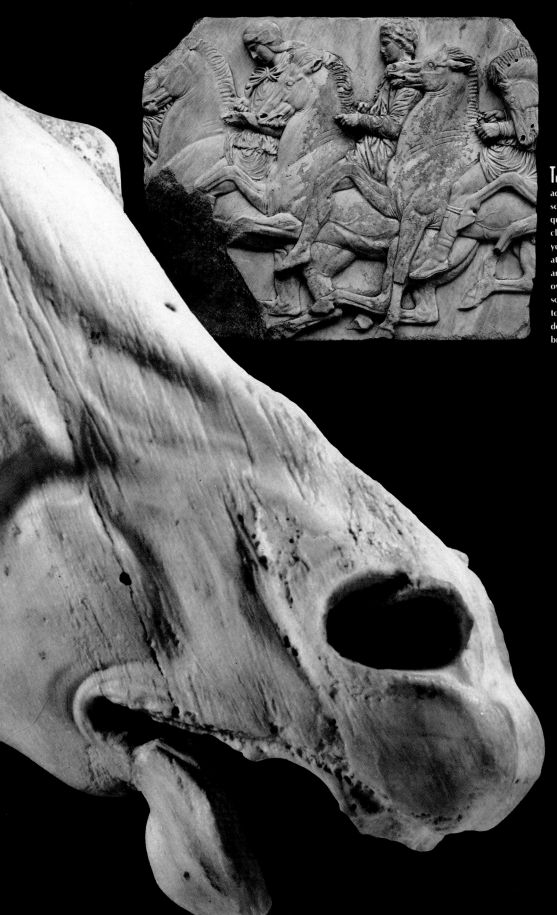

The Parthenon was adorned not only with sculptures but with exquisitely carved reliefs, including this scene of youths riding in the Panathenaic procession. By arraying the horsemen in overlapping rows, the sculptor lent perspective to the relief, adding depth to a scene already vibrant with action.

The head of this life-size bronze warrior reveals the touch of a master. The hair cascading in ringlets around the ears was cast separately and placed over the skull to give the locks a body of their own. And the face was animated with teeth of silver, lips of copper, and eyes of ivory and translucent stone.

CASTING A MASTERPIECE

When an influential Sicilian named Polyzalos decided to commemorate a victory by his chariot team in the Pythian games at Delphi, he commissioned a sculpture not of the traditional marble but of bronze. Judging by the surviving element of that ambitious, early fifth century work *(near left)*, Polyzalos probably was not disappointed. Thanks to a recently perfected process of hollow-casting, bronze had come to rival stone as a sculptor's medium. The artist began by molding wax around a solid core to the exact shape desired. The wax was next studded with metal pegs that reached from its outer surface to the core, then covered with clay; as the clay was baked hard, the wax liquefied and escaped, leaving the pegs to maintain the gap between the core and the clay shell. Molten bronze was poured into this space. Once it hardened, the clay mold was broken to free the hollow figure.

One of the advantages of this process was that large and complex works could be cast in parts and soldered together. In the case of Polyzalos's charioteer, the arms were forged separately, then inserted in sockets deep within the sleeves of the chiton so that the garment would hang free, in a lifelike way. And each arm was light enough to remain outstretched without a supporting element. A sculptor striving for a similar effect in marble would have been forced to rest each arm on a prop.

A victorious charioteer stands with rein in hand in this commemorative work, which once included horses, chariot, and groom. The figures were installed in the sanctuary of Apollo at Delphi by the owner of the team, to thank the god for the win.

Greek myth and Greek expertise are reflected in this Etruscan bronze — a chimera with elements of a lion, a goat, and a serpent. Inscribed on the beast's foreleg is a dedication to Tinia, the chief Etruscan deity. Tales of such animals and advice on the art of bronzeworking reached the Etruscans through the Greek colonies of southern Italy.

This Greek bronze of
the second century BC,
portraying a boy jockey
astride a galloping race-
horse, offers a dramatic
contrast to the serene
works of earlier times.
In the Classical era, before
the rise of Alexander,
sculptors generally depicted athletes as perfectly
composed. But here the artist, true to the spirit of
his age, has evoked an
intense moment, show-
ing the boy hunched down
over his mount to avoid
the wind whipping at his tunic, with lines of con-
centration furrowing his
cheeks and brow.

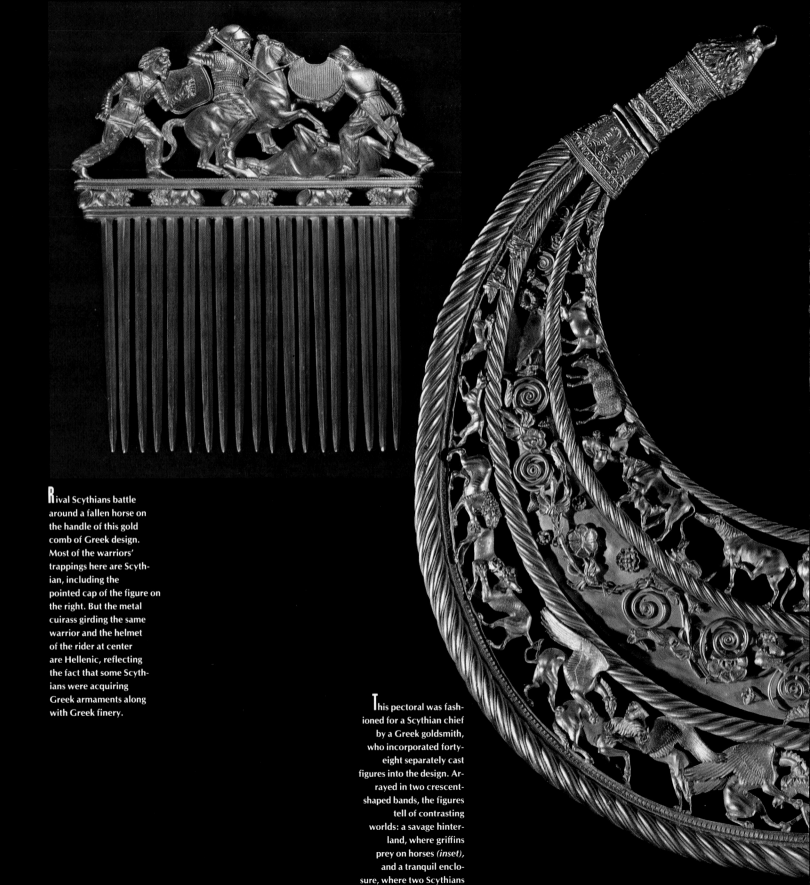

Rival Scythians battle around a fallen horse on the handle of this gold comb of Greek design. Most of the warriors' trappings here are Scythian, including the pointed cap of the figure on the right. But the metal cuirass girding the same warrior and the helmet of the rider at center are Hellenic, reflecting the fact that some Scythians were acquiring Greek armaments along with Greek finery.

This pectoral was fashioned for a Scythian chief by a Greek goldsmith, who incorporated forty-eight separately cast figures into the design. Arrayed in two crescent-shaped bands, the figures tell of contrasting worlds: a savage hinterland, where griffins prey on horses (inset), and a tranquil enclosure, where two Scythians

A GOLDEN TRIBUTE

The commercial bond between the Greeks and the Scythians, which yielded the gleaming ornaments shown here, was supported by Hellenic craftsmanship on the one hand and the natural resources of the Scythian heartland on the other. After making a visit to the Greek colony of Olbia, near the mouth of the Dnieper River, the historian Herodotus marveled at the bounty of that Scythian-dominated waterway: "It has upon its banks the loveliest and most excellent pasturages for cattle; it contains abundance of the most delicious fish; its water is most pleasant to the taste; its stream is limpid, while all the other rivers near it are muddy; the richest harvests spring up along its course." Such plenty was tantalizing to the Greeks, whose burgeoning cities sometimes strained the productive capacity of their outlying districts. But the shrewd Scythian chiefs were not about to surrender their meat and grain for trinkets. They wanted sumptuous offerings, preferably of gold. Greek metalsmiths complied. They learned to enhance the appeal of their work by casting miniature figures that were then soldered to the frame of an ornament to create entire tableaux. Many of the scenes rendered in such painstaking fashion were portraits of Scythian life — evidence that the artists studied their clients as intently as they did their craft.

Two gilded Scythian warriors strike a relaxed pose on this silver drinking cup, obtained in trade with the Greeks and later put into the tomb of a wealthy Scythian along the Dnieper River. Like the Celts, the Scythians drank their wine straight, a practice that left a deep impression on the Greeks, who diluted theirs with water. When Spartans wanted a lift, they ordered wine "Scythian fashion."

A wedding party circles the base of this vase while dancers and musicians surround the handle. As detailed at top, the wedding procession is shown approaching the home of the groom, where a woman waits at the door with torch in hand; the bride sits beside her husband in the lead cart, her back to the best man. In executing the scene, the master Amasis first coated the unfinished clay vessel with a slip that lent a yellow cast to the entire surface. He then painted his figures and incised the sharp details before firing the vase.

CANVASES OF CLAY

Greek heroes enjoy moments of ease on this vase, decorated in Athens by Exekias and exported to the Etruscan city of Vulci. On one side, a helmeted Achilles plays a board game with his comrade Ajax; on the other, the Spartan champion Castor *(center)*, a renowned trainer of horses, and his brother Polydeuces *(far left)*, a prize boxer, are welcomed home by their parents. The artist relied as much on his incising tool here as on his brush, achieving rich details that stand out on the black figures.

This fifth-century Athenian
bowl offers an intimate
view of bronze sculptors at
work. While workmen
stoke the furnace, artisans
to their right assemble
the individually cast segments of a male figure;
the head rests on the floor,
and models for a hand
and a foot hang on the wall.
Farther along, two men
are polishing a bronze warrior as critical observ-
ers — including, perhaps,
the master of the stu-
dio — look on. By the time
this bowl was painted,
most Athenian vase paint-
ers had abandoned the
austere black-figure style,
reserving black paint
for the background and for
the delicate line work
that had once been incised.

ENLIGHTENMENT IN THE EAST

Even as the sages of Greece were laying the foundation for Western philosophy and political thought, inspired teachers in China and India were articulating doctrines that would transform the great civilizations of the Far East. In time those doctrines would help to unify the societies that nurtured them, but they were conceived in an age of divisiveness. By the sixth century BC, both China and India were in the throes of change: In both regions, rival states were vying for supremacy, class conflict was on the rise, and old creeds that had long provided rulers and their subjects with a sense of their proper place in the spiritual and social hierarchy were being called into question. At the same time, cities were growing and trade was flourishing, and with that expansion came an extraordinary burst of intellectual enterprise.

In both lands there arose learned thinkers who embodied the ferment of the times — inquisitive souls seeking order and harmony in a discordant world. Two of those philosophers would have a profound effect: the Chinese teacher Kongfuzi, or Kong the Master, known to Westerners as Confucius; and the Indian sage Siddhartha Gautama, celebrated by his followers as the Buddha, or the Enlightened One.

In one respect, the two could not have been more different. The worldly Confucius longed for political influence and found inspiration in the venerable customs of China's ruling class. The ascetic Buddha turned his back on the life of privilege and power that was his by birth and attacked some of the very premises on which that life had been based. Yet both men set high ethical standards for their followers, recognizing that there could be no inner peace in a community wracked by violence and deceit. And both were universal in their appeal, transcending barriers of rank and region. It was no accident that each was embraced by the dynasty that succeeded in uniting his native land: Theirs were creeds that inspired emperors as well as those who served them. Such was the allure of the two sages that although neither set out to found a religion, both became objects of worship. The priests and the temples would come later, however, after the two had died and the triumphant spirit of their thought had been set free from the troubled age of its birth.

The crisis that faced China at the time of Confucius had roots that extended back several hundred years — centuries marked by a drastic decline in the influence wielded by the Zhou, China's ruling clan. When the Zhou had wrested power from the Shang dynasty around 1100 BC, they had taken over a relatively compact kingdom, centered around the Yellow River and its tributaries. Five centuries later, civilized China extended from the fringes of the hinterland known later as Mongolia to well south of the Yangtze River. The sheer size and diversity of the realm made it all but impossible for a single ruler to control. Along the northern and western borders were truculent nomads. Some had been drawn into the web of Chinese civilization, but others remained beyond the pale — a literal barrier, in places, as the Chinese began erecting walls as defense against their hostile neighbors. Unlike the temperate region along the Yellow River, where millet and barley were the staples, the southern tier of China was a wet, rice-growing region whose inhabitants had once been culturally alien — the northerners incorporated the derogatory symbol of a worm into their characters for the names of the southern tribes.

At first, the Zhou had controlled their expanding domain through nepotism. Once a new territory was secured by force of arms, the Zhou king generally installed one of his relatives as chief of the fledgling state. Such devotion to family, always an important factor in Chinese society, was an article of faith with the Zhou. They claimed descent from the god Di, who was thought to dwell in heaven. Thus, each successive king was called the Son of Heaven. The state rulers who were related to the king shared in this glorious lineage; they in turn often installed their own close relatives as high ministers. Those who could boast only distant ties to the ruler had to make do with minor positions in the state, forming a class known as the *shi* — the nucleus of the educated bureaucracy that would later play such an important part in Chinese government.

Some of the shi may have been freeholders, who worked their own land, but most of the cultivating was done by serfs laboring on estates. At the center of the typical estate was the walled residence of the lord, a vassal of the state's ruler. Outside the walls the peasants toiled throughout the year to meet their own needs and those of their master. A ballad of the era described the seasonal cycle on an estate in northern China: "In the days of the first month the wind blows cold;/ In the days of the second, the air is cold./ Without coats, without garments of hair,/ How could we get to the end of the year?/ In the days of the third month we take our plows in hand;/ In the days of the fourth we make our way to the fields./ Along with wives and children,/ We eat in those south-lying acres./ The surveyor of the fields comes and is glad."

Through spring and summer, the serfs camped in the fields, most likely making do with flimsy thatch huts for shelter. In addition to the sowing and reaping of grain, peasants in many areas harvested huge quantities of mulberry leaves to feed to silk-worms. The business of nurturing the worms and unraveling the fine thread of their cocoons — a secret that would remain confined to China for many centuries to come — was relegated to the women, who then spun the silk into the sheer fabrics favored by the lords and their ladies. Nor was that the only duty a young peasant woman might be expected to fulfill for her lord, as the same ballad revealed: "With the spring days the warmth begins,/ And the oriole utters its song./ The young women take their deep baskets/ And go along the small paths,/ Looking for the tender leaves of the mulberry trees . . ./ The girl's heart is wounded with sadness,/ For she will soon be going with one of the young lords."

To go with the young lord could only mean to become his concubine, for the nobles were careful to marry within their class. Some time after the leaves were gathered and the grain harvested, the peasants retreated to their permanent, earthen dwellings to wait out the winter with its chill north winds: "In the tenth month the cricket/ Enters under our beds./ Chinks are filled up, and rats are smoked out;/ The windows facing north are stopped up./ 'Come, wife and children,/ The change of the year is at hand./Let us live inside the house.' "

It was a hard regimen, and sometimes a cruel one, but as long as the lords protected the serfs from attack and kept them from destitution, life on the estate remained orderly. By the eighth century BC, however, changes were taking place at the highest levels of the social order, changes that would eventually work their way down to the roots, depriving the peasants of any semblance of security.

Time had eroded the bonds of kinship that once ensured the adherence of the various state chiefs to the Zhou king. Ensconced in his palace at the royal capital of Hao, along the Wei River in western China, the king was cut off from the affairs of the states and thus was ill-equipped to fend off challenges to his authority. Matters came to a head in 771 BC, when King Yu announced his intention to bypass the legitimate claims of his own son and heir, Ping Wang, and install the son of his concubine as his successor. Several disgruntled chiefs then allied themselves with a band of border nomads to overthrow the king. The capital was sacked, and Yu was slain. Ping Wang was escorted eastward to the relative security of the Luo River valley. There, at the newly designated capital of Luoyang, the prince was enthroned as the first ruler of the so-called Eastern Zhou dynasty; his predecessors would be remembered as the Western Zhou.

Although the Zhou king was now nearer to the center of his realm, he found himself doomed to political impotence. Owing his position to the chiefs who had saved his life, he could do little more than preside over official ceremonies and ratify the decisions of others. The decline of royal authority led inevitably to a power struggle among the sundry states — there were scores of lesser states and a dozen major ones. Most of the major powers were situated on the periphery of civilized China, where they could expand outward and subjugate thousands of so-called barbarians, who might then serve as soldiers and serfs. Prominent among these rising border states were several with names that seem confusingly similar to Westerners: Chu, to the south; Qin, along the western fringe; Jin, to the northwest; and Qi, to the northeast.

By the early seventh century, Qi was China's most advanced power. It produced ample quantities of salt by evaporating seawater in large ponds along the shore and had rich reserves of iron, a new discovery in China. And it was gifted with a farsighted ruler who recognized the importance of centralized government and introduced uniform systems of taxation and military conscription. His name was Huan Gong — or Duke Huan, as he would be labeled later by Western historians, borrowing a title from feudal Europe. Aided by a shrewd adviser named Guanzi, Duke Huan commanded the respect of his subjects and of his peers in neighboring states.

With the decline of the Zhou dynasty in the eighth century BC, the Chinese world splintered into hundreds of states, their borders and alliances constantly shifting as kingdom battled kingdom for power and survival. By the fifth century BC, the seven states named on the map — their boundaries changed too frequently to show here — dominated scores of smaller kingdoms. Three of the dominant states were locked in a struggle for supreme power: Chu in the south, Qi in the northeast, and Qin in the northwest.

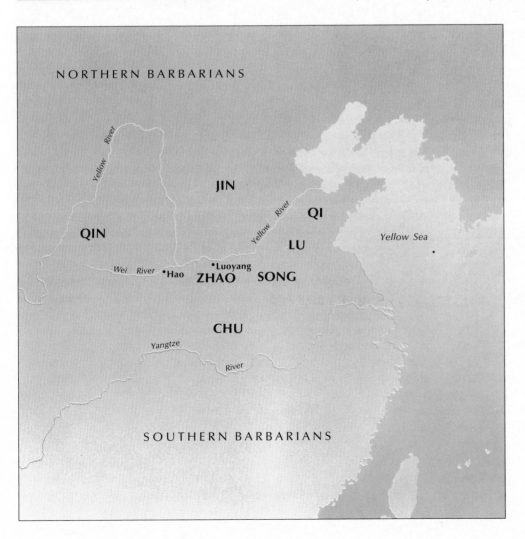

NORTHERN BARBARIANS

Yellow River

JIN

QI

QIN

Yellow River

LU

Yellow Sea

Wei River • Hao • Luoyang
ZHAO SONG

CHU

Yangtze

River

SOUTHERN BARBARIANS

Around 680 BC, several small states in central China were attacked by Chu, and turned to Duke Huan for protection. He soon hammered together a league comprising many northern and central states and sanctioned by the Zhou king. Duke Huan assumed the title of hegemon, or overlord, of the league, a position he held for thirty years. In 656 BC, he compelled Chu to sign a peace treaty and to send regular tribute to the Zhou court. But it was only a lull in the storm; before long the states were warring again. Over the next century, other hegemons would follow in his footsteps and attempt to impose order, but none would achieve lasting peace.

Indeed, the period between 650 and 550 was one of increasingly bitter feuding; dozens of states ceased to exist during the era, swallowed up by ambitious rivals. In earlier days, battles had been limited in scale. Few lasted longer than a day, and they were circumscribed by a gentlemanly code that required the warrior to show respect to a kinsman or to someone of superior rank, whether friend or foe. The aristocratic combatants who followed this code rode to battle in light chariots drawn by four horses, surrounded by a small number of foot soldiers. Before dueling, the charioteers might exchange courtesies; on one occasion, a warrior honored his foe with a slain deer. The clashes that ensued could be fierce — charioteers were expert at drawing a bow while riding on their swaying vehicles — but the vanquished were often treated mercifully, particularly if they were kin to the victors.

As the rivalries between the states grew more heated, however, ambitious chiefs began to ignore the old code, replacing gestures of courtesy with acts of treachery. An ominous example of this occurred in 655 BC, when the ruler of Jin, one of the powerful border states, sought permission to pass through the state of Yu to assault the state of Guo. The rulers of all three states were descended from the royal house of Zhou and were thus kinsmen. Assessing the situation, a minister to the chief of Yu advised his master not to allow the army of Jin to pass through, pointing out that if Jin's chief was willing to attack his kinsman in Guo, he would have no scruples about assaulting Yu as well. The chief of Yu disregarded this logical advice and paid the consequences: The army of Jin moved unopposed through his territory, conquered Guo with ease, then sacked Yu mercilessly on the way back, taking its hapless ruler prisoner.

Along with a new ruthlessness on the part of commanders came a fundamental change in the nature of warfare. Armies grew larger, and foot soldiers began to crowd out the elite corps of charioteers. Drawn largely from the ranks of the peasantry, these infantrymen were equipped with double-edged swords of bronze or forged iron, and many carried a deadly weapon devised in China: the crossbow. Most of the crossbows shot metal-tipped arrows, but some were equipped to launch vicious little pellets made of iron or bronze. Later, in the fifth century, another formidable factor would be introduced to the battlefield: cavalry. Mounted bands from the Eurasian steppes had been harrying China's northern and western borders for some time. Eventually, the soldiers of Zhao, a northern border state, adopted the art of fighting on horseback, and before long cavalry units became standard across China. Warriors rode to battle wearing pointed, Scythian-style riding caps, golden belt buckles, boots, and trousers, the last an article of dress that ultimately caught on among the populace.

The increased reliance on infantry transformed the typical engagement from a brief series of chariot duels to a drawn-out struggle involving tens of thousands of men. When a commander was badly outnumbered or outmaneuvered, his entire army might be crushed and his state subjugated. So fierce were the retributions that on at least two occasions, the rulers of small states overrun by the army of Chu brought coffins with them to the surrender ceremony. They were spared, as it happened, but other defeated rulers were sacrificed. Equally vulnerable were the prominent ministers and lords who had served the fallen chief; they might avoid death, but their land would almost certainly be taken away. Many a great landholder ended his days in captivity, enduring conditions worse than those of his former serfs. To be sure, the peasants of a defeated state were in no enviable position. At worst, they might become the outright slaves of their conquerors, to be uprooted and divided among the victorious lords. But more often, the subject populace remained in place and toiled for alien masters.

Even in militarily successful states, the old rural order was eroding. The needs of the army drew so many lords and serfs away from the land that the estates ceased to function as cohesive, self-sufficient establishments farmed communally; much of the land became the property of certain wealthy lords, who purchased the holdings of others. By the sixth century BC, the typical peasant family worked a small plot, turning over a fixed percentage of the produce as rent to the landlord. In some areas, the levy could be as high as 20 percent, and the effect on some families was devastating. If the father or one of his sons was conscripted to serve in the army or labor on one of the roads needed to speed troop movements, those who remained behind still had to meet the levy — and struggle to fend off starvation throughout the winter.

While many were suffering in these tumultuous times, a few were discovering fresh opportunities. Chief among those to benefit were the merchants, who had formerly played but a minor role in the economy. Peasant communities no longer met all their own needs. They required such items as cloth, pots, and farm implements, including iron blades for their plows. Traveling merchants seized on the opportunity, plying routes that had been improved and extended in recent years for military purposes. Even states at war acknowledged the importance of such traffic, reaching agreements that permitted merchants to cross contested borders unimpeded. The introduction of bronze coinage, first minted by various states late in the sixth century, provided another powerful inducement to trade, furnishing merchants with a practical alternative to such exotic mediums of exchange as strings of cowrie shells and lengths of silk fabric.

Towns that were located at the junctions of trade routes naturally flourished, and some became fledgling cities. Urban areas in the more powerful and secure states became thriving manufacturing centers, where fabric was woven, pots molded, and bronze and iron vessels cast. Some of the workshops were true factories. Iron was smelted in great furnaces, fanned by massive bellows operated by scores of workmen. Inscribed bronzes cast during this era were numerous; to avoid having to carve the characters time and again, artisans came up with the world's first moveable type — characters that could be rearranged and transferred from one mold to another.

All of this activity required an ample supply of labor, and in some cases prisoners of war were put to work in state-run shops. The peasants provided another source of labor, as those who could not make ends meet in the countryside migrated to the cities. To cope with the expansion, some cities established separate residential, industrial, and commercial districts marked off by walls.

Along with the merchants and industrialists, a second class was faring well in the ferment — the bureaucrats and officials referred to collectively as the shi. By tradition, a shi was a faithful retainer who was schooled to serve his lord in any number of capacities — as a warrior in the field, perhaps, or as a bailiff on the estate. As conflict increased among China's states, these versatile underlings weathered the storms far better than their superiors; if their lords were defeated, their talents were of no less use to the victors. Rarely of high birth, they lived by their wits and worked hard for their promotions. In the sixth century, such men were ardently sought by state rulers, who, caring little for the pretensions of the nobility, preferred to entrust the running of their increasingly complex governments to individuals with acquired ability. Indeed, the demand was greater than the supply, and teachers arose whose primary mission was to educate men to govern.

Kongfuzi — Confucius — was one of those teachers. But if he had simply contented himself with providing caretakers for the bureaucratic machines that were being shaped in China, his lessons would soon have been forgotten. Far from counseling his disciples to adapt themselves to the needs of the rulers, he inspired them to look critically at their society and those who commanded it. He called on his followers to transcend the selfish, parochial interests that had embroiled the land in conflict, and to embrace a philosophy of self-discipline and tolerance. And in the process, he inaugurated a system of thought that went beyond the question of how to govern successfully to a more fundamental problem — how to live honorably.

Confucius was born in 552 BC in Lu, one of the smaller central states that had managed to hold its own through the bitter centuries of struggle. Respect for the Zhou king remained high in Lu — its rulers still proudly claimed descent from the royal house — and Confucius grew up with a nostalgic reverence for the golden age when the Zhou had reigned supreme. He himself was the product of an aristocratic family that had seen better days. His followers would contend that he was a legitimate descendant of the ruler of a neighboring state, Song, while detractors would claim that Confucius's forebears were merely the children of concubines at the Song court.

Contradictions abounded in the biographical accounts of Confucius, whose life would be known only in broad outlines to future generations. Confucius's father evidently possessed little wealth, but was said to have been a warrior of great courage and strength, vital enough to conceive a son at the age of seventy. He died shortly before the boy was born, it was said, leaving his wife to rear the future sage alone.

Determined to furnish Confucius with an education, his mother entrusted him to the village tutor. To be educated meant first of all to be literate — no mean accomplishment in a written language with several thousand characters. Many Chinese characters were ideographs, combinations of symbols that expressed abstract concepts with poetic ingenuity. The ideograph for "peace," for example, consisted of the symbol of a woman beneath the outline of a roof, while the concepts of goodness and affection were expressed by the symbol of a mother beside that of a child. Studying such characters and sketching them with brushes on strips of bamboo, students took to heart the lessons of their culture.

As he mastered the language, Confucius would have taken up the literature of his land, including the various ballads that were collected in a great anthology called the *Shijing*, or Classic of Songs. "Have you studied the Songs?" the mature Confucius reportedly asked one of his disciples. "If you have not studied the Songs, you will not be able to converse." Dating back to the tenth century BC, the ballads surveyed the entire pageant of Chinese life through a turbulent epoch, including plaintive glimpses

When this Chinese nobleman of the fifth century BC led his men into battle, he traveled in style, thundering along in a chariot pulled by ornately caparisoned horses and steered by an expert driver. Although his role was basically that of a general directing his troops, a nobleman sometimes was in the thick of the fight, so the axle caps of his chariot might be fitted with protruding serrated blades to slice at the legs of his foes. He was also outfitted with the finest battle gear available. The nobleman wielded both a double-edged bronze sword called a *jian*, and a *ge*, or dagger-ax, the bronze-bladed weapon for hacking and stabbing that he is gripping here. He carried a lightweight leather shield, coated with multiple layers of lacquer for hardness. His iron-and-leather helmet offered some protection for his head, and his upper body was covered by armor constructed of contoured sections of leather stiffened with lacquer, decorated, and bound together with silk.

of those who had been sundered from loved ones by the incessant fighting: "My lord is on army duty./Not for a day or a month./When shall we be together?/The chickens have roosted on their perches;/It's the end of the day./The cows and sheep have come in./But my lord is on army duty./If only he doesn't hunger and thirst."

Along with poetry, there were historical texts to be scrutinized. Those relating to the early days of the Zhou dynasty had been collected by the time of Confucius under the title *Shujing,* or Classic of Writings. Other texts pertaining to more recent times would be brought together in the fifth century as the *Chunqiu,* or Spring and Autumn Annals. Some disciples would later claim that Confucius himself compiled those annals: They covered a period beginning in 722 BC and ending in 481 BC, or two years before his death. Whether or not he was the compiler, Confucius was certainly familiar with the various written accounts of China's past. Pondering them, he acquired a long view of the crisis confronting his homeland.

Literature and history formed the core of his education, but as a young man aspiring to high places he also mastered the art of music, intended to inculcate in the pupil a sense of rhythm and proportion. Instruments included the zither, drums, and chimes — and, of course, the human voice, for the poetry of the day was sung. All of this made up the cultural equipment of the shi, the consummate civil servant.

Confucius embarked on that career in his late teens by accepting a minor post in the Lu state government, administering land held by the ruling family. By one account, he was promoted to the position of family tutor within a few years. Around this time he married and fathered a son, but little more is known of his domestic life. His mother died when he was in his midtwenties, it was said, and obeying an ancient custom, he mourned her for three years, leaving the bottom of his robe unhemmed to signal his bereavement. The remainder of his career was devoted primarily to teaching. He left his official post after a while to tutor students in his own home or to travel from place to place, preparing young men for positions of responsibility.

The enlightenment that earned Confucius the title of Master did not come to him in a blinding flash; he moved toward it slowly and deliberately. "At fifteen I set my heart on learning," he would tell his disciples; "at thirty I took my stand; at forty I came to be free of doubts." In midlife, then, he realized his true mission, which was not to mold himself or his students to the requirements of the world, but to set a standard for the world to follow. He insisted that those seeking office put aside any ambition to wield power for its own sake. The only legitimate motive for governing was to provide an example for the people. By some accounts, Confucius did just that in his native state of Lu, accepting a high post there around the age of fifty. During his virtuous tenure, crime became a thing of the past: A purse dropped in the street would go untouched for days. Such success naturally inspired jealousy, it was said, and conspirators at court succeeded in ousting him.

To be sure, Confucius would have welcomed such an opportunity to put his principles to the test, but his political role seems to have been limited to counseling rulers and those who hoped to serve them. Statements attributed to him in the *Analects,* a collection of his sayings assembled not long after his death, portray a figure who had to resign himself to life on the outskirts of power: "I have never been proved in office. That is why I am a jack-of-all-trades." On another occasion, he insisted that the true leader "does not mind failing to get recognition; he is too busy doing the things that entitle him to recognition."

Recognition would come in full for Confucius, but not in his lifetime. When he died in 479 BC, in his early seventies, he had acquired a small but devoted following of disciples who would preserve and elaborate on his sayings in the decades to come. But the immediate impact of his teachings was limited by the paradox of his place in history, for this was a man both behind his times and ahead of them. His vision of China's past led him to celebrate the virtues of a bygone era when great kings had exercised genuine authority, and that vision would not be fully and widely appreciated until centuries after his death, when an imperial family once again dominated the land.

At the heart of Confucius's conservative outlook lay the concept of *li*, or "rituals." To observe the rituals was to honor traditions rooted in the proud days of the early Zhou and their royal predecessors, the Shang—customs linking children to their parents, lords to their king, and the king to the will of heaven. China's most sacred rite was one in which the Zhou king made sacrificial offerings to Di, his ancestral spirit in heaven. That observance had its humble counterpart in the homage that every devout individual owed to his elders and betters in life and in death. "When your parents are alive, comply with the rites in serving them," Confucius commanded his disciples. "When they die, comply with the rites in burying them; comply with the rites in sacrificing to them." Those who failed to honor their parents were rejecting the lessons of the past, which taught that social harmony depended on acknowledging certain hierarchies and the obligations that flowed from them: "Let the ruler be a ruler and the subject a subject; let the father be a father and the son a son."

The traditionalism of Confucius was anything but hidebound, however. He was aware of the countless instances in which those endowed with authority had betrayed that trust over the centuries. Indeed, his main concern was not that too little respect was being shown to superiors, but that too many of those in a position to command respect were of inferior character. He realized that the nobles who had wielded power in China through the ages were not inherently virtuous, so he redefined the concept of nobility to connote something that could only be acquired through study and self-discipline. Traditionally, those entitled to govern in China were called *Junzi*, or "ruler's sons." With Confucius, that term lost its hereditary associations and came to mean a man of truly noble character whatever his lineage, a gentleman in the broadest sense of the word. The opposite of the gentleman, in Confucius's terms, was the "small man," one who might be touted in his city or state but who lacked the wisdom to see beyond its confines: "While the gentleman cherishes benign rule, the small man cherishes his native land."

To be worthy of the title "gentleman," it was not enough simply to observe the rites, for practicing them was only the outward sign of the superior man. The inward expression of nobility, Confucius insisted, was a generous spirit, a whole-hearted concern that impelled the ruler to deal generously with his subjects, or the landlord to see to the needs of his tenants. Known to the Chinese as *ren*, this benevolent spirit was not unlike the concept of charity later embraced by the early Christians. And in his moral teachings, Confucius anticipated another Christian precept: the Golden Rule. When asked to state the single principle that should govern one's conduct in life, he replied: "Never do to others what you would not like them to do to you."

A ruler who heeded this principle and who was truly benevolent of heart would naturally be slow to resort to force. Confucius once chided two disciples for advising the ruler Jisun to send his army against Zhuanyou, a rebellious province of his state. "When distant subjects are unsubmissive, one cultivates one's moral quality in order to attract them," Confucius argued. "Instead, you propose to resort to the use of arms within the state itself. I am afraid that Jisun's worries lie not in Zhuanyou but within the walls of his palace." On another occasion, Confucius spelled out the steps by which the wise ruler could avoid unrest among his subjects: "Approach your duties with reverence and be trustworthy in what you say; avoid excesses in expenditure and love your fellow men; employ the labor of the common people only in the right seasons."

Confucius recognized the difficulty of applying such enlightened policies in the chaotic conditions of his day. He once repeated wistfully an old saying: "Only if the right sort of people had charge of a country for a hundred years would it become really possible to stop cruelty and do away with slaughter." But the enormity of the task did not exempt those in power from the obligation to make the attempt. And even the disciples who failed to win influence — or lost it to small men appealing to base instincts — would be ennobled by heeding the teachings of the Master. The pursuit of virtue was its own reward, promising peace to the soul if not to the world. Confucius had little to say about the realm of the spirits or the prospects of an afterlife. "May I ask about death?" a disciple once inquired of him. To which he replied: "You do not understand even life. How can you understand death?" Nonetheless, Confucius and his disciples brought a religious intensity to their quest for the honorable life. And their faith in the power of tradition leavened by human kindness would in time inspire millions of Chinese who lived out their lives far from the corridors of power.

A compelling alternative to Confucianism was presented by a school of Chinese mystics who referred to themselves as Taoists, or Followers of the Way. They traced their movement to a legendary figure called Laozi, or the Old Master, said to have been a contemporary of Confucius who abandoned the pursuit of power for a life of meditation. The Way of Laozi was altogether different from the path of civic obligations that had been charted by Confucius. Taoists called for a retreat to nature and to the primitive state of society, pictured as an idyllic rural community where there was no place for envy or exploitation. The fact that this state existed only in the imagination did not deter the Taoists, for they were always more concerned with immutable ideals than with shifting realities. By celebrating the contemplative life over one of restless striving, they prepared the ground in China for another philosophy that would seek enlight-

By the middle of the third century BC, the bulk of the vast Indian subcontinent was unified for the first time under the ruthlessly efficient rule of the Mauryan dynasty. Stretching from the Hindu Kush in the west to Bengal in the east, and from the foothills of the Himalayas to the arid south, the Mauryan empire embraced the basins of two major river systems, the Indus and the Ganges. The narrow Indus Valley, hemmed in by rugged terrain, proved secondary in importance to the Ganges, whose broad and fertile plains nourished the expansionist ambitions of Mauryan kings.

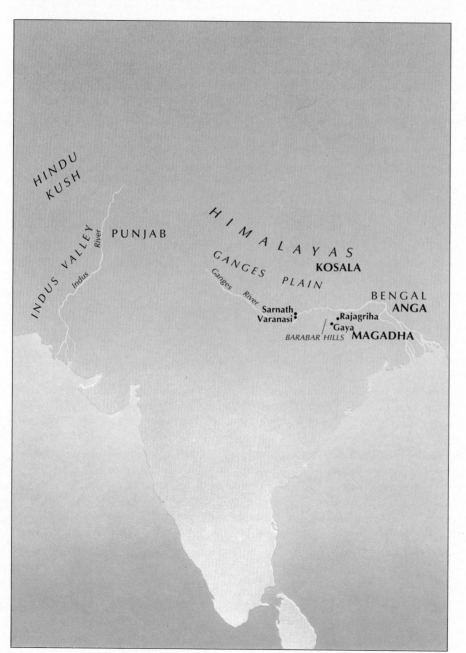

enment through the rejection of worldly ambitions — the Way of the Buddha.

Over the centuries, China would prove receptive to such mystical schools of thought as Taoism and Buddhism without forsaking its attachment to the worldly idealism of Confucius and his disciples. In the mystics, the Chinese heard the strains of a timeless and eternal theme, but in Confucius they confronted the power of history, of lessons culled from the past. It was the study of the past, after all, that had equipped Confucius with many of his insights. And it was the flow of history that would carry his philosophy from the periphery to the very heart of Chinese culture.

Late in the third century BC, the relentless struggle for supremacy in China would at last yield a champion, as the ambitious Han dynasty emerged to govern a united kingdom. Proud of China's imperial heritage, the Han monarchs were to embrace the philosopher who had given that heritage new life and legitimacy in his teachings. The grave of Confucius would become a shrine, where offerings were made to the memory of the sage by no less a figure than the emperor — the Son of Heaven himself.

By the middle of the first millennium BC, India, too, was in ferment. A land of rival kingdoms and castes, it would progress slowly through this period toward cultural unity, helped along by the teachings of another great visionary — the Buddha. Ultimately, the seeds of wisdom nurtured by the Buddha would be borne across Asia, to take root in China, Southeast Asia, and Japan. But this great new creed was first and foremost the fruit of India's complex heritage.

For roughly a thousand years, Indian civilization had been shaped by Aryans. Kin to the nomads who had occupied Persia during the second millennium BC, the Aryans who made their way south through the Hindu Kush range would be remembered as a hardy lot who battled for possession of livestock and pasturage, and offered animal sacrifices to the gods who granted them victories and sustenance. Slowly, however, their nomadic customs had been modified as they progressed first into the Punjab — the alluvial plain of the upper Indus River — and then on to an even more fertile region along the Ganges. Fed by the melting snows of the Himalayas and the summer monsoons sweeping in from the ocean, that river and its many twisting arteries and channels overflowed regularly to irrigate fields of rice and barley, leaving behind a replenishing layer of silt. Amid such prospects, the newcomers set aside their restless ways; the fluid tribal boundaries solidified, and kingdoms took shape. By 600 BC, the Ganges Plain was the acknowledged heartland of Indian civilization. The central and southern portions of the subcontinent, dusty and inhospitable through much of the year, remained the haunt of aboriginal tribes, while the Punjab was subject to repeated incursions from the north. Soon the Persians would follow that path, sweeping down to the Indus Valley to claim it for their empire.

Relatively secure by comparison, the Ganges Plain fostered a settled, largely rural society. There peasants lived in clusters of huts, with a small herd of cattle and a few goats for the needs of the community. Most of those who worked the land were free, but their lot was not an easy one. Variations in the monsoon produced periodic famines, and diseases spread swiftly in the humid climate; even if the peasants themselves remained fit, losses of livestock could be devastating. Misfortune reduced some in the countryside to begging for alms. Others gravitated to the estates of proud rajas, as the Indians called their rulers, to work their land — or migrated to the larger villages, where trade was spawning a merchant class whose members had need of servants and laborers. A few of those settlements were substantial enough to be called cities, including Rajaghra, near the center of the Ganges Plain. It had a fortified perimeter of some twenty-five miles; much of the area within was given over to gardens, which were a source of both nourishment and delight to the residents. Cities and villages were linked by a network of trails and river routes that supported a lively traffic in spices, gems, and fabrics reaching to the Indus Valley and the lands beyond.

Beneath such semblances of unity, however, the political and social fissures ran deep. There were sixteen autonomous kingdoms in the Ganges region alone, and the fact that their rulers shared an Aryan heritage did little to pacify them. Infighting was a tribal tradition of the Aryans, after all, and although the situation in India was not as volatile as that in China, conflict would increase in the centuries to come. No less significant were the racial and class barriers within the society. In the process of settling the land, the Aryans had encountered darker-skinned peoples whose ancestors had inhabited the subcontinent for tens of thousands of years. Some of these aborigines had fallen subject to the Aryans, and dark skin had become associated with low status. Over the centuries, intermarriage and cultural assimilation had blurred the racial distinctions somewhat, but Indian society remained stratified. Indeed, the divisions among the classes were sanctioned by scripture. In the Vedas, sacred verses that harked back to the heroic, tribal days of the Aryans, a strict hierarchy of four classes was spelled out: the Brahmans, or priests, stood at the top, followed by Kshatriyas, or rulers; Vaishyas, or merchants; and Shudras, or servants. Below the Shudras lay the pariahs, outcasts who would be known in a later era as untouchables.

Such was the doctrine. But by the sixth century, Indian society had taken on a complexity that belied the scriptural formula. The Brahmans were still the guardians of the faith as elaborated in the Vedas, and so they naturally kept for themselves the highest rank. Proud priests argued that they should be free from taxation and all secular control, and demanded generous fees and gifts for the rites they performed. Their claims were being challenged, though, by the ambitious rulers who held sway over the various kingdoms. Like the tribal chiefs before them, these kings kept priests at their side to preside over sacrifices meant to strengthen their hand. Yet the kings also derived considerable comfort from more worldly sources: They lived on large estates tended by peasants, and within their palaces courtiers and courtesans vied for their favors. The more secure the kings felt in their privileges, the less inclined they were to defer to the Brahmans. By contrast, the kings were eager to secure the support of certain individuals who ranked lower on the spiritual scale — wealthy Vaishyas, whose coffers were swelling with the profits of trade.

It was not just the rising fortunes of kings and merchants that called into question the old Aryan doctrines. For some time, restless members of the Brahman class itself had been pondering their mission. Some priests joined the ranks of spiritual seekers who were retreating from society altogether or dwelling in huts among the Shudras and outcasts. Such austere holy men saw ample evidence of the suffering wrought by poverty, disease, and famine, and some carried their own ascetic regimens to agonizing lengths, wandering naked through the forests, denying themselves food or drink for days on end, or lying on beds of thorns. Others were more temperate in their self-denial, seeking through asceticism to reach a state of meditative bliss. Those who attained that goal might then share their insights with disciples.

In this way, a tradition of mystical teachings grew up, one that had a profound effect on Indian religion. Ascetics played a leading role in evolving and disseminating the meditative scriptures known as the Upanishads. Unlike the Vedas, with their emphasis on ritual observances, the Upanishads pondered the riddle of the individual's relationship to the divine spirit. They taught that each person's soul harbored a spark of the divine, a spark that sought union with the universal essence, or *brahman*. But the path to that union was long and tortuous; one could only move closer to the goal by leading a good life, and it might take a single soul any number of earthly lives to achieve its end. This was the doctrine of reincarnation and karma, the belief that one's conduct in this life had a bearing on lives to follow. Significantly, although the idea of karma infused Indian religion with a powerful ethical strain, it did little to subvert the traditional hierarchy of classes. It simply offered someone of low rank the hope of climbing another rung up the ladder toward enlightenment in the next life.

Not all found solace there. Some considered the notion of being repeatedly subjected to the vicissitudes of life and the anguish of death profoundly discouraging. One man in particular sought a path to salvation that might break this remorseless cycle — and the trail he blazed would be followed by kings and servants alike.

He was born Siddhartha Gautama around 560 BC to a raja named Suddhodhana and his wife, Maya. Their handsome estate lay in the Himalayan foothills, within the kingdom of Kosala. Of sixteen kingdoms in the Ganges River valley, Kosala was second in power only to neighboring Magadha. Siddhartha's father was head of the Sakya tribe, one of several hill tribes that retained a measure of autonomy by paying tribute to Kosala's king, or maharaja.

The story of Siddhartha's birth and his spiritual quest would not be committed to writing until the second century AD, allowing ample time for legend to intertwine with fact. It was said of Siddhartha's conception that his mother was carried away in a dream to a sacred lake, where a white elephant bearing a lotus blossom in its trunk approached and entered her side with the flower. A wise man said the dream meant she would bear a marvelous son who would grow up to be either a Universal Emperor or a Universal Teacher. Later, after Siddhartha's birth, a soothsayer expanded on that prophecy: Siddhartha would see four signs that would convince him of the misery of the world, and he would choose the path of a teacher. Determined to prevent that from happening, Siddhartha's father vowed to shelter the child from all sickness and decay, and surround him solely with youth and beauty.

As Siddhartha grew to manhood, it seemed that his father's wish would be fulfilled. When he was not being schooled in the arts of war or the traditions of his culture, the young prince rode to hunt, surrounded by a herd of elephants decked in silver ornaments; before him lay thick forests haunted by tigers, verdant meadows sprinkled with saffron crocus, and, far on the horizon, great snowcapped peaks. At the end of the day he might take his ease in the royal park, where, in the lush aftermath of the monsoons, mangoes hung ripe for the picking. And within the palace walls waited further delights: When he assumed the title of raja, Siddhartha would have the run of a sizable harem. His first duty, of course, was to win a suitable mate, one who would exercise authority over the harem as his chief queen, or *mahisi*. In due course he made such a match, wedding his beautiful cousin, Yasodhara. But not long after the ceremony, he was visited by the first of the dreaded signs that had been foretold.

According to the legend, Siddhartha was riding the royal grounds beside his charioteer, Channa, when he came for the first time in his life upon a gnarled old man, who had miraculously found his way into this sheltered precinct. Siddhartha asked Channa what kind of creature stood before them and learned from the answer that to grow old was inevitable. Not long afterward, on another ride, the young prince encountered a man disfigured by sores and shivering with fever, and learned that sickness lay in wait for everyone. The third sign, a corpse being borne to the cremation ground, taught him that death was human fate. But the fourth sign offered the chastened prince hope: He saw a contented holy man, an ascetic who wore nothing but a plain yellow robe and carried a bowl for begging. On seeing him, Siddhartha realized that one could find peace by withdrawing from the world, and he knew the path he must follow.

The palace held no more pleasures for Siddhartha. One night while visiting his father's harem, he beheld some of the kingdom's most beautiful women as they would one day appear — wrinkled and stooped. Soon after, he received word that his wife had given birth to a son, but he felt no pride. That same night, after bidding a silent farewell to his sleeping wife and infant boy, he fled in his chariot with Channa at his side. When they were well beyond the palace grounds, he ordered Channa to halt and stepped from the chariot. He cut his flowing hair with the blade of his sword and sent the locks back to his father with Channa. It was said that as Siddhartha set off alone on foot, his horse dropped dead of grief.

The young man began his quest by sitting at the foot of a learned sage who taught the wisdom of the Upanishads. But those lessons failed to satisfy him, so he joined with five other restless seekers, and together they entered the forest to practice the most rigorous form of asceticism. Siddhartha outdid his companions in self-mortification. He lived for long spells on a grain of rice a day, it was said, eventually growing so thin that when he rubbed his stomach he could feel his spine. He wore garments that scratched his skin, assumed awkward and painful positions for hours, and allowed filth and vermin to accumulate on his flesh. But no torture to which he subjected his body brought release to his soul.

One day, in the sixth year of his penance, he fainted and fell into a stream. The cold water revived him, saving his life, and in the aftermath he determined to abandon his regimen. He walked to a nearby village and began to beg for food. His five companions, following behind, were appalled to see him eating and drinking again with enjoyment. They denounced him as a reprobate and left him.

Siddhartha continued on his uncertain pilgrimage alone. His wanderings took him to Magadha, the powerful kingdom whose rulers would soon aspire to empire. There, in his thirty-sixth year, outside the town of Gaya, Siddhartha one day seated himself beneath a great pipal tree, its branches laden with figs; in time, it would be known to the devout as the *bodhi,* or the Tree of Wisdom. There Siddhartha vowed to remain until he was able to solve the riddle of suffering. For seven weeks he sat beneath the boughs, visited in his reveries by evil spirits who offered him pleasures and powers far greater than those he had chosen to renounce as a youth. Siddhartha spurned them all, until at last he was left in peace, and descended into a timeless meditation. Wrapped in solitary bliss, he entered a state that was neither being nor nonbeing, neither life nor death — a flawless realm that his followers would call nirvana. In that moment he became the Buddha, the Enlightened One.

When he returned to consciousness in the sunlit world around him, the Buddha doubted at first whether he could explain to others the wisdom he had attained, for it seemed to lie outside the bounds of logic and language. He traveled on to the village of Sarnath, near the

A sculpture from northwest India, this skeletal image of the Buddha, emaciated from fasting, contrasts with the usual depictions of a plump, well-nourished master. The Buddha's earliest disciples prohibited any artistic depiction of their transcendent leader, permitting only such symbolic representations of him as footprints or lotus blossoms. But the gradual transformation of Buddhism from a closed, monastic cult to a widespread faith inspired more tangible likenesses of the Buddha for popular devotion. Statues and relics, made by skilled artisans and carried by missionary monks, helped disseminate Buddhism from India to China and Southeast Asia.

modern city of Varanasi, and there, in a sanctuary known as the Deer Park, he met again the five ascetics who had spurned him. They sensed at once the change that had come over him and urged him to speak of his revelation. Words came to him, and he preached to the five his first sermon.

As revealed then and elaborated over the years, the Buddha's message began with the lesson he had learned through bitter experience. The path to wisdom lay neither through self-indulgence nor through self-denial; one should avoid extremes and follow the Middle Way. Such moderation prepared one to receive the Four Noble Truths. The first of these truths was suffering, or *dukka*. In Pali, the language of the first Buddhist scriptures, that word referred to an axle that separates from its wheel or a bone that comes loose from its socket. Such wrenching separations, whether the loss of a loved one or the abandonment of a long-cherished ideal, were intrinsic to life, and no one who clung to the world could escape their pain. The second truth was the cause of that suffering: desire. One's craving for love, for power, for life everlasting, led inevitably to disillusionment and sorrow. Even the craving celebrated by the Upanishads — the longing of the soul to be united with the brahman — was futile, the Buddha insisted, for the soul and the goal it longed for were mere figments of the imagination. The third truth was that the cause of suffering could be transcended — the pain would cease when the desire was forsaken. The fourth truth was the path by which that release was to be obtained, the Eightfold Way. To eliminate suffering, one had to adhere to eight strictures: Hold the right views, harbor the right aspirations, adopt the right speech, demonstrate the right conduct, pursue the right livelihood, expend the right effort, maintain the right mindfulness, and practice the right meditation.

The Eightfold Way was the ethical core of Buddhism, the beacon that guided the faithful toward virtuous behavior much as the doctrine of karma guided those who followed the Upanishads. To speak right, the Buddha explained, was to not lie or slander; to act right was to not kill, steal, drink liquor, or be unchaste; to follow the right livelihood was to make room in one's life for the pursuit of salvation — ideally, to become a monk. But the object of all this was not to improve the next life. On the contrary, those who followed the Eightfold Way hoped soon to achieve nirvana, which literally meant "the blowing out," as of a candle. In blowing out that candle, one escaped the whole sorrowful cycle of human existence into oblivion.

By articulating these ideas, the Buddha set in motion the *dharma:* the Wheel of the Law. The five ascetics to whom he first preached made up his original *sangha,* or monastic order. Soon many more disciples were renouncing home and family to wander the countryside together. They shaved their heads, wore coarse, saffron-dyed robes, and carried with them the beggar's bowl that made up the sum of their worldly possessions. Wherever they went, they told of the Noble Truths and chanted their creed: "I take refuge in the Buddha; I take refuge in the dharma; I take refuge in the sangha." The message was clear and accessible, conveyed not in arcane scriptures intelligible only to priests but in the common parlance of the day.

Men of all classes heeded the call, for the Buddha held that low rank was no barrier to salvation. And before his death around the age of eighty, he assented to the formation of an order of nuns. According to legend, one of its first members was a grief-stricken woman who had lost her child. Having heard miraculous tales of the Buddha, she approached him outside a village with her dead infant in her arms and begged him to bring the child to life. He told her to fetch him a mustard seed from a single household that had not known death. Her search proved fruitless, and realizing that sorrow was the lot of all those who lived and longed, she joined his order. The yellow-clad followers of the Buddha were not alone in renouncing the accepted wisdom of the past. A second group of unorthodox mendicants began to roam the countryside around this time. These mystics, in the colorful phrase of a later day, went "sky-clad," or stark naked. They called themselves Jains, and their leader was another tribal prince, known as the Mahavira, or the Great Hero. Born around 540 BC, the Mahavira, like the Buddha, renounced his privileged status as a young man to become a wandering ascetic. He first joined a sect of nudists called *nigranthas,* or those "free from bonds," staying with them for ten years until their leader died. He then left with a group of his own followers from the sect, and a few years later he experienced the great enlightenment that served as the source of his teachings.

Unlike the Buddha, who held that the soul was a chimera, the Mahavira taught that the soul in the form of tiny particles called *jiva* was present in all living things: men, women, animals, even the flies in the air and the worms in the soil. Humans were caught in the cruel cycle of transmigration because the karma of past misdeeds clung to their jiva like barnacles. The only way to free one's soul and achieve salvation was to renounce destruction of any kind, because even a seemingly innocent action, such as tilling the soil, involved harm to the jiva harbored there.

The nudity practiced by the Mahavira's original followers was just a small part of their system, a symbol of their effort to disencumber the soul. More important were the lengths to which they went to avoid doing harm: They walked about only in daylight to avoid accidentally injuring the soul-laden creatures around them, carried dusters to whisk ants and other insects from mats before seating themselves, and veiled their mouths to keep from inhaling tiny airborne organisms. Eating meat, of course, was strictly forbidden. The Greek historian Herodotus may have had disciples of the Mahavira in mind when he wrote of a group of Indians who "refuse to put any animal to death, sow no corn, and have no dwelling houses. Vegetables are their only food." Presumably, the Mahavira accepted the eating of vegetables as a regrettable necessity for his followers — provided that the cultivation was performed by others. He himself showed little interest in sustaining his own life. Through fasting, he believed, one could liberate one's jiva from its fleshly confinement. His pursuit of this goal, it was said, led ultimately to his death from starvation at the age of seventy-two. To his disciples this ardent opponent of violence became known as a Jain, or "Conqueror," because he had broken the bonds that imprisoned his soul.

The Mahavira had taken old ideas and given them new life, defining the soul and its karma so graphically that he made concrete what the Brahmans had treated as abstractions. The ranks of his followers continued to expand throughout the Ganges Plain after his death, although the rules they followed lost some severity. (In time, the practice of nudity lapsed.) True salvation was possible only to the monks, who renounced all property and sexual activity along with the ways of violence. Most Jains, however, were members of the laity; they retreated periodically to join the monks, then returned to their worldly pursuits. Unwilling to take up the plow, many turned to commerce: Jains formed an important segment of the growing merchant class.

Yet Buddhism would have an even greater impact on India's development in the decades to come, for its teachings had become attached to the rising star of Magadha, the kingdom where the Buddha ended his days. Profiting from its central position in the Ganges Valley, Magadha was a nexus of trade, and it drew as well on a rich mineral resource — the iron ore that lay encrusted at the surface of the Barabar Hills. Magadha's plains were extremely fertile, its forests were thick with the timber needed to fortify villages and royal compounds, and vast herds of elephants — good for work and war — roamed its countryside.

Bimbisara, the king who presided over this flourishing realm during the Buddha's lifetime, was less interested in the proud Aryan past and the traditions of the Vedas than he was in consolidating his wealth and expanding his domain. According to one tale, it was the Buddha himself who convinced Bimbisara to forsake the Brahmans in his court, along with their sacrificial rites. The Buddha was visiting Bimbisara when a priest approached the king and insisted that he sacrifice fifty of his finest goats, assuring him that whatever he offered up would go "directly to heaven." The Buddha then asked the priest if his father was still living. The priest answered that he was, prompting the Buddha to inquire: "Then why not sacrifice him?" Delighted, Bimbisara spared the goats and banished the priest.

Whether or not that conversation ever actually took place, the ambitious Bimbisara clearly found the iconoclastic nature of Buddhism more congenial than the tradition-bound doctrines of the Brahmans. The Buddha had no interest in changing the world or in raising up new gods for the human race to follow. But by rejecting the notion that piety was inherited — by challenging the view of society as a rigid hierarchy — he offered a powerful tool to a man like Bimbisara, who was seeking to break down barriers and forge a cohesive empire.

The fact that Bimbisara and his heirs on the Magadhan throne longed to extend their domain, however, had nothing to do with the lesson of the Buddha. They were inspired rather by the example of the Persians, who demonstrated their power in a way no Indian ruler could ignore. In 521 BC, a few years after the Buddha experienced his enlightenment, the Persian emperor Darius led an invading army south across the Hindu Kush Mountains. Before long the Persians were in firm control of the western Punjab, and the region became the Persian empire's twentieth satrapy. A contingent of Indian troops served under Xerxes when he invaded Greece in 479 BC. Perhaps out of admiration for the Persians, perhaps out of fear of the threat they posed, the kings of Magadha began to piece together their own empire. Bimbisara initiated the process around 500 BC by annexing the small kingdom of Anga, near present-day Bengal, and gaining a foothold in other states through marriage alliances. His successors continued the expansionist policy; late in the fourth century BC, a brilliant adventurer named Chandragupta Maurya came to power in Magadha and proceeded to bring most of the Indian subcontinent under his command. Chandragupta's grandson, the emperor Asoka, proclaimed Buddhism the chief religion of the realm. And with his encouragement, Buddhist monks fanned out along trade routes to the north and east, bringing word of the Noble Truths to much of Asia. The place of the Buddha's enlightenment, the grove of the bodhi tree at Gaya, became the haunt of pilgrims, who arrived from far-away lands to carry off cuttings.

In the end, it was foreign soil that proved most congenial to the teachings of the Buddha. In India itself, an eclectic Hinduism would ultimately prevail — a faith that drew partly on the old Vedic scriptures, partly on fertility cults native to India, and partly on Buddhism and Jainism. Ironically, the Buddha himself — whose Noble Truths made no mention of god — became in time an object of veneration, and not only among those who practiced the Eightfold Way. At Gaya the Hindus maintained their own temple to the Enlightened One, where he was worshiped as an earthly incarnation of the great lord Vishnu, guardian of the good and enemy of evil.

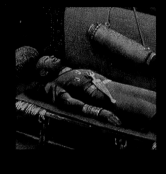

Long before humans learned to record their history, they acknowledged their debt to the past by preserving the remains of the dead in graves, mounds, and caverns. With the coming of civilization, the burial places grew more elaborate. Occasionally, proud kings sought to transcend their prosaic confines by raising pyramids to the heavens or by excavating cavernous shafts to the spirit world below. But over the centuries, the elite of most societies chose to be laid to rest in settings that resembled more closely the dwellings they had lived in. By the middle of the first millennium BC, tomb builders in many lands were reproducing with painstaking fidelity the surroundings that had afforded the deceased pride and pleasure in their lifetimes.

Such realism did not preclude the construction of crypts on a monumental scale. In preparing the awesome facade for the tomb of King Darius I *(pages 162-163),* Persian artisans borrowed motifs from the king's vast complex at Persepolis. In both settings, representatives of the subject nations of the Persian empire were portrayed paying homage to the king. Thus the tomb decoration not only mirrored the surface of mighty Persepolis but assured onlookers that the substance of Darius's policies would live on after his death.

The grave sites of the rich Celtic lords of Europe were more modest in scale, yet they spoke just as eloquently of the earthly ambitions of the occupants. The tomb vaults of Celtic nobles tended to be like their houses, simple structures built of logs and stones. More striking were the objects buried along with the deceased. The far-ranging Celts cherished their vehicles, and few grave goods conferred more honor on the departed than a handsome wagon or chariot. One noblewoman was laid to rest in a ceremonial cart from which the wheels had been removed, transforming it from a hearse into a bier. In addition to such weighty tribute, the corpses of Celtic dignitaries were decked out with fine ornaments from the far corners of the earth: A prince of the Hallstatt culture of Austria was buried in clothing embroidered with Chinese silk.

No ancient people surpassed the Etruscans at fashioning realistic housing for the dead. Even before burial became commonplace in Italy, artisans were creating miniature terra-cotta huts to hold cremated remains. As Etruscan cities grew increasingly prosperous, the leading families commissioned spacious burial villas, excavated out of the region's soft volcanic rock, with individual chambers organized around a common room equipped for the enjoyment of the deceased. The residents of what became San Giuliano could look across a ravine to view the facades of scores of such family vaults carved into a cliffside. Far from being disturbed by the prospect, the inhabitants must have found it reassuring. The necropolis of a large Etruscan community was in effect its sister city, where the dead resided in as civilized a fashion as their living kin.

One of the most spectacular tombs of the ancient world was that of Darius I, king of Persia. Begun about 520 BC, when Darius was thirty years old, the royal sepulcher *(far right)* was the first of such tombs carved into the side of a cliff on the mountain of Naqsh-i Rustam, a few miles north of the royal city of Persepolis. Working under Darius's supervision, architects and sculptors replicated the exterior of the royal palace on the sheer rock face. They crowned the seventy-five-foot facade with the image of the king worshiping the winged god Ahuramazda while standing on a throne supported by vassals from thirty nations subject to Persia. A massive portal gave access to the tomb's interior *(inset)*. In subsequent years, similar resting places for Darius's successors were carved out alongside his own.

The interior of Darius's tomb was tunneled into the solid rock of Naqsh-i Rustam. A sixty-foot-long corridor gave access to three vaults, each containing three burial niches for members of the royal family.

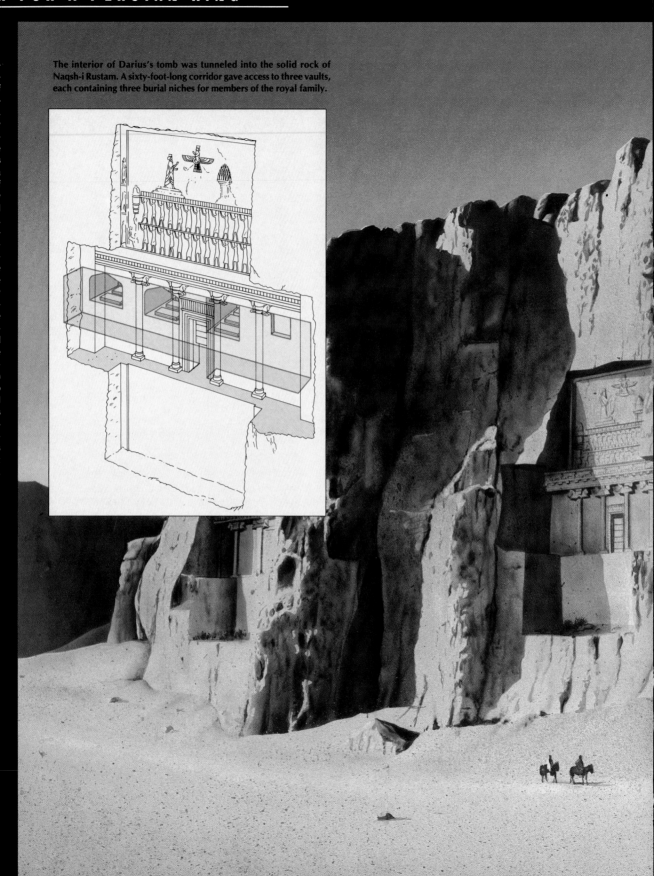

TOMB OF A CELTIC WARRIOR

The vigorous life-style of the Celts was reflected in the tomb setting of a forty-year-old warrior-prince buried in a hillside near what became Hochdorf, Germany. Clad in a flaxen robe adorned with gold, the dead warrior was laid out on an ornate bronze burial couch within a box-like structure of logs and rock, four feet deep and fifteen feet square. The body was surrounded with trappings for the journey to the afterlife: a wooden cart, weapons, crockery, ceremonial drinking horns, and a massive bronze caldron filled with mead.

Believing that the dead had the same daily needs as the living, the Etruscans were careful to equip their family tombs with all the comforts of home. One of the most elaborate Etruscan burial houses was the so-called Tomb of the Reliefs at Cerveteri, twenty-five miles northwest of Rome.

The artisans who carved the chamber out of the porous rock meticulously duplicated the interior of an upper-class Etruscan home. The floor, walls, and hand-hewn columns that supported the ceiling of the tomb were covered with life-size stucco bas-reliefs of common household items. The models were carefully painted to enhance their realistic appearance. In the tomb at Cerveteri the symbolic adornments included furniture, clothing, weapons, tools, cooking utensils, pottery, and foodstuffs.

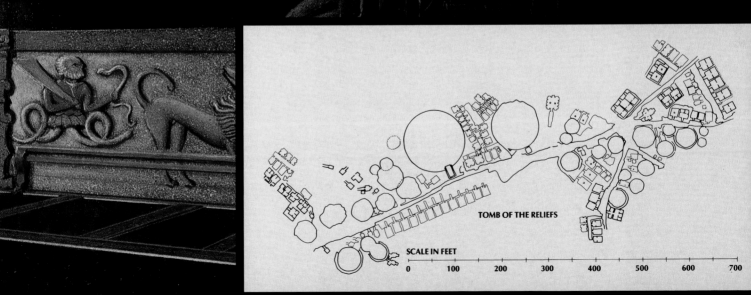

TOMB OF THE RELIEFS

SCALE IN FEET

0   100   200   300   400   500   600   700

The Tomb of the Reliefs was part of the necropolis of Cerveteri, whose hundreds of graves were set along a branching road, much like dwellings in a city for the living. Many of the rectangular tombs were covered with mounds of earth, or tumuli.

King Nebuchadnezzar II of Babylonia burns Jerusalem and deports thousands of Jews to Babylon.

Cyrus the Great conquers Media, Lydia, and Babylonia, and forms the Persian empire.

Cyrus frees the Jews from captivity in Babylonia and aids their return to Israel.

Cambyses, son of Cyrus, conquers Egypt.

Darius I assumes the Persian throne. He extends the empire to the Indus River, introduces a common currency, and regulates taxes.

The palace at Persepolis is begun.

PERSIA

Solon's code lays the foundation of Athenian democracy and stimulates the economy. Coinage is standardized and trade increases.

Constitutional government breaks down after Solon retires from power. The aristocrats refuse political equality to the poor and landless. Three decades of anarchy follow.

Ionian philosophers try to explain the nature of the physical world.

Lyric poetry, celebrating love and valor, is raised to an art form.

The tyrant Peisistratus rules in Athens and encourages industry and the arts. Grape and olive cultivation increases.

First Greek drama performed in Athens.

The sons of Peisistratus continue the tyranny until overthrown by the democratic reformer Cleisthenes.

GREECE

Early Celts work the salt mines at Hallstatt in Austria.

The Celts of inland Europe begin to trade with the Greeks who establish a colony at Massalia (Marseilles).

Roman patricians abolish the monarchy and establish a republic.

EUROPE

Trade and commerce create a merchant class in China. Coins replace barter and cowrie shells. State rulers rely on educated bureaucrats to govern.

In India, Brahman priests preserve the rituals of the Vedas and maintain the caste system.

After experiencing enlightenment, Buddha founds a monastic community and teaches a code of ethics leading to nirvana.

Confucius, a teacher whose moral code emphasizes exemplary conduct, spreads his philosophy.

The Mahavira, founder of Jainism, instructs his followers to renounce destruction of any living thing.

Trade brings wealth to the merchant class of India.

ASIA

TimeFrame 600-400 BC

Darius is defeated in a campaign against the Greeks.

Xerxes, son of Darius, invades Greece and is defeated in land and sea battles. Persia abandons plans to conquer Greece.

Assassinations and palace intrigues weaken the Persian dynasty and the empire declines.

The expansionist Persian empire sends a vast force to invade Greek territory, but is defeated by an inferior number of Greeks.

Athens builds a fleet, employing thousands of landless citizens.

Athens enrolls allies in the Delian League against a future Persian threat, extracting tribute from them.

Pericles' rise begins, followed by five decades of cultural achievement, known as the Golden Age of Greece.

Powerful Athens and its empire wage war against Sparta and other Peloponnesian powers.

Victorious Sparta strips Athens of its holdings but allows the city to stand.

Plebeians strike for a role in governing Rome and establish an assembly with a tribune to protect their rights.

Rome joins neighboring tribes to form the Latin League for mutual defense.

The plebeians' assembly is recognized as part of the Roman state.

Celtic art becomes more imaginative and sophisticated in the La Tène period.

Roman law is codified in the Twelve Tables.

Bimbisara of Magadha establishes an Indian empire.

The feudal states in China are reduced to a dozen, then to seven.

INDEX

A

Achaemenians, 13-14
Achilles (Greek hero), *139*
Acropolis, *68-69,* 77
Aequi, 101, 109
Aeschylus (Greek dramatist), 74, *75,* 77-78, 85; quoted, 88, 90-91
Agamemnon (Aeschylus), 90
Agriculture: Celts, 112-114; China, 144, 147; India, 153; Persia, 29; Rome, 97, 106
Ahmose (Egyptian king), 22
Ahuramazda (Persian deity), 37, 162
Ajax (Greek hero), *139*
Akhenaten (Egyptian king), 37
Akkadian, 32
Alcaeus (Greek poet), 54, 86; quoted, 87
Alcibiades (Greek general), 83, 84
Alcman (Greek poet), 54
Alexander the Great (Greek king), 71
Allia, battle of, 118
Amasis (Greek painter), vase by, *136-137*
Ammianus Marcellinus (Roman historian), quoted, 110
Analects (Confucius), 150
Anatolia, mines in, 31
Anaxagoras (Greek philosopher), 79
Anaximander (Greek philosopher), 54
Anga (Indian kingdom), 160
Animals, art motif, *33-36,* 98, *124-125, 128-129*
Antigone (Sophocles), 89, 92, 93
Aphrodite (Greek deity), *122-123*
Aplu (Etruscan deity), *103*
Apollo (Greek deity), 14, 64, 103
Arabia, 22, 27
Aramaic, 32
Arcadia, 54
Archons, 60, 63, 76
Areopagus, 60, 76
Aristophanes (Greek dramatist), 79, 81, 82
Aristotle (Greek philosopher), 84
Art, animal motifs, *33-36,* 98, *124-125, 128-129;* Celtic La Tène motifs, 114-115; Etruscan sculptures, *98, 102-104, 128-129;* Greek gold ornaments, *132-133;* Greek pottery, *78-79,* 119; Greek sculpture, 77, 119, *120-127, 130-131;* Greek silver drinking cup, *134-135;* Greek vase painting, *136-141;* Persian bas-reliefs, *16-21, 24*
Artaxerxes I (Persian king), 71
Aryans, 10, 153, 154
Asoka (Indian king), 160
Aspasia (Greek concubine), 81
Assur (Assyrian city), 13
Assyrians, 9, 11-13, 22
Astyages (Median king), 13, 14
Athena (Greek deity), 53, *54,* 68, 72, 76, 77, 123
Athenaeus (Greek historian), 117
Athens (Greek city), *map* 52; art and culture, 61, 74, 136; Delian League, 73-77, 84; Peloponnesian War, 39, 47, 82-84; Periclean Age, *68-69,* 77-82; Persian Wars, 63-64, 67, 70; plague in, 82; rise of, 56; trade, 60, 73, 81
Atossa (Persian queen), 31
Attica, 56, 63

B

Babylon, 10, 14, *15,* 16, 20, 66
Babylonia, 13, 23, 27, 31, 54
Bacchae, The (Euripides), 94-95
Bactria, 16, 28
Banking, development in Babylonia, 16
Battle-Ax people (Celts), 110-111
Behistun (Persian city), 23
Bell Beaker people (Celts), 110-111
Belshazzar (Babylonian prince), 17
Bible, 17
Bimbisara (Indian king), 160
Boeotia, 53, 82
Bosporus, 38
Brahmans, 154, 159, 160
Buddha, 143, 153, 156, *157,* 158-160
Buddhism, 10, 143, 156-160

C

Caere (Etruscan city), 99
Callicrates (Greek architect), 77
Cambyses (Persian king), 14, 22-23, 29, 37
Capitoline Hill, 99
Carthage (Phoenician colony), 22, 31, 99
Castor (Greek athlete), *138*
Catana (Greek city), 83
Celts, 10, 97; education, 112; grave sites, 161, *164-165;* iron technology, 111-112, 114, 117; life of, 117; origin, 110-111; sack of Rome, 118; settlements, *map* 101, 111, *112-113;* trophy heads, 115, *116;* wine, 114
Cervetari (Etruscan necropolis), 167
Chalcidice, 82
Chandragupta Maurya (Indian king), 160
Channa (Siddhartha's charioteer), 155, 156
China: bureaucracy, 147-148; Confucianism, 10, 148, 151; growth of, 143-144; life in, 144-145, 147; merchant class, 147; power struggle in, *map* 145, 146, 153
Chu (Chinese state), *map* 145, 146
Chunqiu (Spring and Autumn Annals), 150
Cleisthenes (Greek statesman), 61, 76
Cleomones (Greek king), 61
Clusium (Etruscan city), 107, 118
Coins: Chinese, 147; Persian, 29, 71
Confucianism, 10, 148, 151
Confucius (Chinese philosopher), 143, 148-153
Corinth (Greek city), 31, 54, 60, 136
Council of Five Hundred, 63, 76
Council of Four Hundred, 60, 63
Critias (Greek tyrant), 83, 84
Croesus (Lydian king), 14, 29, 37, 51, 56
Cumae (Greek city), 99
Cyaxares (Median king), 13, 23
Cyprus (Greek island), 136
Cyrus the Great (Persian king), 29, 31, 37, 38, 71; birth and education, 14; conquests of, 14-17; death, 22; tolerance of, 20, 26, 66

D

Damascus (Syrian city), 29
Daniel (Jewish hero), 20
Danube River, 38, 112
Darius I (Persian king), 9, 11, 12, 17, *21,* 23, 71, 160; administrative ability, 26-29, 66; construction projects, 31-32; death, 64; Greeks, conflict with, 37-38; tomb of, 161, *162-163*
David (Jewish king), 20
Deer Park, 158
Delian League, 73-77, 84
Delos (Greek island), 73
Delphi (Greek city), 118
Delphian oracle, 14, 60, 67, 70, 83
Democritus (Greek philosopher), 81
Di (Chinese deity), 144, 151
Diodorus Siculus (Roman historian), 117
Dione (Greek deity), *122-123*
Dionysus (Greek deity), 61, *80,* 85, 88, 94
Divination, 100, 106, 117
Dracon (Greek lawgiver), 56
Druids, 115-117
Duke Huan. *See* Huan Gong

E

Ecbatana (Median city), 13, 14, 32
Education: Celts, 112; Persians, 14
Egypt, 13, 28, 54; Persian rule of, 22, 63, 66; trade, 31
Elam, 11, 13, 14, 23, 31
Elamite, 32
Elephantine (Egyptian city), 22
Elis (Greek city), 53, 76
Empedocles (Greek philosopher), 79
Engineering, 67, 100
Eretria (Greek city), 63
Etruscans, 99-100, 105-107, 110, 114, 118; tombs, 161, *166-167*
Euboea (Greek island), 63, 82
Eumenides, The (Aeschylus), 90, 91
Euripides (Greek dramatist), 57, 77-78, 81, 82, 85, 88; quoted, 89, 94-95
Eurybiades (Greek general), 70
Exekias (Greek painter), 136; vase by, *138-139*

F

Falerii (Etruscan city), 104
Farvartish (Median pretender), 23
Festival of Dionysus, 77, 79, 81, 85
Fidenae (Etruscan city), 110
Food: Celts, 117; Greeks, 81; Jains, 159; Persians, 29; Romans, 97
Fosterage, 112

G

Ganges River, *map* 152, 153
Gauls. *See* Celts
Gaumata (Median usurper), 23
Gaya (Indian city), 156, 160
Gobryas (Babylonian governor), 17
Government: Celtic, 111, 112; Chinese, 144, 147-148, 150-153; Greek, 10, 55-56, 60-63, 76, 84; Indian, 154; Persian, 9, 17-20, 26-27, 37, 66, 73; Roman, 100-101, 105-107
Greece, *map* 52; expansion by, 38, 52-53; life in, 56, 77, 81, *136-137;* Olympian games, 53, 57, *58-59;* Peloponnesian Wars, 39, *map* 46-49, 82-84; Persian Wars, 39, *map* 40-45, 63-64, 70, 73; slavery in, 81-82; trade by, 31, 81, 114; values and character of, 51-54
Guanzi (Chinese adviser), 145
Guo (Chinese state), 16
Gylippus (Greek general), 48

H

Halys River, 13, 14
Han dynasty, 153
Hanging Gardens of Babylon, 16
Harpagus (Median chief steward), 14
Hathor (Egyptian deity), 53
Hellenes. *See* Greece
Hellenic League, 67
Hellespont, crossing by Persian army, 67
Helots (Greek serfs), 55
Hephaistos (Greek deity), 64
Hera (Greek deity), 53, 72
Heraclitus (Greek philosopher), 54
Hermes (Greek deity), 103
Hernici, 109
Herodotus (Greek historian), 79; quoted, 13, 14, 22, 23, 29, 40, 133, 159
Hestia (Greek deity), *122-123*
Heuneberg (Celtic settlement), *112-113*
Hinduism, 160
Hippias (Greek tyrant), 61, 63
Hippocrates (Greek physician), *75*
Histories (Herodotus), 79
History of the Peloponnesian War (Thucydides), 83
Homer (Greek poet), 53, 61, 85, 119
Hoplites, 39, *62,* 76
Horatius Cocles (Roman hero), 107
Huan Gong (Chinese king), 145-146
Hyrcania, 16
Hystaspes (Persian governor), 16

I

Ictimus (Greek architect), 77
Iliad, (Greek epic), 53, 85
India, 27, 28; Buddhism, 10, 143, 156-160; caste system in, 154, 155; life in, 153-154; Mauryan empire, *map* 152, 160; merchant class in, 159; Persian invasion, 160; trade by, 31
Indus River, 26, *map* 152, 153
Insubres, 118
Ionia, Greek cities in, 14, 16, 20, 27, 38, 52, 54, 61, 63, 71, 73
Ishtar Gate (Babylon), 17

*Numerals in italics indicate
an illustration of
the subject mentioned.*

J

Jainism, 159, 160
Jehoiakim (Jewish king), 20
Jeremiah (Jewish prophet), 20
Jerusalem, 20, 27
Jews, 20, 27, 37, 38
Jin (Chinese state), 145, 146
Jisun (Chinese king), 151-152
Judah, 20
Juno (Roman deity), 99
Jupiter (Roman deity), 99

K

Karma, 155, 158
Kea (Greek island), 51
Kongfuzi. *See* Confucius
Kosala (Indian kingdom), 155
Kshatriyas, 154
Kurush. *See* Cyrus the Great
Kush. *See* Nubia

L

Lake Regilius, battle of, 108
Laozi (Chinese philosopher), 152
Lars Porsenna (Etruscan king), 107
Latin League, 108, 110
Latium, 97, 99, 107-108
Law: Greek, 56-60; Persian, 9, 27; Roman, 107
Leonidas (Spartan king), 70
Lesbos (Greek island), 54
Libation Bearers, The (Aeschylus), 90, 91
Literature: Chinese, 148-150; Greek drama, 61, 77-79, 81, 85, 88-95; Greek epic poetry, 53; Greek history, 83; Greek lyric poetry, 54, 85-87; Indian, 154-155
Livy (Roman historian), quoted, 98, 118
Lu (Chinese state), 148, 150
Luoyang (Chinese city), 145
Lydia, 13, 14, 29, 55, 63
Lysander (Greek general), 84
Lysistrata (Aristophanes), 79

M

Macedonia, 38, 63, 70
Magadha (Indian kingdom), 155, 156, 159-160
Magi, 23, 37
Mahavira (Indian ascetic), 159
Manching (Celtic town), 112
Mandane (Persian queen), 14
Mantinea, battle of, *map* 46-47
Marathon, battle of, 39, *map* 40-41, 63-64
Mardonius (Persian general), 44, 71
Marduk (Babylonian deity), 15, 16, 17, 53, 66
Mars (Roman deity), 98
Massalia (Greek colony), 114, 117
Maya (Siddhartha's mother), 155
Medes, 10, 13, 23
Megara (Greek city), 82
Megarians, 56
Melpum (Etruscan city), 110
Menander (Greek dramatist), 72
Meroe (Kushite city), 23
Messenia, 76
Metalworking, 64, 100, 111-112, 114, 117, 127, 140-141, 147
Miletus (Greek city), 63
Miltiades (Greek general), 40, 64, 76
Minerva (Roman deity), 99
Mount Olympus, 53
Music: Celtic, 117; Chinese, 150
Mycenaeans, 52. *See also* Greece

N

Nabonidus (Babylonian king), 16, 17
Napata (Nubian city), 22
Naqsh-i Rustam, Darius's tomb at, *162-163*
Naucratis (Egyptian city), 22, 119, 136
Navigation: Egyptian canal, 22, 31; Egyptian explorations, 22; Persian explorations, 31

Naxos (Greek island), 55, 73, 120
Nebuchadnezzar (Babylonian king), 16, 20
Necho II (Egyptian king), 22, 31
Nicias (Greek general), 48, 83
Nineveh (Assyrian city), 13

O

Odysseus (Greek hero), 51, *55*
Odyssey (Greek epic), 53, *55*, 85
Oedipus at Colonnus (Sophocles), 92, 93
Oedipus the King (Sophocles), 92
Olbia (Greek colony), 119, 133
Old Persian, 32
Olympian Games, 53, 57, *58-59*
Opis (Babylonian city), 17
Oresteia, The (Aeschylus), 90
Oroetes (Persian satrap), 27
Orontes River, 119
Osiris (Egyptian deity), 53
Ostia (Roman city), 99
Ostracism, 63, 76
Oxus River, 16

P

Palatine Hill, 98
Pali, 158
Pallas Athena. *See* Athena
Panathenaic Festival, 61, 85
Panathenaic Games, 57
Paros (Greek island), 120
Parsa, 10-11, 13, 27
Parthenon, *68-69*, 77, 120, 123-125
Parthia, 16
Pasargadae (Persian city), 14, 22, 31, 32; Cyrus's garden at, *30, 31*
Pausanias (Greek general), 44
Peisistratus (Greek tyrant), 60-61, 63, 85
Peloponnesian League, 54, 67, 76
Peloponnesian War, 39, *map* 46-49, 82-84
Pelusium, battle of, 22
Pericles (Greek general), 68, *74*, 76-78, 81, 82, 88
Persepolis (Persian city), 9, 32, 66, 71, 161; architecture of, *24-26*; bas-reliefs at, *16-21*, 24
Persia: court retinue, 32-37; decline of, 71; education in, 37; extent of empire, 9, *map* 11, 26, 153; Greece, conflict with, 39, *maps* 40-45, 63-66, 70, 73; highway network in, 9, *map* 11, 27-28; life in, 37; and Medes, 13, 14; messenger service in, 28-29; origin of, 10-11; political turmoil in, 23; trade, 29-31; tribute processions, 9, *16-21*, 24, 32
Persians, The (Aeschylus), 74, 78, 88
Phidias (Greek sculptor), 77
Phoenicia, 17
Pindar (Greek poet), quoted, 68, 86
Ping Wang (Chinese king), 145
Piraeus (Greek city), 81
Plataea, battle of, 39, *map* 44-45, 71
Plato (Greek philosopher), 84, 86, 119
Plutarch (Roman historian), quoted, 77
Pollaiuolo, Antonio (Italian sculptor), 98
Polybius (Roman historian), quoted, 117-118
Polydeuces (Greek athlete), *138*
Polyzalos (Sicilian), 127
Poseidon (Greek deity), 76
Pottery, *78-79*, 100, 136, 139, 140
Protagoras (Greek philosopher), 83
Psamtik III (Egyptian king), 22
Pteria (Lydian city), 14
Punjab, 153, 160
Pyrgi (Etruscan city), 104
Pythagoras (Greek philosopher), 54

Q

Qanats (aqueducts), 29
Qi (Chinese state), *map* 145
Qin (Chinese state), *map* 145

R

Rajaghra (Indian city), 154
Religion: Buddhism, 10, 143, 156-160; Celtic, 111, 112, 115-117; Chinese, 10, 143, 148, 151-153; Confucianism, 143, 148, 152; Etruscan temples, *102*; funeral rituals, 161, *162-167*; Greece, 53, 83; Hinduism, 160; Indian, 10, 154-160; Jainism, 159, 160; Judaism, 10; Persian, 10, 23, 37-38; Roman, 10, 99-100, 106; Taoism, 10, 152-153; Zoroastrianism, 10, 37-38
Remus (Roman hero), 98
Rhodes (Greek island), 82, 136
Rome, 10; expansion by, *map* 101, 107-110; founding of, 97-99; highway network, 99; life in, 100-101; republic established, 105; sacked by Celts, 118; social unrest in, 106-107, 110
Romulus (Roman hero), 98
Royal Road, *map* 11, 27-28

S

Sais (Egyptian city), 22
Salamis, battle of, *map* 42-43, 70-71
Salamis (Greek island), 56, 70
Salt, 99, 111, 145
Samos (Greek island), 55
Sangha (monastic order), 158
Sappho (Greek poet), 54; quoted, 86
Sardis (Lydian city), *map* 11, 13, 14, 16, 27, 28, 63
Sarnath (Indian village), 156-158
Satricum (Etruscan city), 103
Science: Babylonian astronomy, 16; Greek philosophy, 54, 79-81, 83, 84
Scythians, *12*, 13, 38, 119, 132-134
Senate, 105, 106
Septimontium, 99
Shang dynasty, 143, 151
Shi (Chinese bureaucracy), 144, 147-148, 150
Ships: Athenian triremes, *66-67*, 73; Phoenician fleets, 17, 22, 70
Shudras, 154
Shujing (*Classic of Writings*), 150
Siddhartha Gautama, 143, 155-156. *See also* Buddha
Sikanos (Greek painter), 136
Silkmaking, 144
Simonides (Greek poet), 86; quoted, 87
Sin (Babylonian deity), 16
Smerdis (Persian usurper), 23
Socrates (Greek philosopher), *74*, 83
Solomon (Jewish king), 20
Solon (Greek lawgiver), 51, 56-60, 61, *74*
Song (Chinese state), 148
Sophists, 83
Sophocles (Greek dramatist), 52, 77-78, 85, 88; quoted, 89, 92-93
Sparta (Greek city), 14, *map* 52; 61, 73, 76; expansion by, 54-55; Peloponnesian War, 39, 47, 82-84; Persian Wars, 63-64, 67
Strabo (Greek historian), quoted, 110
Struggle of the Orders, 106-107
Suddhodana (Siddhartha's father), 155
Susa (Elamite city), *map* 11, 14, 28, 31, 32
Syene (Egyptian city), 22
Syracuse, siege of, 39, *48-49*, 83-84

T

Taoism, 10, 152-153
Tarquinii (Etruscan city), 99
Tarquinius Superbus (Etruscan king), 105
Taxes, in Persia, 27
Technology: Celtic, 111-112, 114, 117; Chinese, 144, 147; Etruscan, 100; Greek, *78-79*, 136, 139, 140
Ten Thousand Immortals (Persian warriors), 38, *62*
Thales (Greek philosopher), 13, 54
Thasos (Greek island), 55, 73
Thebes (Greek city), 53, 76
Themistocles (Greek general), 43, 67, 70, 73, 74, 75, 76
Thermopylae, battle of, 70
Thespis (Greek poet), 85
Thessaly, 53, 67, 70, 82
Thrace, 38, 63, 70, 81, 82
Thucydides (Greek historian), 74, 75, 83; quoted, 48

U

Tiber River, 97, 99
Tigris River, 11
Tinia (Etruscan deity), 129
Tomb of the Reliefs, *166-167*
Tomyris (Massagetaean queen), 20
Tower of Babel, *15*
Trade: Babylonia, 16; by Celts, 112, 114; China, 147; by Etruscans, 99; Greece, 31, 60, 73, 81, 119, 133, 136; India, 153-154, 159; Lydia, 13; Persia, 29-31; Rome, 99
Trojan Women, The (Euripides), 89
Turkestan, 10, 16
Turms (Etruscan deity), *102*
Twelve Tables, 107
Tyrtaeus (Greek poet), 54

U

Untouchables, 154
Upanishads (religious meditations), 154-155, 156, 158
Urnfield culture (Celts), 111

V

Vaishyas, 154
Vedas (sacred writings), 154, 160
Veii (Etruscan city), 103, 110
Via Salaria, 99
Vishnu (Indian deity), 160
Volsci, 101, 109
Vulca (Etruscan sculptor), 103
Vulci (Etruscan city), 139

W

Warfare: cavalry, 14, 38, 146; Celtic, *108-109*, 110, 117-118; Chinese, 146-147, *149*; crossbow, 146; Greek mercenaries, 22, 38; helmet, *64*, *65*; hoplites, *62*; India, 154; Lydian, 13; Mede, 13; naval, *map* 42-43, 48, 66-67, 70-71, 83; Peloponnesian War, 39, *map* 46-49, 82-84; Persian, 14, 17, 22, 38, 39, *62*; Persian Wars, 39, *map* 40-45, 63-64, 70, 73; phalanx, 39; Roman, 108-110; Scythian cavalrymen, *12*; seasonal nature of, 14
Wheel of the Law (dharma), 158
Wine, 97, 114, 134
Women: Celtic society, 110, 112-113; Chinese society, 144; Greek society, 72, 81; Roman society, 100-101, 107
Writing: alphabet, 72, 99; Celtic, 117; Chinese, 148; Greek, 52, 53, 72-73; Persian, 32; Roman, 98

X

Xerxes (Persian king), 43, 44, 66, 67, 70, 71, 73, 160

Y

Yahweh (Jewish deity), 20
Yangtze River, 143
Yasodhara (Siddhartha's wife), 155
Yellow River, 143
Yu (Chinese king), 145
Yu (Chinese state), 146

Z

Zagros Mountains, 10, 13, 23, 29
Zarathustra. *See* Zoroaster
Zedekiah (Jewish king), 20
Zeus (Greek deity), 53, 67
Zhao (Chinese state), 146
Zhou dynasty, 143-146, 148, 151
Zhuanyou (Chinese province), 151-152
Zodiac, 16
Zoroaster (Persian prophet), 37
Zoroastrianism, 10, 37-38

BIBLIOGRAPHY

BOOKS

Aero, Rita, *Things Chinese.* New York: Doubleday, 1980.

Ali-Sami, A. L., *Pasargadae.* Transl. by the Rev. R. N. Sharp. Shiraz: 1971.

Allchin, Bridget, and Raymond Allchin, *The Birth of Indian Civilization: India and Pakistan before 500 B.C.* Harmondsworth, Middlesex, England: Penguin Books, 1968.

Banti, Luisa, *Etruscan Cities and Their Culture.* Transl. by Erika Bizzarri. Berkeley: University of California Press, 1973.

Basham, A. L., *The Wonder That Was India.* New York: Hawthorn Books, 1963.

Beazley, Mitchell, *The World Atlas of Archaeology.* London: Mitchell Beazley Publishers, 1985.

Bengtson, Hermann, ed., *The Greeks and the Persians from the Sixth to the Fourth Centuries.* Transl. by John Conway. New York: Delacorte Press, 1968.

Biel, Jörg, *Der Keltenfürst von Hochdorf.* Stuttgart: Konrad Theiss Verlag, 1985.

Bloch, Raymond, *The Etruscans.* Vol. 7 of *Ancient Peoples and Places.* New York: Frederick A. Praeger, 1958.

Boardman, John:
Athenian Black Figure Vases. London: Thames and Hudson, 1985.
Greek Art. London: Thames and Hudson, 1964.
Greek Sculpture: The Archaic Period. London: Thames and Hudson, 1978.
The Parthenon and Its Sculptures. Austin: University of Texas Press, 1985.

Boardman, John, Jasper Griffin, and Oswyn Murray, eds., *The Oxford History of the Classical World.* New York: Oxford University Press, 1986.

Bowra, C. M., *The Greek Experience.* New York: New American Library, 1957.

Brendel, Otto J., *Etruscan Art.* New York: Penguin Books, 1978.

Brown, A. C., *Ancient Italy before the Romans.* Oxford: Ashmolean Museum Publications, 1980.

Bruce-Mitford, Rupert, ed., *Recent Archaeological Excavations in Europe.* Boston: Routledge & Kegan Paul, 1975.

Burn, A. R., *Pericles and Athens.* New York: Macmillan, 1949.

Bury, J. B.:
The Ancient Greek Historians. (Harvard Lectures). New York: Macmillan, 1909.
A History of Greece to the Death of Alexander the Great. London: Macmillan, 1972.

Bury, J. B., S. A. Cook, and F. E. Adcock, eds., *The Assyrian Empire.* Vol. 3 of *The Cambridge Ancient History.* Cambridge: University Press, 1929.

Camp, John M., *The Athenian Agora: Excavations in the Heart of Athens.* London: Thames and Hudson, 1986.

Capon, Edmund, *Art and Archaeology in China.* South Melbourne, Australia: Macmillan, 1977.

Chadwick, Nora, *The Celts.* Harmondsworth, Middlesex, England: Penguin Books, 1986.

Chang, Kwang-chih, *The Archaeology of Ancient China.* New Haven: Yale University Press, 1977.

Cheng, Te-K'un, *Chou China.* Vol. 3 of *Archaeology in China.* Toronto: University of Toronto Press, 1963.

Coarelli, Filippo, *Roma Sepolta.* Rome: Armando Curcio Editore, 1984.

Colonna, Giovanni, *Santuari d'Etruria.* Milan: Electa Editrice, 1985.

Cowell, F. R., *The Garden As a Fine Art from Antiquity to Modern Times.* Boston: Houghton Mifflin, 1978.

Creel, Herrlee G.:
The Birth of China: A Study of the Formative Period of Chinese Civilization. New York: Frederick Ungar, 1967.
The Western Chou Empire. Vol. 1 of *The Origins of Statecraft in China.* Chicago: University of Chicago Press, 1970.

Cristofani, Mauro:
I Bronzi Degli Etruschi. Novara, Italy: Istituto Geografico de Agostini, 1985.
The Etruscans. Transl. by Brian Phillips. London: Orbis, 1979.

Cunliffe, Barry, *The Celtic World.* New York: McGraw-Hill, 1979.

Dalton, O. M., *The Treasure of the Oxus with Other Examples of Early Oriental Metal-Work.* London: British Museum, 1926.

Delaney, Frank, *The Celts.* London: Hodder and Stoughton, 1986.

De Sélincourt, Aubrey, *The World of Herodotus.* Boston: Little, Brown, 1962.

Deubner, Ludwig, *Attische Feste.* Darmstadt: Wissenschaftliche Buchgesellschaft, 1966.

Dontas, George, *The Acropolis and Its Museum.* Transl. by Alexandra Douma. Athens: Clio Editions, 1979.

Douskou, Iris, ed., *The Olympic Games in Ancient Greece.* Athens: Ekdotike Athenon, 1976.

Duval, Paul-Marie, *I Celti.* Milan: Rizzoli Editore, 1978.

Eberhard, Wolfram, *A History of China.* Berkeley: University of California Press, 1977.

Finley, M. I., ed., *The Legacy of Greece: A New Appraisal.* New York: Oxford University Press, 1981.

Flacelière, Robert:
Daily Life in Greece at the Time of Pericles. Transl. by Peter Green. New York: Macmillan, 1965.
A Literary History of Greece. Transl. by Douglas Garman. Chicago: Aldine Publishing, 1964.

Frye, Richard N.:
The Heritage of Persia. Cleveland: World Publishing, 1963.
The History of Ancient Iran. Munich: Beck, 1983.

Gardiner, Edward Norman, *Athletics of the Ancient World.* Oxford: Clarendon Press, 1930.

Gershevitch, Ilya, ed., *The Median and Achaemenian Periods.* Vol. 2 of *The Cambridge History of Iran.* Cambridge: Cambridge University Press, 1985.

Ghirshman, Roman, Vladimir Minorsky, and Ramesh Sanghvi, *Persia: The Immortal Kingdom.* New York: New York Graphic Society, 1971.

Grant, Michael:
The Etruscans. New York: Scribner's, 1980.
Myths of the Greeks and Romans. New York: New American Library, 1962.

Grant, Michael, ed., *Greece and Rome: The Birth of Western Civilization.* New York: Bonanza Books, 1986.

Green, Miranda, *The Gods of the Celts.* Totowa, N.J.: Barnes and Noble, 1986.

Greer, John P., *The Armies and Enemies of Ancient China.* Wargames Research Group Production, 1975.

Hamblin, Dora Jane, and the Editors of Time-Life Books, *The Etruscans* (The Emergence of Man series). New York, 1975.

Hamilton, Edith, *The Greek Way.* New York: Franklin Watts, 1958.

Hammond, N. G. L., *A History of Greece to 322 B.C.* Oxford: Clarendon Press, 1967.

Han, Zhongmin, and Hubert Delahaye, *A Journey through Ancient China.* New York: W. H. Smith, Gallery Books, 1985.

Hawkes, Christopher, and Sonia Hawkes, eds., *Greeks, Celts and Romans.* Vol. 1 of *Archaeology into History.* Totowa, N.J.: Rowman and Littlefield, 1973.

Herington, John, *Poetry into Drama.* Berkeley: University of California Press, 1985.

Herodotus, *The History of Herodotus.* Transl. by George Rawlinson. Chicago: William Benton, Encyclopaedia Britannica, 1952.

Herzfeld, Ernst E., *Iran in the Ancient East.* New York: Oxford University Press, 1941.

Heurgon, Jacques, *The Rise of Rome to 264 B.C.* Transl. by James Willis. London: B. T. Batsford, 1973.

Hicks, Jim, and the Editors of Time-Life Books, *The Persians* (The Emergence of Man series). New York: Time-Life Books, 1975.

Homer, *The Odyssey.* Transl. by Robert Fitzgerald. New York: Doubleday, 1963.

Houser, Caroline, *Greek Monumental Bronze Sculpture.* London: Thames and Hudson, 1983.

Hsu, Cho-yun, *Ancient China in Transition: An Analysis of Social Mobility, 722-222 B.C.* Stanford: Stanford University Press, 1965.

Hucker, Charles O., *China's Imperial Past: An Introduction to Chinese History and Culture.* Stanford: Stanford University Press, 1975.

Kendall, Timothy, *Kush: Lost Kingdom of the Nile.* Brockton, Mass.: Brockton Art Museum, 1982.

Keuls, Eva C., *The Reign of the Phallus.* New York: Harper & Row, 1985.

Kitto, H. D. F., *The Greeks.* Harmondsworth, Middlesex, England: Penguin Books, 1951.

Koch, Heidemarie, and D. N. MacKenzie, eds., *Kunst, Kultur und Geschichte der Achämenidenzeit und Ihr Fortleben.* Berlin: Dietrich Reimer Verlag, 1983.

Krefter, Friedrich, *Persepolis Rekonstruktionen.* Berlin: Gebr. Mann Verlag, 1971.

Kruta, Venceslas, *The Celts of the West.* Transl. by Alan Sheridan. London: Orbis, 1985.

Li, Xueqin, *Eastern Zhou and Qin Civilizations.* Transl. by K. C. Chang. New Haven and London: Yale University Press, 1985.

Megaw, J. V. S., *Art of the European Iron Age.* New York: Harper & Row, 1970.

Menghin, Wilfried, *Kelten Römer und Germanen.* Munich: Prestel-Verlag, 1980.

Meskill, John, ed., *An Introduction to Chinese Civilization.* Lexington, Mass.: D. C. Heath, 1973.

Moretti, Mario, *Cerveteri.* Novara, Italy: Istituto Geografico de Agostini, 1977.

Morrison, J. S., and J. F. Coates, *The Athenian Trireme.* New York: Cambridge University Press, 1986.

Moynihan, Elizabeth B., *Paradise As a Garden in Persia and Mughal India* (World Landscape Art & Architecture series). New York: George Braziller, 1979.

Myres, John L., *Herodotus: Father of History.* Oxford: Clarendon Press, 1953.

Needham, Joseph, *History of Scientific Thought.* Vol. 2 of *Science and Civilisation in China.* Cambridge: Cambridge University Press, 1969.

Norton-Taylor, Duncan, and the Editors of Time-Life Books, *The Celts* (The Emergence of Man series). New York: 1974.

Oates, Joan, *Babylon.* Vol. 94 of *Ancient Peoples and Places.* London: Thames and Hudson, 1979.

Pallottino, Massimo, *The Etruscans.* Bloomington: Indiana University Press, 1975.

Parke, H. W., *Festivals of the Athenians*. Ithaca, New York: Cornell University Press, 1986.

Piggott, Stuart, Glyn Daniel, and Charles McBurney, eds., *France before the Romans*. London: Thames and Hudson, 1974.

Pope, Arthur Upham, ed., *A Survey of Persian Art*. New York: Oxford University Press, 1938.

Powell, T. G. E., *The Celts*. New York: Frederick A. Praeger, 1958.

Rawson, Jessica, *Ancient China: Art and Archaeology*. London: British Museum Publications, 1980.

Reich, John, *Italy before Rome*. Oxford: Elsevier Phaidon, 1979.

Rice, Tamara Talbot, *The Scythians*. New York: Frederick A. Praeger, 1957.

Rodzinski, Witold, *The Walled Kingdom: A History of China from Antiquity to the Present*. New York: Free Press, 1984.

Rolley, Claude, *Greek Bronzes*. Transl. by Roger Howell. London: Sotheby's Publications, 1986.

Root, Margaret Cool, *The King and Kingship in Achaemenid Art*. Vol. 9 of *Textes et Mémoires*. Leiden, Holland: E. J. Brill, 1979.

Ross, Anne, *The Pagan Celts*. London: B. T. Batsford, 1986.

Salmon, E. T., *The Making of Roman Italy*. Ithaca, New York: Cornell University Press, 1982.

Schmidt, Erich F.:
Persepolis I: Structures, Reliefs, Inscriptions. Vol. 68 of *The University of Chicago Oriental Institute Publications*. Chicago: University of Chicago Press, 1953.
Persepolis III: The Royal Tombs and Other Monuments. Vol. 70 of *The University of Chicago Oriental Institute Publications*. Chicago: University of Chicago Press, 1970.

Scullard, Howard H.:
The Etruscan Cities and Rome. Ithaca, New York: Cornell University Press, 1967.
A History of the Roman World from 753 to 146 B.C. New York: Macmillan, 1939.

Sherratt, Andrew, ed., *The Cambridge Encyclopedia of Archaeology*. Scarborough, Ontario: Prentice-Hall of Canada / Cambridge University Press, 1980.

Stronach, David, *Pasargadae*. Oxford: Oxford University Press, 1978.

Swaddling, Judith, *The Ancient Olympic Games*. London: British Museum Publications, 1980.

Thompson, Homer A., and R. E. Wycherley, *The Agora of Athens*. Vol. 14 of *The Athenian Agora*. Princeton: The American School of Classical Studies at Athens, 1972.

Thucydides, *The History of the Peloponnesian War*. Transl. by Richard Crawley. Chicago: William Benton, Encyclopaedia Britannica, 1952.

Trigger, B. G., et al., *Ancient Egypt: A Social History*. New York: Cambridge University Press, 1983.

Trippett, Frank, and the Editors of Time-Life Books, *The First Horsemen* (The Emergence of Man series). New York: Time-Life Books, 1974.

Vallardi, A., *Gli Etruschi*. Italy: Garzanti Editore, 1985.

Vickers, Michael, *Greek Vases*. Oxford: Ashmolean Museum, 1982.

Von Bothmer, Dietrich, *The Amasis Painter and His World*. New York: Thames and Hudson, 1985.

Walser, Gerold, *Persepolis*. Tubingen: Ernst Wasmuth, 1980.

Ward-Perkins, John B., *Roman Architecture*. New York: Harry N. Abrams, 1977.

Warry, John Gibson, *Warfare in the Classical World*. New York: St. Martin's Press, 1980.

Watson, William, *China before the Han Dynasty*. Vol. 23 of *Ancient Peoples and Places*. New York: Frederick A. Praeger, 1966.

Wedgwood, C. V., *The Spoils of Time: A World History from the Dawn of Civilization through the Early Renaissance*. New York: Doubleday, 1985.

Wells, Peter S.:
Culture Contact and Culture Change: Early Iron Age Central Europe and the Mediterranean World. Cambridge, Mass.: Cambridge University Press, 1980.
The Emergence of an Iron Age Economy. Bulletin 33. Cambridge, Mass.: American School of Prehistoric Research, Harvard University, 1981.
Rural Economy in the Early Iron Age: Excavations at Hascherkeller, 1978-1981. Bulletin 36. Cambridge, Mass.: American School of Prehistoric Research, Harvard University, 1983.

Woodford, Susan, *An Introduction to Greek Art*. London: Gerald Duckworth, 1986.

Zimmer, Heinrich, *The Art of Indian Asia: Its Mythology and Transformations*. Ed. by Joseph Campbell. Princeton: Princeton University Press, 1983.

Zoelly-Kartalides, Lila, *The Ancient Greek Theatre*. Athens: D. G. Kalofolias. No date.

OTHER SOURCES

"The Athenian Agora: An Ancient Shopping Center." Princeton: American School of Classical Studies at Athens, 1971.

"Bronzeworkers in the Athenian Agora." Princeton: American School of Classical Studies at Athens, 1982.

Crumley, Carole L. "Celtic Social Structure: The Generation of Archaeologically Testable Hypotheses from Literary Evidence," *Anthropological Papers* (Ann Arbor), 1974.

Mansfield, John Magruder, "The Robe of Athena and the Panathenaic Peplos." Dissertation, University of California, Berkeley, 1985.

Petruccioli, Attilio, ed., "Water and Architecture," *Environmental Design: Journal of the Islamic Environmental Design Research Centre* (Rome). No date.

Vickers, Michael, "Greek Symposia." The Joint Association of Classical Teachrs. No date.

ACKNOWLEDGMENTS

The following materials have been reprinted with the kind permission of the publishers: Page 86: "You are the herdsman of evening" from *Sappho: A New Translation* by Mary Barnard, © 1958, 1986 Mary Barnard, published by The University of California Press. "First Olympian Ode" from *Pindar's Victory Songs* by Frank J. Nisetich. © 1980 The Johns Hopkins University Press. Page 87: "Winter Scene" by Alcaeus, "Epitaph #10" and "Danae and Perseus" by Simonides from *Greek Lyrics*, translated by R. Lattimore, © 1960 R. Lattimore, published by The University of Chicago Press. Page 88: "The Persians" from *The Greek World* by Peter Levi, photographs by Eliot Porter. First published 1980 in the U. S. by E. P. Dutton. All rights reserved by International and Pan-American Copyright Conventions. Published by E. P. Dutton, a division of NAL Penguin Inc. Page 89: "Antigone" from *Sophocles I*, translated by Elizabeth Wyckoff, © 1954 The University of Chicago Press. "The Trojan Women" from *Euripides III*, translated by R. Lattimore, © 1955 The University of Chicago Press. Page 90: "Agamemnon" from *Aeschylus I*, translated by R. Lattimore, © 1953 The University of Chicago Press. Page 91: "The Libation Bearers" and "The Eumenides" from *Aeschylus I*, translated by R. Lattimore, © 1953 The University of Chicago Press. Page 92: "Oedipus the King" from *Sophocles I*, translated by David Greene, © 1954 The University of Chicago Press. "Oedipus at Colonus" from *Greek Tragedies*, translated by Robert Fitzgerald, © 1941 Harcourt, Brace & Co., published by The University of Chicago Press. "Antigone" from *Sophocles I*, translated by Elizabeth Wyckoff, © 1954 The University of Chicago Press. Pages 94-95: "The Bacchae" from *Greek Tragedies*, translated by William Arrowsmith, © 1959 The University of Chicago Press.

The editors also wish to thank the following individuals and institutions for their valuable assistance in the preparation of this volume:

Austria: Vienna — Fritz Eckart Barth, Naturhistorisches Museum, Vienna.

England: London — Richard Blurten, Department of Oriental Antiquities, British Museum; Lucilla Burn, Department of Greek and Roman Antiquities, British Museum; Robert Knox, Department of Oriental Antiquities, British Museum; Ellen Macnamara, Department of Greek and Roman Antiquities, British Museum; T. C. Mitchell, Keeper of Western Asiatic Antiquities, British Museum; Ian Stead, Department of Prehistoric and Romano-British Antiquities, British Museum; Judith Swaddling, Department of Greek and Roman Antiquities, British Museum; Brian A. Tremain, Photographic Service, British Museum; Sheila Vainker, Department of Oriental Antiquities, British Museum; Geoffrey Waywell, Reader in Classical Archaeology, King's College, London. Oxford — Brian Gilmore, Oxford Univesity; P.R.S. Moorey, Keeper, Department of Antiquities, Ashmolean Museum; Michael Vickers, Department of Antiquities, Ashmolean Museum.

Federal Republic of Germany: Berlin — Peter Calmayer, Archaeologisches Institut; Heidi Klein, Bildarchiv Preussischer Kulturbesitz; Gabrielle Kohler-Gallei, Archiv für Kunst und Geschichte; Gertrud Platz, Antikenabteilung, Staatliche Museen Preussischer Kulturbesitz. Göttingen — Walther Hinz. Heidelberg — Karl Jettmar, Südasien Institut, Universität Heidelberg. Herbertingen-Hundersingen — Dieter Gaertner, Heuneburg Museum. Karlsruhe — Michael Maasz, Oberkonservator Badisches Landesmuseum. Munich — Irmgard Ernstmeier, Hirmer Verlag; Friedrich Wilhelm Hamdorf, Oberkonservator, Staatliche Antikensammlung und Glyptothek; Raimund Wünsche, Oberkonservator, Staatliche Antikensammlung und Glyptothek. Stockdorf — Claus Hansmann. Stuttgart — Hilmar Schickler, Württembergisches Landesmuseum. Trier — Hartwig Löhr, Hans Nortman, Rheinisches Landesmuseum. Tübingen — Franz Fischer (Direktor), Egon Gersbach, Wolfgang Kimmig, Institut für Vor- und Frühgeschichte, Universität Tübingen; Heinz Luschey. Würzburg — Guntram Beckel, Akadademischer Direktor, Martin-von-Wagner-Museum der Universität Würzburg.

France: Paris — Michel Amandry, Conservateur au Cabinet des Médailles; François Avril, Curateur, Département des Manuscrits, Bibliothèque Nationale; Christophe Barbotin, Conservateur du Département des Antiquités Egyptiennes, Musée du Louvre; Laure Beaumont-Maillet, Conservateur en Chef du Cabinet des Estampes, Bibliothèque Nationale; Catherine Bélanger, Chargée des Rélations Extérieures du Musée du Louvre; Jeannette Chalufour, Archives Tallandier; Béatrice Coti, Directrice du Service Iconographique, Editions Mazenod; Antoinette Decaudin, Documentaliste, Département des Antiquités Orientales, Musée du Louvre; Michel Fleury, Président de la IV Section de l'École Pratique des Hautes Études; Marie-Françoise Huygues des Étages, Conservateur, Musée de la Marine; Françoise Jestaz, Conservateur, Cabinet des Estampes, Bibliothèque Nationale; Marie Montembault, Documentaliste, Département des Antiquités Grecques et Romaines, Musée du Louvre; Marie-Odile Roy, Service Photographique, Bibliothèque Nationale; Jacqueline Sanson, Conservateur, Directeur du Service Photographique, Bibliothèque Nationale.

German Democratic Republic: Berlin — Max Kunze, Direktor, Antikensammlung, Staatliche Museen zu Berlin.

Greece: Athens — Judith Binder, American School of Classical Studies at Athens; Daphne Gondicas; Manolis Korres, Architect to the Ministry of Culture and Sciences, responsible for Parthenon restoration.

Italy: Perugia — Filippo Coarelli, Dipartimento di Antichita Greche e Romane, University of Perugia. Rome — Paola Pelasatti, Superintendent, Soprintendenza alle Antichita per l'Etruria Meridionale; Ann Britt Tilia, Giuseppe Tilia.

People's Republic of China: Beijing — Cultural Relics Publishing House; Cultural Relics Department, Hebei Province, Shijiazhuang, Hebei Hubei Provincial Museum, Wuhan, Hebei.

U.S.A.: Connecticut: New Haven — David Goodrich. Maryland: Fort Washington — Melva M. Holloman. North Carolina: Chapel Hill — Carole Crumley, Department of Anthropology, University of North Carolina. Texas: Lubbock — Clifford Ashby, Texas Tech. University. Virginia: Charlottesville — University of Virginia.

PICTURE CREDITS

The sources for the illustrations that appear in this book are listed below. Credits from left to right are separated by semicolons; from top to bottom they are separated by dashes.

Cover: Detail of the Delphi Charioteer, photo by Ronald Sheridan, The Ancient Art and Architecture Collection, London / Delphi Museum, Greece. **2, 3:** Maps by Carol Schwartz of Stansbury, Ronsaville, Wood, Inc., background map by R. R. Donnelley. **8:** Detail from bas-relief of Median nobles, photo by Ronny Jacques © 1979 / Photo Researchers. **11:** Map by Carol Schwartz of Stansbury, Ronsaville, Wood, Inc. **12:** Art by Greg Harlin of Stansbury, Ronsaville, Wood, Inc., inset from Werner Forman Archive, London / Hermitage Museum, Leningrad. **15:** The Oriental Institute, University of Chicago. **16:** G. Dagli Orti, Paris (2) — SEF / Art Resource. **17:** Picturepoint, East Molesey, Surrey — G. Dagli Orti, Paris (2). **18, 19:** Picturepoint, East Molesey, Surrey (2) — Robert Harding Picture Library Ltd., London; MacQuitty International Collection, London — G. Dagli Orti, Paris; Robert Harding Picture Library Ltd., London, background, © Nino Cirani / Ricciarini, Milan. **20:** Sybil Sassoon / Robert Harding Picture Library Ltd., London — G. Dagli Orti, Paris (2). **21:** MacQuitty International Collection, London — G. Dagli Orti, Paris; Giraudon, Paris. **24, 25:** Art by Lana Rigsby, Lowell Williams, Inc., based on reconstruction by Professor Friedrich Krefter. **26:** Art by Lana Rigsby, Lowell Williams, Inc., based on reconstruction by Professor Friedrich Krefter — Lauros-Giraudon, Paris / Musée du Louvre, Paris. **28:** Art by Greg Harlin of Stansbury, Ronsaville, Wood, Inc. **30:** Art by Rob Wood of Stansbury, Ronsaville, Wood, Inc. **31:** Drawing by Fred Holz, based on reconstructions by Professor Friedrich Krefter and Professor David Stronach. **33:** Tim Harrison / Susan Griggs Agency, London — Picturepoint, East Molesey, Surrey. **34, 35:** © Lee Boltin — C. M. Dixon, Canterbury, Kent / Hermitage Museum, Leningrad; Pan Binyuan / Hubei Provincial Museum, People's Republic of China; "Archéologia," courtesy *Archeo* magazine, Rome; © Lee Boltin — Ingrid Geske, West Berlin / Antikenmuseum Staatliche Museen Preussischer Kulturbesitz, West Berlin. **36:** Hirmer Fotoarchiv, Munich / Museo Nazionale, Tarquinia. **39-49:** Battle maps by Rob Wood of Stansbury, Ronsaville, Wood, Inc., diagrams and inset maps by John Drummond. **50:** Detail of the head of the Artemision Zeus, photo by Nimatallah / Artephot-Ziolo, Paris / National Archaeological Museum, Athens. **52:** Map by Carol Schwartz of Stansbury, Ronsaville, Wood, Inc. **54:** Nimatallah / Artephot-Ziolo, Paris / Museo Archeologico del Piero, Greece. **55:** Michael Holford, Loughton, Essex / British Museum, London. **57:** Foto Koppermann / Staatliche Antikensammlungen, Glyptothek, Munich, inset, The Metropolitan Museum of Art, Rogers Fund, 1916 (16.71).

58, 59: Christa Begall / Staatliche Museen zu Berlin, Antikensammlung, East Berlin — © Michael Holford, Loughton, Essex / British Museum, London (3); Emmett Bright, Rome / Musei Vaticani, Rome; Scala, Florence / Agora Museum, Athens — Detail from Attic Red Figure Kylix from H. L. Pierce Fund / Museum of Fine Arts, Boston (01.8020) — Martin-von-Wagner Museum der Universität, Würzburg, background, drawing by Fred Holz. **62:** Art by Greg Harlin of Stansbury, Ronsaville, Wood, Inc. **64:** Michael Freeman, London / Ashmolean Museum, Oxford. **65:** Erich Lessing Culture and Fine Arts Archives, Vienna / National War Historical Museum, Sofia, Bulgaria. **66, 67:** Drawing by Fred Holz — Susan Mulhauser, Athens / Hellenic Maritime Museum, Piraeus. **68, 69:** Art by Lana Rigsby, Lowell Williams, Inc. **72:** Antikenmuseum der Staatlichen Museen Preussischer Kulturbesitz, West Berlin; Nikos Kontos, Athens / Acropolis Museum, Athens. **74, 75:** Scala, Florence / Galleria degli Uffizi, Florence; Scala, Florence / Musei Vaticani, Rome; Scala, Florence / National Archaeological Museum, Athens — Mauro Pucciarelli, Rome / Musei Vaticani, Rome; G. Dagli Orti, Paris / National Archaeological Museum, Naples — Giraudon, Paris / Musei Capitolini, Rome; Stephen Natanson, Rome / Museo Ostiense, Ostia, Italy, background, École Nationale Supérieure des Beaux-Arts, Paris. **77:** Bildarchiv Preussischer Kulturbesitz, West Berlin / Staatliche Antikensammlungen, Munich. **78, 79:** Michael Freeman, London / Ashmolean Museum, Oxford, G.287 (V. 526); drawings by Fred Holz. **80:** © Caecilia H. Krüger-Moessner, Munich / Staatliche Antikensammlungen, Munich. **85:** Detail from Attic red figure vase of youth playing the kithara, The Metropolitan Museum of Art, Fletcher Fund, 1956 (56.171.38). **86:** Detail from Attic red figure vase of Sappho and Alcaeus, photo © by Caecilia H. Krüger-Moessner, Munich / Staatliche Antikensammlungen, Munich. **87:** Youth before a grave stele on an Attic vase, photo from Ekdotike, Athens / National Archeological Museum, Athens. **91:** Detail of the murder of Aegisthus on an Attic Red Figure Calyx Krater, from William Francis Warden Fund / Museum of Fine Arts, Boston (63.1246). **92:** Detail from Attic red figure vase of Oedipus and Sphinx, photo from Scala, Florence / Musei Vaticani, Rome. **95:** Detail from Attic vase of Maenad, photo © by Caecilia H. Krüger-Moessner, Munich / Staatliche Antikensammlungen, Munich. **96:** Detail from Etruscan sarcophagus at Cerveteri, Italy, photo from Scala, Florence / Museo Nazionale di Villa Giulia, Rome. **98, 99:** Nimatallah / Ricciarini, Milan / Musei Capitolini, Rome. **101:** Maps by Carol Schwartz of Stansbury, Ronsaville, Wood, Inc.

102: Drawing by Fred Holz — Hirmer Fotoarchiv, Munich / Museo Nazionale di Villa Giulia, Rome. **103:** Stephen Natanson, Rome / Museo Nazionale di Villa Giulia, Rome; Hirmer Fotoarchiv, Munich / Museo Nazionale di Villa Giulia, Rome. **104:** © Mauro Pucciarelli, Rome / Museo Nazionale di Villa Giulia, Rome — Mario Carrieri, Milan / Museo Nazionale di Villa Giulia, Rome. **108, 109:** Trustees of the British Museum, London (P&RB P1986 9-1 1); Erich Lessing, Vienna / Staatliche Museum zu Berlin, East Berlin; Bulloz, Paris / Museum of Baia Mare, Rumania. **112, 113:** Drawing by Fred Holz; art by Greg Harlin of Stansbury, Ronsaville, Wood, Inc., based on reconstructions by Wolfgang Kimmig and model in the Neuneburg Museum, Hundersingen, West Germany. **116:** Erich Lessing Culture and Fine Arts Archives, Vienna / Musée Granet, Aix-en-Provence, France. **119:** Detail of bust from the Acropolis, photo from T.A.P. Service, Athens / Acropolis Museum, Athens. **120, 121:** Luisa Ricciarini, Milan / National Archeological Museum, Athens; T.A.P. Service, Athens / Acropolis Museum, Athens. **122, 123:** Trustees of the British Museum, London / East Pediment of the Parthenon (K,L&M). **124, 125:** Trustees of the British Museum, London / East Pediment of the Parthenon (O); © Michael Holford, Loughton, Essex / British Museum, London. **126, 127:** Nimatallah / Ricciarini, Milan / Museo Nazionale, Reggio Calabria, Italy; Luisa Ricciarini, Milan / Delphi Museum, Greece. **128, 129:** Nimatallah / I.G.D.A., Milan / Museo Archeologico, Florence. **130, 131:** Nimatallah / Ricciarini, Milan / National Archeological Museum, Athens. **132, 133:** Dmitri Kessel, Time-Life Picture Agency, © 1972 Time Incorporated / Hermitage Museum, Leningrad; David Lees, Florence / Kiev State Historical Museum, (2). **134, 135:** © Lee Boltin / Kiev State Historical Museum. **136, 137:** The Metropolitan Museum of Art, Walter C. Baker Gift Fund, 1956 (56.11.1) — Justin Kerr / The Metropolitan Museum of Art, Walter C. Baker Gift Fund, 1956 (56.11.1). **138, 139:** Emmett Bright, Rome / Musei Vaticani, Rome. **140, 141:** Jürgen Liepe, West Berlin / Antikenmuseum Staatliche Museen Preussischer Kulturbesitz, West Berlin. **142:** Statue, "The Teaching Buddha," photo by Claus Hansmann, Stockdorf / Russek Collection, Switzerland. **145:** Map by Carol Schwartz of Stansbury, Ronsaville, Wood, Inc. **149:** Art by Greg Harlin of Stansbury, Ronsaville, Wood, Inc. **152:** Map by Carol Schwartz of Stansbury, Ronsaville, Wood, Inc. **157:** Robert Harding Picture Library Ltd., London / Lahore Museum, Pakistan. **161:** Art by Greg Harlin of Stansbury, Ronsaville, Wood, Inc. **162, 163:** Art by Rob Wood of Stansbury, Ronsaville, Wood, Inc., inset, drawing by Fred Holz. **164, 165:** Art by Greg Harlin of Stansbury, Ronsaville, Wood, Inc. **166, 167:** Art by Rob Wood of Stansbury, Ronsaville, Wood, Inc., inset, drawing by Fred Holz.